Early Literacy Work with Families: policy, practice and research

**Cathy Nutbrown, Peter Hannon
and Anne Morgan**

⑤ SAGE Publications
London ● Thousand Oaks ● New Delhi

First published 2005

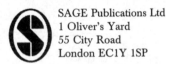

SAGE Publications Ltd
1 Oliver's Yard
55 City Road
London EC1Y 1SP

SAGE Publications Inc.
2455 Teller Road
Thousand Oaks, California 91320

SAGE Publications India Pvt Ltd
B-42, Panchsheel Enclave
Post Box 4109
New Delhi 110 017

British Library Cataloguing in Publication data

A catalogue record for this book is available from the British
Library

ISBN 1-4129-0374-2
ISBN 1-4129-0375-0 (pbk)

Library of Congress Control Number: 2005921541

Typeset by TW Typesetting, Plymouth, Devon
Printed on paper from sustainable resources
Printed in Great Britain by Athenaeum Press Ltd, Gateshead,
Tyne & Wear

Contents

Acknowledgements   vii

Biographical details   viii

**PART 1   EARLY CHILDHOOD EDUCATION AND FAMILY LITERACY:
            POLICY CONTEXTS**   **1**

    Chapter 1 *Policy contexts*   3

    Chapter 2 *Family literacy programmes*   18

**PART 2   DEVELOPING A FAMILY LITERACY PROJECT:
            PRACTICE AND EXPERIENCE**   **33**

    Chapter 3 *Building a framework for family literacy practice*   35

    Chapter 4 *Using the ORIM framework to develop a family literacy
           programme*   52

    Chapter 5 *Opportunities for parents as adult learners*   97

    Chapter 6 *Professional development for family literacy work*   104

PART 3   EVALUATION AND THE PERSPECTIVES OF PARTICIPANTS   **115**

    Chapter 7 *The importance of evaluation*   117

    Chapter 8 *Teachers' experiences of family literacy*   123

    Chapter 9 *Parents' experiences and views of a family literacy programme*   133

    Chapter 10 *Children's perspectives on family literacy*   147

    Chapter 11 *Making a difference?*   168

**PART 4   THE FUTURE FOR EARLY CHILDHOOD EDUCATION
            AND FAMILY LITERACY**   **173**

    Chapter 12 *Developing practices and processes*   175

REFERENCES   187

INDEX   198

ANNOTATED BIBLIOGRAPHY

A briefly annotated list of practical and accessible texts and some key texts in family literacy and work with parents.

Available at: sagepub.co.uk/resources/nutbrown_bibliography.pdf

APPENDIX: Parents' Accreditation Handbook

Available at: sagepub.co.uk/resources/nutbrown_appendix.pdf

APPENDIX: Language for Literacy jigsaw

                 Literacy word web

Available at: sagepub.co.uk/nutbrown_appendix.pdf

Acknowledgements

This book is based upon what we have learned from a project in which the University of Sheffield collaborated with the Sheffield Local Education Authority and schools and centres across the city. It builds on the work that colleagues in many schools and nurseries have developed with us over some years, particularly in a preparatory phase during 1995–1997, and we acknowledge the contribution of all involved in the early stages of the study. The Raising Early Achievement in Literacy (REAL) Project involved hundreds of people: some 300 families, over 50 schools, over 100 teachers, nursery nurses, and other professionals (policy-makers, academics, secretaries, technicians) who helped us at different points during the life of the Project. Without their collective effort and commitment there would be no book. We want to thank them all. Not everyone can be named but we particularly want to thank the following, several of whom played more than one role in the Project.

All the families – children and parents – in the programme as well as many others who also participated in the research. The programme teachers: Judith Butler, Fran Ford, Diane Hetherington, Anne Kirkpatrick, Chris Mackintosh, Sally Rowland, Sue Senior, Anne Stafford, Sean Stanley, Denise Summerhayes. Kath Hirst, who developed, delivered and evaluated the bilingual strand of the REAL Project and Shaheen Kahn for her translation work. Colleagues who assisted us with independent assessments and interviews: Linda Davis, Kathy Evans, Chris Harrison, Jean Hayes, Anne Newton, Judy Paget, Eileen Pratt, Kay Roe, Linda Rowland, Pat Smith, Margaret Lee, Phillipa Thompson. The headteachers of the 21 programme and control schools. Margaret Fitter, for her support in assessing children, her work with parents following the OCN accreditation, her indefatigability in tracking families who had moved, and her interviewing. Mary Marken, Eileen Fawcett, Steve Anwyll, Sue Hoban, Howard Griffiths, Deidre Eastburn, from Sheffield LEA and other members of the Project Steering Group (Roger Adams, Ian Clifford, Margaret Fairclough, Peter Joynson, Arline Kersey, Steve Farnsworth, Rob Poole). Colleagues in the University of Sheffield School of Education: Len Barton, Greg Brooks, Wilfred Carr, Judi Duffield, Lou Hughes, Heather Scott, and Jo Weinberger. The Open College Network. Madeleine Lindley Books.

We are grateful for funding from the Nuffield Foundation, the University of Sheffield, the Sheffield LEA and the Sheffield Strategic Education Forum and to individuals who facilitated access to funding (Helen Quigley, Catrin Roberts, Kathy Sylva, Neil McClelland, and Raymond Douglas, former Master Cutler)

Finally, our thanks to Marianne Lagrange and all members of the SAGE publication team.

Biographical details

Cathy Nutbrown, Peter Hannon and Anne Morgan work at the University of Sheffield where the REAL (Raising Early Achievement in Literacy) Project has been central to their family literacy research. Dr Cathy Nutbrown is Senior Lecturer in the School of Education where she directs a Masters' programme in Early Childhood Education. She has many publications in the field of early childhood and literacy. Peter Hannon is a professor in the School of Education. He has directed several projects, and published extensively, in the field of family literacy. Dr Anne Morgan is a Research Fellow in the School of Education and worked as a teacher on the REAL Project family literacy programme.

PART I

Early Childhood Education and Family Literacy: Policy Contexts

The first part of this book documents the range of policies which contribute to the context for developing early literacy work with parents of young children. Chapter 1, Policy contexts, tells the story of early childhood education and its changing nature. It sets the scene for the book and gives examples of a variety of settings and services where parental involvement in their children's learning is integral to practice. This is followed by Chapter 2, Family literacy programmes, which provides an overview of a parallel set of developments which since the early 1980s have led to a range of practices in schools and other early childhood education and care settings to support parents in their roles as early literacy educators of their children.

Policy contexts

Chapter summary
- Introduction
- The changing nature of early childhood education
  - policy developments in curriculum and pedagogy; observing the literacy hour
  - policy developments in systems and services
- Parental involvement in their children's learning
  - parents and early literacy development; developing a home-school writing project

---

Introduction

This chapter sets the scene for the book through discussion of the many policy developments through the 1990s and early 2000s that have been responsible for a reshaping of early childhood education in the UK, both in terms of settings and services and in terms of the curriculum children experience. The breadth and range of programmes and initiatives to involve parents in their children's learning, and specifically in early literacy learning, are illustrated with examples from a range of settings and services.

The changing nature of early childhood education

Early childhood education policies of the 1990s and early 2000s have brought radical change to curriculum and pedagogy and to state-funded systems in all four countries in the UK, for example:

- *Sure Start* (Glass, 1999) represents massive investment and innovation in early years provision across the UK.
- *Birth to Three Matters* (QCA, 2003) has established a framework for effective practice in work with babies and toddlers.
- The *Review of Preschool Education* in Northern Ireland (DENI, 2004) is an indication of how curriculum can be developed to support the fulfilment of key aims for a society. This review examines structures, systems and practices in settings.
- The *Foundation Stage* for 3–5 year olds is being developed with the creation of Foundation Stage units where children aged 3–5 years are taught together through a curriculum which favours play as an approach to learning and where educators

assess children's learning through observation rather than formal assessment (QCA, 2000).

● The *Foundation Phase* 3–7 being developed in Wales (QCAAW, 2004) shows how a country can draw in various experiences across the world, firstly to redefine 'the early years' and secondly to propose a system of early education which is designed to enable all children to reach their potential and limit the possibility of creating educational failure.

● In Scotland (Scottish Executive, 2003), refreshing approaches to assessment in the early years have been informed by a view of early education curriculum which is informal, individualistic and diverse.

These large-scale initiatives demonstrate how central policy-makers now recognise the importance of strategic investments in early childhood education and care. Amidst this nationwide interest on a scale never before witnessed, and at a time of great investment – of money, energy and belief – early childhood educators are charged with multiple responsibilities. They must maintain and develop the quality of education and care experienced by young children and, in many cases, develop new programmes of provision for families, pioneer new approaches and enhance their own professional knowledge and development.

This section summarises some of the policy developments that have changed the landscape of early childhood education and care; first in terms of curriculum and pedagogy and second in terms of systems and services.

Policy developments in curriculum and pedagogy

The recent history of state-prescribed curricula for children below the statutory school starting age began in 1996 with *The Desirable Outcomes of Nursery Education on Entry to Compulsory Schooling* (SCAA, 1996). Subsequent revisions (perhaps in the context of unrelenting challenge and persistent lobbying by some early childhood educators) resulted, in 2000, with new government 'guidelines' for a curriculum for children aged 3–5+ years (QCA, 2000). These guidelines, while not compulsory, were the focus of inspection of provision. State-required assessment was introduced in 1998 (SCAA, 1997) under the National Framework for Baseline Assessment. Four-year-old children in England and Wales (below the age of compulsory schooling) were to be assessed a few weeks after entry to school. The system was heavily criticised (Nutbrown, 1997) and, in 2003, National Baseline Assessment was replaced with the Foundation Stage Profile, a system of assessment based on practitioner observation over time, to be completed by the time children leave their reception classes. This marked an improvement on the brief summative assessment administered at the start of the reception year. Though some schools chose to maintain an 'on-entry' assessment in order to calculate the value added by the school to the child's achievement at a later date, this was no longer nationally required or reported. These changes were, arguably, a result of early childhood educators remembering important lessons from previous experience and philosophy, and refusing to reject what they learned from the writings and influences of earlier pioneers.

During this period (from 1996 to 2002) other policies influenced what was taught and how it was taught in the early years. The National Literacy Strategy (DfEE, 1998) and, in the following year, the National Numeracy strategy (QCA, 1999) strongly influenced pedagogy, promoting whole-class and differentiated independent work for small groups – even for the youngest children. A key feature of these policies, too, was the 'pace' of the lesson. Teachers were encouraged to keep the lesson moving. Whole-class teaching, groups of young children working at set, 'pencil and paper' tasks, often without adult support, and fast pace were alien teaching strategies for many early years teachers and the children they taught, and the impact on many reception classes was strongly felt. The daily 'literacy hour', which usually took place in the early part of the morning each day, changed the face of literacy teaching. Although the 'hour' was not compulsory in the reception class, the high-profile introduction of the National Literacy Strategy and the intensive work of local literacy consultants meant that most reception teachers and headteachers felt obliged to introduce the literacy hour in the reception class.

The following observation (made by Cathy Nutbrown in 1999) of a reception class literacy hour shows how some children were receiving this (then) new form of literacy teaching.

Observing the literacy hour
(names and identifying details changed)

9.10 a.m.   Reception children (children who began reception in January, 3 weeks ago, all aged 5:1–5:4).

Teacher: 'You did 'T' brilliantly yesterday. We'll do a new letter today. We will do this letter: [writes Ss on the whiteboard]. What letter is this?'

Danny: [thrusts his hand in the air] 'S and s' [saying the letter name and sound].

Teacher: 'Well done – you said the letter name and sound – well done. Which one is a capital?'

Someone eagerly identifies the capital.

It is a minute into the lesson – three boys sit to the right of the group of 21. One picks his nose, one reaches between his legs and plays with his trousers, the third plays with the cord on his jumper. A single girl – alone in the middle of the group plays with her hair – adjusts and re-adjusts her Barbie hair band. Another boy – also sitting apart from the group – plays with his ear. The arc of eight children in the front thrust their hands in the air and list words beginning with S: *Sun Snake Sunflower Six Snooker* (winning a 'that's a good one' from the teacher).

The boy in the trio at the far right stops playing with his trousers and starts twiddling with his hair – his hand as if raised to offer a word beginning with S (but it is not). More words: *Seven Salmon.*

Teacher: 'Salmon' [pulls a face as if to say 'what made you think of salmon?'].

Leighton (playing with his hair) is picked to offer a word – he looks blank and says 'Zebra' (I think – *not bad*).

Teacher: 'Not quite – good try.'

Someone else offers 'sugar', *sugar* is listed.

They are all asked to read the whiteboard while the teacher points to the words:
Sun Snake Sunflower Six Snooker Seven Salmon Sugar.

Teacher: 'We need two more words beginning with S to make ten.'

Yusef offers: *submarine.*

Aaron says: *stairs.*

They are added to the list. The class is asked to read the list: *Sun Snake Sunflower Six Snooker Seven Salmon Sugar Submarine Stairs.*

I notice that Leighton (still playing with his hair) is puzzled; perhaps he's wondering what happened to his *Zebra* – his teacher had said 'good try' but still his Zebra was not on the list.

The teacher begins work with the big book. He points to the title: 'What is it called?'

Children chant out the title.

Teacher holds up a speech bubble: 'What is this?'

Josh has his hand up: 'Speech bubble.'

Teacher: 'Let's read it.'

The children chant this (now) familiar text – it is Wednesday and they have been using this book since Monday. Most of them have learned some of the repetitive lines. Children at the back are chanting the words – they know the words – they are not looking at the text, or at the teacher's pointer. Aaron is yawning. Andrew returns to his trousers. Danny puts the speech bubble on the page. Danny is with this – into it – saying every word – pushing his hand into the air at every opportunity to respond to a question.

The chorus of confident readers starts the text on the next page. The back row of this haphazard arc join in, a phoneme or so behind.

Reece removes and checks his glasses, checks his shoelaces (glasses in hand). Children are repeating the text 'by heart' – but many are not even looking in the direction of the book. A few heads are being scratched. Several cardigans are being buttoned and unbuttoned. Aaron is still yawning.

The emphasis on the current page is on the letter 'h' – with 'huh' sound (not easy in the dialect of this northern city).

Eventually the teacher says; 'Mark – where does this [speech bubble] go?'

'Near the 'en [hen]' says Mark.

Teacher: 'Well done Mark – near the 'en' [pointing to the picture of the hen].

Alex sticks the next speech bubble on the page – confident and swift. Alex, it seems, knows about speech bubbles.

Last page – Aaron gets to stick on the speech bubble – in the wrong place.

(He had not realised that it matters where on the page these speech bubbles go.)

Aaron looks puzzled when the teacher asks another child to try. He looks puzzled and then he looks at his feet. Then he helps Reece check his shoelaces. Alex places the speech bubble on the right place (yes, she knows about speech bubbles).

Aaron misses this – he is still sorting out Reece's shoelaces.

Mikala fixes her Barbie hair band.

It is time to go into groups. The teacher announces 'Jobs for Today'. Yellow group will make a picture of S words using paper in the shape of stairs (the ten 'S' words written on the board are rubbed off). Children work with dictionaries – they have a helper who explains their task and keeps them going. Yellow group start.

The teacher is sorting out the rest of the groups. Green group are starting on a 'T' poem – they are waiting . . . Blue group are at their table . . . waiting. Green group must highlight all the *T*'s and *t*'s in the *T* poem. Three children are listening at the listening station – wearing headphones. Two children have an alphabet jigsaw on the carpet.

Tina and Hanna bump heads – Tina cries – she's banged her nose. The two adults are engaged with their groups – they do not notice Tina (I alert the helper). Tina sits with the helper while the helper continues with her group. The teacher is using single words on cards.

This is

Tina goes to the '*This is*' table but she has missed the two minutes of teaching *This is* so she sucks her hair – she does not seem to know what she is doing.

The children have finished their T poem and go to the two adults, who break off from their groups to check their work. One girl plays with a jigsaw alphabet game alone – saying letter sounds and names of objects (correctly) as she fits them together.

Corey rolls on the floor and intermittently fits pieces of an alphabet jigsaw together – he does more rolling than fitting – rolling between a set of number dominoes and the 26 pieces of the alphabet jigsaw.

The *S* pictures are going well – with continued adult support.

Corey is now playing with the plastic bag which contained the alphabet jigsaw – he rolls around the carpet – picks up a few letter pieces – tries to match them to the baseboard of the jigsaw – he now has two pieces in.

The teacher tries to teach Tina *This is* (she missed that when she banged her nose and has since struggled with the activity).

Lindsay is staring – staring straight ahead – in her own daze ... She adjusts her knickers – pulls up her left sock (different in pattern from the right). She fits a picture of a *ball* with the letter *d* – a bit of pressure makes it go – so that must be OK then ...

The teacher talks to the children on the carpet: 'I'll be there in two seconds ...' [He has perhaps realised that the two boys doing the letter dominoes have done nothing yet – but roll.]

It is 10 minutes to 10 – they have been rolling for 15 minutes.

The '*This is*' group are trying to find the word *horse* out of a choice of *horse, bull, boy*.

Yusef is correct – he looks surprised! He got it right – but has no idea why he's right.

The domino boys find the plastic bags.

Corey stops rolling and calls the teacher (calls his name eight times). He has found *S* in the jigsaw – which he has now two-thirds complete (in the last 60 seconds).

Corey tells his teacher: 'Look – a "S".'

'Well spotted' says the teacher (he's distracted – he needs to get to the domino boys).

The teacher moves to the domino boys 'You need to match them'. He goes back to the '*This is*' table.

(It strikes me that he is like a conductor, trying to conduct an orchestra – as yet untuned and in need of practice – but he has 21 soloists – all playing different instruments – all playing their own unique tunes – each one something of itself – but each needing its own audience.)

Lindsay is still having trouble with her knickers – and has fixed '*a*' with an apple picture – she rests her chin on her fist and removes something from her eye – examines it with some interest.

The 'T' table are now all practising writing their names. Copies from the teacher's model.

Lindsay holds on to her ankles and checks her (odd) socks – she smiles at them – I imagine how she did battle with her mother this morning to get to wear both favourites, and how her mother eventually gave in rather than have her be late for school.

Tina and Reece are on the computer, typing letters and enjoying the configurations which appear rapidly on the screen:

zsdosoihvgndspaoijs
\\aosifnrufghdsln\\dlvlgildjfv
dssbnsdjdhoeoi349867fnas;vgh.

'Let's do it reet fast' says Tina. They do – strings and strings of letters and numbers appear on the screen – the two shout out the symbols they recognise as they appear – they are animated with their creation . . . (and mostly correct).

wuierihv nsaojigugohmd r9ert r 82485q4t
b3tw89tpqh394t qy4t8qy49 t8   9p48   2y948 9yp248t
2p4a;odfnso8th othe82hwo;ehw
84'OHEFOWLSGHO8SHGS;G W[w[Rq9w9 t8w9p
ehrgpeh gpehejvrurtohagm

The teacher returns to the domino boys: 'Can you find the "duh"? – What goes with "duh"? We'll soon have to stop.'

Lindsay re-adjusts her knickers and looks through the big book. Mary picks up the pointer and the two girls take roles of teacher and pupil. Lindsey reads – Mary points. They know this book and read it happily.

The teacher speaks to the class: 'There are too many children in the sand. Everyone stop now. It is tidying-up time. Tidy up and sit on the carpet.'

Lindsay puts away her letter jigsaws. Corey has finished his alphabet jigsaw – it took two minutes of fitting and 14 minutes of rolling on the carpet.

Children have 'tidied' and are sitting on the carpet, in time for the 'whole class' plenary.

Class plenary

Yellow group come to the front. They stand up and with the helpers help show the other children the *S* pictures they have made. Five children stand at the front (Terri has gone to the toilet so misses this 'showing and sharing time').

Children on the carpet are at various levels of engagement with literacy. Andrew returns to his trousers. Aaron twiddles his hair. Reece checks his glasses again.

The little front-row band are keen and *S* words flow from their lips – they shout out more *S* words for the teacher to write (five are wanted this time – not ten as before).

Children from yellow group are invited to say together the '*S*' words in the pictures. They are told they have worked really hard and get a clap.

Alex's finger is bleeding – he has bitten it . . .

The teacher holds up some more words – red letters on laminated yellow cards.

at

all say *at* – (this is OK for those who know *at*. It is tough on those phoneme laggers who join in part way and provide a little echo of the front-row band).

It goes on.

in

am

my

many say 'y'(eye) (as in 'my' with the 'm' missing – phoneme laggers set the pace on this one)

dog

(held upside-down – some know it is upside-down – others don't notice and guess at a word – how will they know it's upside-down?)

and

is

(upside-down again – many know – some don't)

mum

Alex says 'Mum', others are silent.

can

I wonder what is happening here? Those who know say – those who don't still don't. They scratch their backs – wriggle – sort out shoelaces . . . Danny (Danny who was into it 50 minutes ago) screws up his T-shirt. Lindsay adjusts her knickers again. Ten children – half the class – are not looking at the teacher (or the words).

cat

Mary says *cat* – the rest shout *cat* – close behind her.

dad

Kelly gets this; the rest chorus after her.

Teacher: 'Brilliant – you're really good at these everyone.' [I think – 'everyone?']

Corey says 'I got belly ache'. The helper takes him from the room. He is in tears.

Back to the whiteboard: *S*s written by the teacher.

Eight children raise their hands (the rest check T-shirts, socks, noses, knickers, etc.)

Sunflower

Sun

The same eight hands go up

Seven

(Alex's '*S*' sounds like f's. The teacher thinks she says *feathers* – she has said *seven*.)

Six

Sunshine

More nose-picking and shoelace fiddling.

Alan says to the teacher 'We haven't had milk yet' (his first spoken contribution during the time on the carpet).

They have moved on to 'T'. Five words beginning with *T*:

Tina

Tiger
Tea
Terri
Teddy bear
Aaron: 'I'm not coming tomorrow.'
Teacher: 'One more minute. What letter is this?'
He writes '*Aa*'.
Aaron says: '*A*'.
Teacher: 'Good'.
Alex is screwing up his eyes – pulling down his eyelids.
Teacher: 'Alex stop that please!' [almost shouted].
Five beginning with *A*.
Aaron
Alex
Adam
Lindsay tunes into names – she says 'Lindsay'.
Teacher: 'NO we're looking for *A*'s.'
(Lindsay perhaps thought they were looking for names.)
Teacher: 'Andrew – can you think of a word beginning with *A*?'
Andrew: 'No.'
Teacher writes 'Andrew' on the board.
(Lyndsay is puzzled now; what was wrong with her name?)
The hour is over. Children start to line up by the door to go to assembly. Then it will
    be milk time and Alan will be happy.

This observation illustrates the tight structure and pace of a literacy hour which occurred
in 1999. The emphasis on 'moving along' and whole-class group teaching meant that
understanding, for some children, was sacrificed in order to cover a range of concepts
and activities. The lesson moved on even if some children could not and the pace of
teaching meant that some were left behind.

Teachers have revised the literacy hour in the seven years since that account was
written and it is unlikely that such observations could be made now. Teachers, it seems,
no longer slavishly follow instructions and repeat the words printed in model lessons but,
without doubt, the National Literacy Strategy and its literacy hour was fundamental in
reforming the literacy curriculum and related pedagogies. The question remains,
however, as to the impact of this experience on the children who were the recipients of
the new government-prescribed literacy curriculum and pedagogy in 1998. What did the
children make of this 'new' literacy, surely so alien from that which they experienced at
home or in the nursery classes they attended previously? Studies have shown that the
literacy many children experience at home is often quite different, contextualised and
more meaningful (Baghban, 1984; Green, 1987; Goodman, 1980; Nutbrown, 1999a;
Hirst, 1998). Later chapters will consider the interface between home and school literacy
and ways in which home literacy can be exploited in the early years to introduce,
meaningfully, other aspects of school literacy.

Policy developments in systems and services

The pace and extent of policy development left no aspect of state-funded early childhood education provision untouched, and just as curriculum and pedagogy were the focus of revolution in settings, so too were the settings themselves subject to change as policy (and with it substantial funding) brought about change in the systems through which early childhood education and care were provided.

The formation of local Early Years Development and Childcare Partnerships (EYDCP) in 1999 made training and advice available for all settings providing education and care for 4- and 5-year-olds, including voluntary and private as well as local authority run state provision. Groups wishing to be part of the EYDCP in their locality committed themselves to OFSTED (Office for Standards in Education) quality standards and received support to achieve these standards. The EYDCP structure was a system devised to achieve quality of experience for children within a framework of increasing diversity of provision. However, as Webster (2002) warned, further support for voluntary-sector providers, in the form of remuneration and management structures, may well be necessary to achieve the goal of assured quality across a diverse network of provision.

Perhaps the most far-reaching and significant change in the development of diverse, multi-agency and 'holistic' provision was the Sure Start initiative which, since its inception in 1998 (Glass, 1999), has developed programmes across the whole of the UK, with responsible government departments in England, Northern Ireland, Scotland and Wales. The distinctiveness of Sure Start lies in its locally (and community) defined projects within national targets; the multi-agency focus on marginalised and disadvantaged communities where educational achievement is low and young children and their families experience multiple difficulties; and unprecedentedly high funding to support this huge country-wide policy development.

Nationally (and, more importantly, within local communities) Sure Start has brought together existing initiatives and developed new services to address issues of, for example; poverty, ill-health, addiction, teenage pregnancy – all the elements in communities and lives which create exclusion and gheto-ise families and communities.

Within Sure Start – and administered and developed under the Sure Start umbrella – is another far-reaching project which is a major early intervention policy development. Birth to Three Matters (QCA, 2003) disseminated a widely, multi-disciplinary approach to considering and providing for the capabilities and needs of children under three. Extensive networks of training for workers who care for children under three (childminders in homes and practitioners in group settings) have begun to be established. Birth to Three Matters emphasised quality and equality and was a major, innovative and creative approach to providing for living and learning opportunities for children in the first three years. Described as 'a framework to support children in their earliest years', Birth to Three Matters stressed four 'components': a strong child; a skilful communicator; a competent learner; a healthy child. The emphasis throughout is on recognising and supporting young children's developing competence from the beginning.

Every Child Matters was the title of the Green Paper in 2003 which became the basis of the Children Act 2004, described as:

A legislative framework: For improving outcomes for all children; To protect them; To promote their well being; To support all children to develop their full potential.

Prompted by the need to reform child-protection systems following the Laming Inquiry into the death of Victoria Climbié, the Act sought to address 'causes' and to prevent so many young children being 'in need'. It was in this context that proactive development of the kind of 'one-stop-shop' provision for families and young children was high on the agenda. Initiatives promoted in *Every Child Matters* included: Sure Start Children's Centres ('one-stop' nursery education, family support, employment advice, childcare, health services); full service extended schools (pre- and post-school care); speech and language therapy; homelessness; support for parents and carers; early intervention and effective provision; accountability and integration (locally, regionally, nationally); work-force reform to bring about flexibility in working and appropriate qualification and remuneration. There were parallel policy developments in Scotland, Wales and Northern Ireland to address the same issues.

The first years of the 2000s saw early childhood education across the whole of the UK as the focus of increased and intensive recognition. Policy-makers in all four countries of the UK were speaking with increasing frequency and verve of young children and their needs, of the importance of multi-agency, 'joined-up' services. Viewed from this perspective, despite interest in curriculum and pedagogy seeming to forget the historical legacy of early childhood pioneers, the heightened political recognition and substantial increase in funding were responsible for expansion of provision, development of services and a reshaping of the activities in early childhood settings. Though many of these policy initiatives were in their early stages and their impact had yet to be evaluated, it was possible to think of a new era in early childhood education and care in the UK. It is in this context that parental involvement needs to be viewed and understood.

Parental involvement in their children's learning

There are today many examples of parental involvement in children's learning, and the aim of this section is to give a flavour of the kinds of work being undertaken in early childhood settings. For example, throughout the 1990s, Sheffield Local Education Authority (LEA), like many others, promoted partnership with parents in schools throughout the city and 'partnerships' took many forms, with workshops, open days, opportunities for adult learning, and special events being offered in many schools across the whole age range from nursery to secondary.

In one school a 'Parents in Partnership' project led to the development of a programme of accredited learning designed to help parents learn more about their children's education in order better to support them. An accredited course was designed for the parents, tailored to their needs, with four units: sharing your child's school; sharing your child's reading; sharing your child's maths; sharing your child's science. Parents' comments confirmed the usefulness of the project and the aspirations of many to continue lifelong learning. Some said:

I've got a greater awareness of child centred learning and primary education.

I think that it is easy to sit back and let school and teachers get on with doing their jobs but when I think back to when I was younger and how easy it was not to do any work I want to help my child realise that learning could be fun.

Just being involved helps children because it shows your interest in what they do and helps them to understand it is worthwhile.

The headteacher of the school at the time reported:

A key aim is to raise achievement of pupils. Through being involved in the project parents can learn alongside their children and develop better understanding of the expectations of school learning and there is shared understanding of where children's education is coming from and going to. Parents are continuing on their paths of *lifelong* learning too and many have yet to discover where those paths will lead. The potential is tremendous.

(Firth, 1997)

Hurst and Joseph (1998) viewed the coming together of parents and practitioners as 'sharing education'. They argued for understanding of the complex cultural differences and shifts which children, parents and practitioners experienced when they entered each other's worlds and opportunities for each to 'share' the others. However,

The sharing of intentions and perspectives between parents and practitioners is not easy in a busy classroom. There has to be a rationale for it, and it needs links with a curriculum model which sets a value on children's experiences at home with family and friends. It requires just as much commitment as sharing intentions with children does. Contacts with the home should be seen as a part of the curriculum, and a part of the practitioner's responsibility to provide for children's learning in ways that suit them. The first step is to consider what kind of contact with parents is most valuable, and to find out what kind of contact with the setting is needed by the parents.

(Hurst and Joseph, 1998, p.89)

Specific initiatives to involve parents in the early years have often focused on young children's learning or aspects of curriculum and helping parents learn more about their children's ways of learning. In the late 1980s the Froebel Early Learning Project (Athey, 1990) identified ways of helping parents to understand their children's learning interests so that they could better support them. This theme was further developed by Nutbrown (1999b), who argued that the more parents knew about how children's learning developed, the better placed they were to understand what their children were doing and how they might further enhance learning opportunities for them. More recently, the PEEP Project (Peers Early Education Partnership) in Oxfordshire has developed ways of involving parents with babies and young children in several aspects of their learning and development (Evangelou and Sylva, 2003).

Some settings have developed an international reputation for their work in involving parents in their children's learning; for example, the Penn Green Centre (Arnold, 2001; Whalley *et al.*, 2001), the Coram Children's Centre in London and the Sheffield Children's Centre. Many settings develop their own specific projects to help parents learn more about their children's learning, such as that reported by Parker (2002), who explains how sharing work with parents on children's drawing and mark-making lead to enhanced understanding and enthusiasm from parents. Parker records the views of some parents who remarked:

> I have been able to enter her imagination and see the world through her eyes.

> Now I'm fascinated by the way she develops a drawing, rather than just looking at the end result.

> I have learnt that Brandon is more capable of mark making than I first thought.
> (Parker, 2002, p.92)

Parker notes:

> The parents learned from observing their children and developed an appreci-ation of their children's high levels of involvement, discussing their children's achievements at home with confidence, clarity and joy . . . The children have been the primary beneficiaries of this collaboration between parents and practitioners. We all had valuable knowledge and understanding to share. This was a group which enjoyed mutual respect, shared understandings, political awareness and a commitment to extending learning opportunities for young children.
> (Parker, 2002, pp.92–3)

In some cases initiatives have been targeted specifically at minority groups, including families for whom English is not the language of the home. Karran (2003) describes work with parents who are learning English as an additional language and the importance of bilingual support for such parents who want to understand more of education systems and how to help their young children. Siraj-Blatchford (1994) has argued that in some cultures 'education' and 'home' are distinct and separate and time may need to be given to explaining how home–school partnerships can support young children's learning and development. Baz *et al.* (1997) have discussed the importance of bilingual early childhood educators working bilingually with parents and young children using books, early writing, rhymes and poems in families' homes and in group settings.

Parents and early literacy development

Given the strong interest in parental involvement in their children's learning in the early years and the strength of national interest in literacy, it is no surprise that many specific initiatives to focus work with parents on early literacy have been developed. Such work builds on strong foundations of research and practice (a theme which will be further developed in Chapter 2). Several examples of work with parents to promote early literacy development demonstrate how effective and pleasurable (for all concerned) such work can be. The Sheffield Early Literacy Development (SELD) Project (Hannon *et al.*, 1991) worked with parents to explore how together parents and the research team could promote children's early literacy. After home visits and group meetings the parents saw more of their children's capabilities and they understood more of what they saw. The SELD Project demonstrated how children's homes and members of their families could offer powerful learning encounters. It made sense for professional educators and families to work in collaboration, sharing their knowledge, insights and questions. Since the SELD Project other initiatives have been developed; some small-scale and others larger in reach. The work of the Raising Early Achievement in Literacy (REAL) Project will be a focus of later chapters in this book, but first we should examine what is possible on a smaller scale where just one teacher wants to do something to develop work with parents.

Recent work in Tameside Local Education Authority, Greater Manchester, has resulted in a range of projects to involve parents, from work to include parents in the general experiences of the children in a reception class, to specific projects to involve parents in assessment, in early literacy and in early numeracy activities with their children. The following account describes one such project, run by Helen Hickson, a nursery teacher.

Developing a home–school writing project

The Project started with an initial information meeting, the aim of which was to inform parents of the progression they could expect to see as their children experimented with mark making. I wanted to share with parents the importance of letting their children 'have a go' rather than writing everything for them to copy.

I used overheads of progressive examples of children's independent writing to illustrate the points I was making. I also emphasised the importance of the fact that children develop at different rates and what was important was that children developed the confidence to have a go.

Parents could become involved in this process by providing meaningful opportunities for writing and children would have the opportunity to develop their skills and become confident writers.

The Project ran over four weeks and revolved around a teddy bear! To begin with all the children were given a teddy along with a selection of writing materials. Each week parents had the opportunity to come to school on either a Tuesday or Wednesday morning and see me modelling the weekly writing task. This was followed by the parents working with their children on the writing task with me and the nursery nurse on hand to offer help or guidance.

Every Friday the teddies went home, along with another writing task which was similar to the task completed in school during the week. This ensured that all the parents had an opportunity to be involved in the project if they wanted to, even if they could not get to the weekly sessions in school. (Table 1.1 shows the programme.)

Outcomes and achievements

The children and parents became very involved in the project. In total, 17 out of 30 children had their parent or grandparent come into school to work with them and almost everyone in the class worked at home on the weekly task.

Table 1.1 A four-week writing programme for parents and children

Week	Focus
1	Teddy wrote a letter to his/her new friend and the children each wrote a reply
2	Teddy invited his/her friend to his/her birthday party. Each child wrote a reply
3	Writing a shopping list for the birthday party
4	Teddy's birthday party! The children made and wrote birthday cards for their teddy.

As a result of the Project it was possible to see how children developed as confident writers who were prepared to have a go. Parents were now more aware of how they could encourage their children as independent writers rather than dismissing their independent attempts and writing things for the children to copy in a more perfect form.

Parents were also trying to find ways of involving their children in meaningful writing tasks at home.

The project emphasised the importance of providing parents with the necessary information to enable them to work effectively with their children. I am looking forward to developing an annual programme of work with parents that will enable them to work with their children in other areas of the Foundation Stage curriculum (Hickson, 2003).

The above example of linking home and school is a far cry from the situation described by Anning and Edwards (2003, p.13):

> . . . our education system is still geared to promoting literacy with an emphasis on 'conventional' reading and writing and this model is increasingly 'colonising' pre-school settings. The sign systems of school literacy – alphabet charts, words Blu-tacked onto doors, chairs and tables, workbooks and worksheets – which set the boundaries of literacy in the formal settings of many early years classrooms are infiltrating the informal settings of day care centres, childminders and even some young children's bedrooms or playrooms at home. Parents are pressurised into joining this version of 'the literacy club' by a burgeoning industry in 'out-of-school'/homework educational materials. In supermarkets parents are urged to invest in an array of workbooks, videos and educational games, all designed to improve children's basic skills in reading and writing.

What Hickson's example shows is how, when theory is shared with parents, literacy learning at home can be contextualised and meaningful. 'Theory' is not on sale in supermarkets, but once parents are given an insight into theories of literacy development and can see those theories brought to life in their own children, they can use the supermarket to support children's literacy. For then, as we shall see later, parents can see that the range of print on show, for free, is useful, contextualised and meaningful reading material.

This chapter has given an overview of recent policy developments in early childhood education and introduced the theme of parental involvement in early childhood education. In Chapter 2 issues of policy specifically related to family literacy are discussed.

2 Family literacy programmes

Chapter summary
- Introduction
- Conceptualising family literacy programmes
- Rationale for family literacy programmes
- The development of family literacy programmes
- Research issues in the field
  - Deficit approaches
  - Targeting of programmes
  - Evidence of effectiveness
  - Gender
  - Bilingualism
  - Training and professional development
  - Policy relevance and policy research
- Conclusions

Introduction

Family literacy research has become indispensable for a full understanding of how young children learn literacy and how they may be taught or helped to acquire it. This chapter focuses on family literacy programmes. These are approaches to teaching literacy that recognise the family dimension in individuals' learning. The aim of the chapter is, first, to offer a way of conceptualising family literacy programmes and the research base that provides their rationale. The development of such programmes – so far in English-speaking countries – over the past two decades or so will then be summarised. Family literacy programmes belong to the field of adult education as well as to early childhood education but, for our purposes, programmes are viewed mainly from the perspective of early childhood education. There are several research issues in the field. Seven key ones will be reviewed: deficit approaches, targeting of programmes, evidence of effectiveness, gender, bilingualism, training for practitioners, and policy research. Some of these have attracted considerable research interest and activity; others remain under-researched or under-conceptualised. The chapter makes suggestions about what we know about family literacy programmes and what we still need to know.

Conceptualising family literacy programmes

The term 'family literacy' has had two basic meanings. In the first it refers to interrelated *literacy practices within families.* Taylor (1983) appears to have coined the term with this meaning. Her original research, which involved qualitative case studies of middle-class white families in the United States, showed how young children's initiation into literacy practices was shaped by parents' and other family members' interests, attitudes, abilities and uses for written language. Many other studies have shared this focus even if they have not all used the term 'family literacy' (Heath, 1983; Teale, 1986; Taylor and Dorsey-Gaines, 1988; Hannon and James, 1990; Baker *et al.*, 1994; Moss, 1994; McNaughton, 1995; Purcell-Gates, 1995; Gregory, 1996; Voss, 1996; Weinberger, 1996; Barton and Hamilton, 1998; Cairney and Ruge, 1998; Hirst, 1998). These studies can generally be classed as descriptive-analytic in that they have sought to understand existing family literacy practices rather than to evaluate any attempt to change them (although Cairney and Ruge, 1998, combined this approach with a study of innovative literacy programmes). All studies have involved qualitative methods but some have also made use of quantitative survey or longitudinal data (e.g. Hannon and James, 1990; Baker *et al.*, 1994; Weinberger, 1996; Hirst, 1998). This body of research, now covering different societies – and different social classes and ethnic groups within those societies – constitutes a rich archive which opens our minds to the variety of language and literacy practices that can be found in families and therefore the many ways in which children can be drawn into literacy without the direct agency of schools.

It is the second meaning of 'family literacy' that is the focus of this chapter. Here the term refers to certain kinds of *literacy programmes involving families.* The origin of this meaning is not so clear but it appears to have emerged (again in the United States) in the late 1980s, one of the earliest documented instances being the University of Mass-achusetts English Family Literacy Project (Nash, 1987). This meaning is now so common as almost to obliterate the first – a matter of some regret for, as Hannon (2000a) has argued, it was very useful to have a term which referred to literacy practices which occur independently of any programme. Without such a term, programme designers and practitioners can easily overlook valuable language and literacy activities in which family members engage, separately and interactively, independently of any programme.

Family literacy programmes can be defined as programmes to teach literacy that acknowledge and make use of learners' family relationships and engagement in family literacy practices. An obvious example of a programme fitting this definition would be a school involving parents in the teaching of reading to their children. This acknowledges that many parents do, to some degree, assist their children's reading development, makes use of their motivation to do more, their opportunities at home to do so and the likelihood that, because of their relationship to their parents, children will enjoy and benefit from the experience. Another example would be an adult literacy programme for parents that made use of their desire to help their children learn to write and which created shared writing activities to enable both parent and child to learn together.

It may be helpful to contrast family literacy programmes with non-instances of the concept, i.e., programmes in which members of families may participate but in which no account is taken of their being family members. Most traditional schooling and adult education of the past century or two has been of this character. This is not necessarily a bad thing where it is desirable or appropriate to treat learners as individual children or adults. For example, if some parents value adult literacy classes because they offer a respite from childcare rather than an extension of it, it is sensible to take account of their wishes. It should also be noted that not all learners – especially in the case of adults – are members of families and in these cases the question of providing family literacy programmes does not arise.

At this point it is necessary to acknowledge that the terms 'family', 'literacy' and 'teaching' can have many different meanings. The concept of *family* employed in this book is intended to include the full range of groups within which children are cared for and grow up. Carers of young children can be biological parents, step-parents, foster parents, grandparents, siblings or others in the home. Children learn from carers and *vice versa*. Family literacy programmes are sometimes based on a narrow concept of family and unexamined assumptions about its structure; for example, the assumption that children in programmes have fathers at home. Regarding *literacy*, current research and theory tend to conceptualise it either as a set of social practices involving written language or as a skill. These conceptions are not necessarily mutually exclusive since social practices do involve skills (often transferable ones) but it does still matter whether one gives primacy to the social practices or to the skills. Although some family literacy programmes focus mainly on skills, the approach underlying this chapter is that it is the social practices that matter. Reference will be made later to literacy inequalities. By this is meant unequal access to those literacy practices associated with power in society or those literacy practices valued in formal education. Teaching literacy cannot by itself reduce literacy inequality but it can contribute to that goal. Finally, the concept of *teaching* itself needs unpacking. It includes many ways in which those engaged in literacy practices can help others – whether children or adults – to become proficient in those practices. Hannon (2000b) has suggested that there is a teaching spectrum, with 'instruction' at one end and 'facilitation' at the other. *Instruction* involves deliberate, planned teaching to meet curricular objectives, often carried out with one instructor teaching many students in settings distanced from real-life contexts. *Facilitation* is support of on-task learning, embedded in real-life contexts – well captured by the Vygotskyan notion of learners doing in cooperation with others today what tomorrow they will be able to do on their own. Broadly speaking, instruction can be said to be characteristic of schools and other formal learning situations; facilitation is characteristic of learning in out-of-school settings, particularly families. Family literacy programmes vary in the balance struck between instruction and facilitation, those giving primacy to teaching literacy skills being more likely also to emphasise instruction.

A consequence of there being different concepts of family, literacy and teaching is that, depending upon which ones are applied, there can be many different kinds of family literacy programmes. A further source of variation among programmes concerns their aims. These can be limited to teaching children and adults how to participate in specific literacy practices or they can be broader, aiming to enhance families' awareness of their own literacy and that of others in society and how literacy may play a part in maintaining or changing their position in society. This issue will be considered in a later section on 'deficit approaches'.

A wide variety of family literacy programmes over the last two decades have been documented (McIvor, 1990; Nickse, 1990; ALBSU, 1993b; Dickinson, 1994; Meek and Dombey, 1994; Cairney and Munsie, 1995; Hannon, 1995; Morrow, 1995; Morrow *et al.*, 1995; Wolfendale and Topping, 1996; Taylor, 1997; Tett, 2000; Auerbach, 2002; Cairney, 2002; Wasik, 2004). A fundamental way in which programmes vary is in whose literacy they aim to change. Some focus on children, some on adults, some on both. Programmes vary in aiming for outcomes in individuals' literacy in homes, schools, other educational institutions, communities or workplaces. Then there are variations in whether programme input is to children, adults or both. If both, there may be separate inputs to each or they may be combined in shared activities. Inputs may be to one family member with outcomes sought in another (e.g. work with parents to affect children's literacy). The location of work with families can vary. In some programmes work is carried out in families' homes; in others it is in centres/schools, libraries, workplaces, football clubs or elsewhere in the community. The workers can be early childhood educators, adult educators, para-professionals or volunteers. Teaching can involve different mixes of instruction and facilitation. There are variations in the target populations for programmes, e.g. bilingual or ethnic groups, fathers, adolescent mothers, prison inmates. The underlying concept of literacy varies from an emphasis on conventional activities within written language to broader conceptions involving media texts, oral language and additional language learning. Some programmes extend literacy to health awareness, parenting and life skills. Some make critical awareness of literacy itself the object of learning.

How might we conceptualise this complexity, and the potential for countless permutations of focus, input, location, workers, target populations and conceptions of literacy? It is hardly surprising that such categorisations of programmes as have been proposed tend to be illuminative rather than comprehensive. Nickse (1990) suggested that 'Family and intergenerational literacy programs are organised efforts to improve the literacy of educationally disadvantaged parents and children through specially designed programs' with the basic idea that 'parents and children can be viewed as a learning unit and may benefit from shared literacy experiences' (p.2). She proposed a fourfold typology according to whether programmes target the adult directly and the child indirectly, vice versa, both directly or both indirectly. This is helpful as far as it goes but clearly leaves out many features that could be important to researchers, practitioners and policy-makers. Morrow and Paratore (1993) distinguished two categories of programmes: home–school partnerships and intergenerational interventions. Cairney (2002) suggested similar categories (home/school program initiatives, intergenerational literacy programs) but added a third, termed 'partnership programs', in which the focus is on links at the level of schools, families and communities. Some agencies – notably, in the United States, the National Center for Family Literacy (Darling, 1993), and in England, the Adult Literacy and Basic Skills Unit (ALBSU, 1993b) – have insisted on a specific definition of family literacy that refers to programmes which combine basic skills and parenting input for parents with early literacy education for their children and joint parent–child activities. This definition, while having the virtue of clarity, has been so restricted as to exclude most programmes other than those that the agencies themselves promoted (Hannon, 2000a). It excludes 'home–school partnerships' or 'parental involvement', leaving only what Morrow and Paratore (1993) and Morrow *et al.* (1995) term 'intergenerational' programmes. The confused and contested status of the term led Morrow *et al.* (1995) to conclude rather weakly that 'family literacy refers to a complex concept associated with many different beliefs about the relationships between families and the development of literacy' (p.2). Wolfendale and Topping (1996) characterised family literacy as a broadening of parental involvement in early literacy to include a wider range of activities often also concerned with the needs of parents and carers. Auerbach (1997b) proposed that programmes be grouped according to three paradigms whose assumptions, goals and practices are informed by different ideological and theoretical perspectives: the 'intervention prevention' approach, the 'multiple literacies' approach and the 'social change' approach. Categorisation according to these three paradigms is not straightforward but the categories rightly draw attention to the fundamental aims and purposes of programmes, and the extent to which they enable families to challenge social forces that marginalise them. Taylor (1997) argued for a redefinition of family literacy programmes as ways to 'organize the advantaged and disadvantaged to read, write, and do other kinds of work together to increase the opportunities available to all' (p.4). Recent reviewers (Purcell-Gates, 2000; Wasik *et al.*, 2001) have accepted that it is extremely difficult to impose any overall conceptualisation on the field. Given the heterogeneity of current family literacy programmes, and the continuing inventiveness of practitioners in developing new ones, it is probably best to work with the general definition offered earlier, that we are dealing with a class of programmes to teach literacy that acknowledge and make use of learners' family relationships and engagement in family literacy practices. The programmes thus encompassed vary considerably; some of their variations are significant for research, practice or policy.

From the viewpoint of early childhood educators, family literacy programmes could be conceptualised simply as another method for achieving historic aims regarding teaching literacy to young children. This, however, would be a rather narrow view because the concept, fully appreciated, means educators shifting their focus from the individual child to the family, acknowledging that their role may be secondary to that of parents, recognising pre-existing family literacy practices, and seeing that teaching aims might be better achieved by also taking an interest in the learning of other family members. It means rethinking some pedagogical assumptions in early childhood education and a two-way professional exchange with adult education. This has research implications to be discussed later.

Rationale for family literacy programmes

What is the justification for taking seriously the concept of a family literacy programme? We can look to studies in literacy, language, child development and education for a rationale. The research of most relevance concerns children's, rather than adults', literacy and was carried out in the period leading up to the emergence of family literacy programmes in the late twentieth century. That emergence no doubt owed much to political and ideological factors but the ground for it had been well prepared by research.

The most influential research is that showing the importance of home (for which one can generally read 'family') factors in school literacy achievement throughout all the years of schooling. Achievement in school literacy and in reading tests reflects proficiency in only one kind of literacy practice but it is one valued by many families. Compelling evidence comes from large-scale surveys. In the USA, for example, studies within the National Assessment of Educational Progress have shown the very strong association between the extent of literacy materials (newspapers, magazines, books, dictionaries) in homes and children's reading test scores at ages 9, 13 and 17 (Applebee et al., 1988). By the end of schooling, children in families having 'many', as opposed to 'few' such materials enjoyed approximately four years' superiority in reading achievement. In the UK one could cite the National Child Development Study, which showed that the likelihood of children being 'poor' readers or 'non-readers' at age 7 was very strongly related to social class (Davie et al., 1972). It can be argued from such evidence that efforts to reduce literacy inequalities are unlikely to be successful if they are confined to school learning; literacy education needs also to address learning at home – in families.

Research concerning parental involvement in children's early literacy development also underpins family literacy programmes. In the UK, for example, studies have shown such involvement – not necessarily encouraged by specific programmes – to be very common (Newson and Newson, 1977; Hannon and James, 1990) across all social groups and that within disadvantaged groups it is strongly associated with literacy achievement (Hewison and Tizard, 1980; Hannon, 1987; Bus et al., 1995). It should not be surprising that parents involve themselves in this way. For most parents, it is intrinsically motivating to be involved in their children's development – it being one reason for becoming a parent in the first place – and literacy is a part of that development. That alone might be considered sufficient justification for family literacy programmes.

Parental motivation matters particularly in the case of parents who feel they have literacy difficulties. Adult literacy tutors are familiar with the situation where an adult decides to do something about their literacy at the point when their young children are beginning to learn to read and write. The fact that parents' motivation to help their children and to help themselves can peak at the same time, and reinforce each other, suggests that family literacy programmes that provide opportunities for both could be very effective.

Another line of research serving to justify family literacy programmes is that from the 1980s which showed the previously overlooked extent of young children's knowledge of literacy before formal schooling. Some of this work has been in the emergent literacy tradition (Goodman, 1980; Goelman et al., 1984; Teale and Sulzby, 1986; Hall, 1987). Knowing about literacy practices and skills valued by schools confers advantages on some children starting formal education just as lack of it disadvantages others (Heath, 1983; Harste et al., 1984). The relevant knowledge can include awareness of the purposes of literacy (Heath, 1983), awareness of story (Heath, 1982; Wells, 1987), knowledge of letters (Tizard et al., 1988), or phonological awareness (Bryant and Bradley, 1985; Maclean et al., 1987). If children have this knowledge at school entry it seems reasonable to infer that they have acquired it in their families. If they do not have it (and if it is desirable that they should), there is a case for family literacy programmes to help them acquire it.

More generally, research into pre-school language and literacy learning has forced a re-evaluation of the power of home learning. On the basis of studies such as that by

Tizard and Hughes (1984) comparing children's early language experiences at home and in pre-school classes, Hannon (1995) identified many ways in which home learning can be more powerful than school learning (for example, in being shaped by immediate interest and need, in often seeming to be effortless, in spontaneity, in being a response to real rather than contrived problems, in being of flexible duration, in having a high adult–child ratio, in being influenced by adult models, and in allowing a 'teaching' role for younger family members). Hannon further suggested that families can provide children with four requirements for early literacy learning: (1) *opportunities* to read texts and attempt writing; (2) *recognition* of early literacy achievements; (3) *interaction* with more proficient literacy users, usually through facilitation rather than instruction; and (4) *models* of what it is to use literacy. Nutbrown and Hannon (1997) and Hannon and Nutbrown (1997) have shown that this framework (generally abbreviated to 'ORIM') can be used to construct family literacy programmes. Chapter 3 will further explain the ORIM framework and Chapter 4 will demonstrate how it was used in practice to develop and implement a family literacy programme.

Finally, a strong research justification for family literacy programmes comes from those studies, cited at the beginning of this chapter, which have revealed the nature and extent of families' uses for literacy and family members' interrelated literacy practices. Once these practices are recognised, children's literacy learning is de-individualised. It is seen as part of a larger system – a system moreover that from a social learning perspective has the capacity to scaffold and otherwise facilitate young children's literacy development.

The development of family literacy programmes

Early childhood educators tend to see family literacy programmes as the latest form of parental involvement in early literacy education. That is true up to a point but fails to do justice to the contribution of adult educators who, not unreasonably, tend to see such programmes as a new form of their practice. It is better to see the development of family literacy programmes as stemming from both of these strands of education.

Taking first the early childhood education strand, it is worth noting at risk of some oversimplification that parental involvement in the teaching of literacy is a fairly recent development. In industrialised countries, mass compulsory schooling, since its beginnings in the late nineteenth century and throughout most of the twentieth, was characterised more by parental exclusion than by involvement (Hannon, 1995). This was probably not planned or even conscious and can be attributed, at least in the early years of the system, to lack of space and physical resources in schools, to a lack of cultural resources (an educated teaching force, literature for children), and to an ideology that took it for granted that children should be educated outside their homes, in large groups, in specially dedicated educational institutions (i.e., schools) where it was assumed that school teaching methods, often characterised by rote learning, was superior to home learning. Even when more sophisticated methods were developed later (for example, systematic reading schemes), the effect was often to privilege professional knowledge and distance parents further from their children's literacy development.

It was not generally until the last quarter of the twentieth century that, in industrialised societies, early literacy educators began to see parents differently. The change reflected interest in parental involvement as a tool for reducing persistent educational inequalities, increased adult literacy in society, rethinking of professional knowledge concerning literacy development, more print in the environment (including children's books), and a recognition of families as active users, rather than passive beneficiaries, of educational services.

Parental involvement in the teaching of literacy developed gradually. Parents were enjoined to support their children's school literacy learning through encouragement and showing an interest. To this end they were informed about schools' policies and practices. Parental involvement was often seen as a matter of coming into school, it being assumed that school, not home, was the key site for literacy learning. Reading was prioritised over writing (with the term 'literacy' at first rarely used). Later, involvement became more direct, for example in the UK, when schools began encouraging and supporting parents of young children to 'hear' children read aloud books that they brought home from school. A pioneering programme with 6- to 7-year-olds in Haringey, London, was found to have measurable outcomes in terms of children's reading test performance (Tizard *et al.*, 1982) and had a national impact on practice. Parents in the Haringey programme were not given any particular method for assisting their children's oral reading but other, more prescriptive programmes most importantly 'paired reading', were developed and also spread rapidly (Bushell *et al.*, 1982; Topping and Lindsay, 1991, 1992). In New Zealand, another prescriptive programme, 'pause, prompt and praise', was developed and evaluated (McNaughton *et al.*, 1981). In the US, prescriptive programmes have included giving quite explicit directions to parents (Edwards, 1994) and 'dialogic reading' (Whitehurst *et al.*, 1994). The 'hearing reading' programmes (whether 'open' or 'prescriptive') have been the most clearly documented and evaluated but they emerged at the same time as a multitude of less easily catalogued approaches to involving parents and families (Dickinson, 1994; Hannon, 1995; Wolfendale and Topping, 1996). Some programmes have reached into the pre-school years (Hannon, 1996) and a few have gone beyond books to focus also on writing and oral language (Wade, 1984; Green, 1987; Hannon, 1998). A recent national initiative in England has involved several thousand parents in courses to familiarise them with changes in the school literacy curriculum and to help them support their children's learning (Brooks *et al.*, 2002).

In summary, within the early childhood education strand, parental involvement in the teaching of literacy began, after a long period of routine parental exclusion, with a focus on parents helping children's oral reading. It has gradually evolved to take on a broader concept of literacy, pre-school as well as school-aged children, and support for a wider range of at-home as well as in-school activities. These actions by schools can be counted as family literacy programmes in that they clearly 'acknowledge and make use of learners' family relationships' but it must be admitted that the learners with which they are concerned are mainly young children and that on the whole programmes have not so much been concerned with 'engagement in family literacy practices' as families' engagement in school literacy practices.

Within the adult education strand there has been, as one would expect, more concern for parents as learners. In the United States, McIvor (1990) documented eight family literacy programmes, all of which were devised and delivered by agencies whose mission was primarily to do with adults (libraries, colleges, adult education services, prison organisations, services to users of day care or Head Start). In England, it was the Adult Literacy and Basic Skills Unit that did more than any other organisation to promote 'family literacy' by securing and distributing government funding for a particular model of family literacy – taken from the US – that clearly aimed to aid parents' literacy development as well as children's (ALBSU, 1993a, 1993b). The introduction of adult literacy educators into family literacy reinforced concern for families' own literacy values and practices. For example, in the US, Nickse, in a foreword to McIvor (1990), pointed out that family literacy programmes required extra sensitivity from providers who had to become aware of different cultural and literacy practices in families. She suggested, 'When families are involved together for literacy, more of their lives are shared with us, and adults become more vulnerable. This is a trust not to be taken lightly' (p.5). These considerations are not always uppermost in the minds of early years educators whose focus is the child in a school setting.

Family literacy programmes in the twenty-first century can thus be seen as a merging of literacy teaching in early childhood education and in adult education. Future development will depend upon success in combining the strengths and avoiding the weaknesses of each strand. Future research in the field also needs to draw upon traditions associated with each strand.

Research issues in the field

Family literacy programmes now constitute a large field of educational activity in which can be found, in some form or other, most issues of interest to early childhood literacy researchers. The following are singled out because, to us, they seem to have high theoretical or practical interest.

Deficit approaches

It has already been noted that family literacy programmes developed by early childhood educators tend to emphasise the engagement of families in school literacy rather than the engagement of schools in the families' literacy. Some adult educators do the same but many take a more sceptical view of the value of school literacy (which has often been problematic in their students' lives) and a more positive view of the strengths of parents and families in relation to everyday life and literacy. There have been critiques (by Auerbach, 1989, 1995, 1997b; Grant, 1997; Taylor, 1997) of what is termed a 'deficit approach' in family literacy programmes. Families may be heavily engaged in literacy practices and have many literacy skills but these may not be the practices and skills valued by schools. Cairney (2002) points out that many family literacy programmes are about taking school literacy into families. Further, it is probable that there are family literacy programmes that proceed on ignorant, and even offensive, assumptions concerning what certain families do not do or what they are supposed to be incapable of doing. That is, some programmes ignore the family literacy research cited earlier in the 'Rationale for family literacy programmes'. They are also ignoring research that has shown more generally the extent to which families' knowledge is undervalued by schools (Moll *et al.*, 1992). Such assumptions, as well as being educationally unsound, have political consequences in 'explaining' the situation of poor families in terms of their literacy being less than, rather than simply different from, that of the powerful in society whose hegemonic definition of what counts as literacy goes unchallenged.

This issue may not, however, be quite as straightforward as stated and it is one that could benefit from further research – both conceptual and empirical. The term 'deficit approach' is not entirely helpful, because there is a sense in which there is nothing wrong with deficits – with learners acknowledging they have them or with teachers seeking to remedy them. None of us would ever engage in any conscious learning if we did not feel we had some deficit we wanted to make up. Problems arise if differences (e.g. in literacy practices) are uncritically viewed as deficits, if deficits are imputed to learners without their assent, if deficits are exaggerated or if deficits are seen as all that learners have (i.e., their cultural strengths are devalued). These problems can arise in any form of literacy education – indeed in any form of education – but they are more exposed in the case of family literacy programmes within which the cultural values and practices of homes and schools are brought together. The challenge for family literacy educators is to value what families bring to programmes but not to the extent of simply reflecting back families' existing literacy practices (for it is patronising to suppose families need help with their existing literacy practices). Somehow programmes must offer families access to some different or additional literacy practices – but through collaboration and negotiation rather than imposition. If educators fail either to facilitate families' entry into powerful literacy practices or to empower them to challenge those practices, they will simply perpetuate families' continued exclusion from whatever benefits participation in those practices confers. Some family literacy programmes do take up this challenge (e.g. several in Taylor, 1997) but their efforts are documented rather than rigorously evaluated. Using and valuing what families already know in order to teach them what they do not know is a subtle process that can easily go wrong. Research can help by elucidating teaching possibilities and pitfalls. Studies of particular programmes by Delgado-Gaitan (1990), Moll *et al.* (1992) and Tett (2000) – as well as others discussed by Auerbach (1997a) – have begun to provide insights into this but more research in a wider range of cultural settings is needed.

Targeting of programmes

A recurrent idea in family literacy discourse is that there are families in which parents have literacy difficulties and in which it is supposed the children are consequently destined to have low literacy achievement, at least by school measures. The policy and professional literature in family literacy, if not the research literature, abounds with claims that there is a 'cycle of underachievement' which be can be broken, but only by targeting parents' and children's literacy at the same time and in the same programmes. Conspicuous advocates of this view in the US have included Nickse (1990) and Darling (1993), and in the UK the Adult Literacy and Basic Skills Unit (1993a). It leads directly to the idea that targeting intergenerational family literacy programmes on families where parents have literacy difficulties will have a major impact on literacy levels in society.

Despite a certain common-sense appeal this idea is poorly supported by research evidence. It is actually two propositions wrapped together: (a) that parents with literacy difficulties will have low-achieving children; and (b) that low-achieving children have parents with literacy difficulties. Both have to be true for the 'cycle of underachievement' claim to be accepted as an explanation for literacy inequalities in society (and for targeted family literacy programmes to be seen as the remedy). It is not easy to conduct research into the literacy of parents and children in a representative sample large enough to permit statistical analyses but one such study has been carried out in the UK and reported by the Adult Literacy and Basic Skills Unit (1993c). 'Low literacy achievement' for children was operationalised in terms of performance in the lowest quartile of a nationally standardised reading test and for adults in terms of whether or not they reported having reading difficulties. The research claimed to have found 'the first objective evidence of the link between a parent's competence in basic skills and the competence of their children' (p.3) but a re-interpretation of the data by Hannon (2000b) showed that, even if one were to accept the validity of the measures used, the link is far weaker than first appears. According to ALBSU (1993c), those few children who had parents reporting reading difficulties were three times more likely than other children to have reading test scores in the lowest quartile. This might appear to support proposition (a) were it not for the fact that around half the children in these families did not have low scores. There was practically no evidence for proposition (b) since the overwhelming majority (92%) of children in the lowest quartile did not have parents reporting reading difficulties. Literacy inequalities among children in a society such as the UK therefore, on the available evidence, cannot plausibly be attributed to parental literacy difficulties. It follows that targeting family literacy programmes only on those families where parents acknowledge that they have literacy difficulties can make no more than a modest contribution to reducing literacy inequalities among young children.

Evidence of effectiveness

The effectiveness of parental involvement in the teaching of early literacy (the early childhood strand of family literacy programmes) has been known for some time. A review of over 30 studies by Hannon (1995), which also built upon several earlier reviews of the literature by other authors, concluded that there was substantial evidence of benefits, and no reports of negative consequences, of involving parents. Most evaluations concern open or prescriptive approaches to parents hearing children read. It must be admitted, however, that there have been relatively very few randomised control trial (RCT) evaluations (Baker et al., 1998; Wagner et al., 2002). One does not have to believe RCTs are the only way of conducting evaluations, or that they are the gold standard, to wish that now and again they could be used in comparing family literacy programmes to alternatives in this way, especially in view of the bold claims made for their effectiveness (Hannon, 2000b). Many evaluations have relied upon quasi-experimental controls (Griffiths and Edmonds, 1986; Jordan et al., 2000) or pre-test/post-test comparisons using standardised tests (in effect using a test standardisation sample as a quasi-experimental control group). Nevertheless, the sheer weight of positive findings is probably sufficient to conclude that parental involvement generally 'works'. What is harder to judge, given the weakness of research designs, is how well it works. There is no evidence that any programme so far developed is guaranteed to have profound effects for all families involved. Some programmes in some circumstances appear to have considerable impact on some families but in other cases effects may be rather modest. The problem of take-up has often been overlooked in evaluations even though, from a policy perspective, programmes with low take-up cannot make much impact at community level. Apart from Hewison (1988), Brooks *et al.* (1997) and Wagner *et al.* (2002), there is a lack of follow-up studies of parental involvement programmes. Neither is there sufficient evidence to compare the effectiveness of different kinds of programmes. In practice the conditions for direct comparison do not often arise. However, research has helped identify factors to be kept in mind in choosing between programmes. For example, Hannon (1995) concluded that some programmes were costly in professionals' time but could be helpful for older children having continued difficulties with reading; others might be suitable for all children at a younger age but may not be sustainable over a long period. Little is known about the effects of combining different forms of involvement. Another gap concerns involvement in writing, the predominant focus having been book reading. In summary, a great deal still needs to be researched but enough has been done to conclude that the parental involvement form of family literacy programme is effective.

What about family literacy programmes that aim to change parents' literacy, too? Here there are numerous small-scale, largely qualitative studies but probably no more than two well-designed quantitative studies. The former are interesting in revealing issues in programme design, the nature of effects and factors limiting effectiveness (e.g. Finlay, 1999; Tett, 2000). The latter have found positive effects for both children and parents (St. Pierre *et al.*, 1995; Brooks *et al.*, 1996). Brooks *et al.* (1997), in a follow-up study, also found that effects persisted. However, there is as yet no evidence that intergenerational programmes combining provision for adults with provision for children (including parent–child sessions) have greater effects, or are more cost-effective, than separate child-focused or adult-focused programmes (Hannon, 2000b). One seriously under-researched issue in those family literacy programmes that require parents' participation as literacy learners is take-up. If take-up is low (and Hannon, 2000b, suggests there are signs that this is often the case), the value of such programmes is greatly diminished. Finally, it is unfortunate, and perhaps a little surprising, that no study has yet set out directly to test the strong claims made for the synergistic benefits of intergenerational programmes as compared to stand-alone programmes.

Gender

This chapter has consistently referred to 'parents' in programmes when generally it would be more accurate to talk of 'mothers'. This is not to say that fathers or male carers are never involved in programmes, only that the numbers are generally low (typically well under 10% in centre-based programmes). Using the word 'parent' is inclusive and helps maximise the number of fathers who are involved (if programmes referred only to mothers, the gendered nature of parental involvement would be reinforced and it is likely that there would be even fewer fathers). Sticking to 'parent', however, must not blind us to the highly gendered nature of parental involvement. Many programmes are sensitive to this issue and have made serious efforts to include men, in some cases adopting this as a primary goal (Haggart, 2000; Lloyd, 2001; Millard, 2001; Karther, 2002).

There are at least three research challenges here. First, it would be helpful to understand more about the gendered nature of family literacy practices and how they vary in different economic and family circumstances (e.g. as men in industrialised countries respond to increased literacy demands in the workplace). Quantitative, as well as qualitative, studies could make a contribution. It would be interesting to know whether men's lower involvement is an artefact of school-based programmes where employment and cultural expectations reduce fathers' attendance; they may be more involved, if less visibly so, in home-based programmes. Second, research could usefully distinguish different kinds of family structure referred to earlier in this chapter and the different roles that men and women now perform as parents, step-parents, grandparents, foster parents, carers within them, or whether or not they are in daily contact with children. Third, it would be helpful to have detailed evaluations of those programmes that have made special efforts to involve men. To be really helpful, such studies need to go beyond documentation of interesting cases to a quantitative evaluation of key issues such as take-up and outcomes.

Bilingualism

More research is needed into programmes for bilingual or multilingual families. There have been valuable reports of research programmes (Auerbach, 1989, 2002; Delgado-Gaitan, 1990; Hirst, 1998, 2001; Brooks et al., 1999; Blackledge, 2000; Kenner, 2000; Cairney, 2002) which point out how such families can be different (for example, in relation to the gendering of parenting, expectations of children) but also how they can often be similar (such as in parents' aspirations for their children). What also emerges is how families are perceived by educators (who may grossly underestimate the cultural resources of homes). However, much of the literature concerning family literacy programmes concerns monolingual, English-speaking families. As we enter the twenty-first century and take an international perspective, it becomes ever clearer that bilingualism and multilingualism, rather than monolingualism, will be the norm. Some of the issues to be investigated are very complex. For example, the first language of some families may not have a written form or, if it does, it may not be much used by family members. Parents' literacy can appear limited in comparison with what is familiar in industrialised countries. Parents' aspirations for their own and their children's literacy may or may not accord with the assumptions of programme designers and national policy-makers. Different cultures, different concepts of childhood and different pedagogies may require their own programmes and desired outcomes. Research still needs to catch up with global realities.

Training and professional development

If early childhood educators are to play a full part in family literacy programmes, they need appropriate training and professional development opportunities. In Chapter 5 we argue that working with adults demands a different awareness and set of skills than does working with groups of children. Nutbrown et al. (1991) proposed a framework for pre-service and in-service provision within which early childhood educators could become better equipped to meet the demands of family literacy programmes and they urged research into key issues. Since then there has been very little progress either in the provision of training and professional development or in associated research. Hannon and Nutbrown (1997) investigated teachers' use of the ORIM framework referred to earlier and further work is reported later in this book, but that is only one variety of family literacy work. Potentially, there are as many issues worth researching in training and professional development in relation to family literacy work as there are in relation to wider aspects of early childhood and adult education. There is the issue, for example, of whether family literacy teachers/tutors should be reflective practitioners or technicians implementing – and obediently following – prescriptions of programme designers (Hannon *et al.*, 2000). Another issue is the role of organisations providing or accrediting training who may use the opportunity to impose their particular models of family literacy. We shall visit this theme in Chapter 6. As we hope this book will demonstrate, research can enable a more open and critical approach to programme development and to related professional development.

Policy relevance and policy research

It is by no means clear what role family literacy programmes should play in relation to mainstream, compulsory early childhood education. It could be argued that all education should take a family approach; alternatively that family literacy programmes can never be more than an adjunct to mainstream provision, perhaps only in areas of disadvantage. Research has a role to play here, not only in providing evidence – particularly about take-up and effectiveness – to inform family literacy policies but also in examining and critiquing those policies. One area where there is scope to do this concerns the claims made for family literacy programmes. Some of these seem rather extravagant. In the US, the National Center for Family Literacy (1994) has claimed that family literacy programmes enable 'at risk families with little hope to reverse the cycle of undereducation and poverty', bringing about changes that 'pave the way for school success, and thereafter life success' (p.1). Brizius and Foster (1993) have claimed that family literacy 'provides disadvantaged children with educational opportunities that can enable them to lift themselves out of poverty and dependency' (p.11). Although it is to be hoped that family literacy programmes can make a useful contribution to these goals, promising more than the research evidence warrants may store up trouble for the future.

Conclusions

This chapter has shown that family literacy programmes have, over the past two decades, come to occupy an important role in early childhood literacy education. There is fuzziness in the conceptualisation of family literacy programmes but this reflects the variety that has been, and continues to be, developed. The effectiveness of programmes is reasonably well established in a general sense but there remain significant unanswered questions about the extent and duration of effects, the benefits of combining the different components of programmes, and the limiting effect of low take-up. There are also other areas to be developed, relating for example to implied deficits, gender, bilingualism, training and policy. These are to be expected in any field of education but may be more exposed in family literacy programmes and all of them can be illuminated by future research, including research to be reported in later chapters of this book

Taken together, Chapters 1 and 2 set the policy and research contexts for family literacy work in early childhood education. In Part II of this book we describe the theoretical basis for the REAL project, the design of the project and practical activities engaged in by parents, children and teachers.

Note

A version of this chapter was originally published in Hall, N., Larson, J. and Marsh, J. (eds) *Handbook of Early Childhood Literacy Research.* London: SAGE (2004).

PART II

Developing a Family Literacy Project: Practice and Experience

This part of the book explains how one particular family literacy programme was developed by the REAL (Raising Early Achievement in Literacy) Project.

Chapter 3, 'Building a framework for family literacy practice', explains the particular view of early literacy and family literacy work developed through the REAL Project. It describes the theoretical underpinnings of key strands of literacy and four important roles that parents can play. The chapter demonstrates how the conceptual framework ORIM was constructed. Chapter 4, 'Using the ORIM framework to develop a family literacy programme', draws on examples from over 800 home visits made by teachers to families to answer the question 'What did they do?' Each cell of ORIM is addressed, with examples showing what teachers and families actually did. The chapter concludes with a profile of work with one family, showing how the programme was developed with them over the duration of the project.

Having focused on how parents and teachers together supported children's early literacy development, Chapter 5 moves on to discuss 'Opportunities for parents as adult learners'. It describes a view of adult learning, its differences from young children's learning and how a family literacy programme might appropriately support parents who want opportunities to further their own learning as adults. This part of the book concludes in Chapter 6 with a descriptive evaluation of the ways in which the family literacy workers were supported through a professional development programme. It gives details of the approach taken to offering professional development to family literacy workers and makes some suggestions about how it might be offered and what such a programme might include.

3 Building a framework for family literacy practice

Chapter summary
- Introduction
- The story of the REAL Project
- The ORIM framework
- Four strands of early literacy development
- Four key roles for parents in their children's early literacy development

Introduction

This chapter shows how a family literacy programme might be developed using families' existing knowledge as a starting point. It details how the programme can be devised (whatever its duration) using the ORIM framework developed by Nutbrown and Hannon (1997) and, as Chapter 12 will illustrate, now widely used in the UK and other countries.

The story of the REAL Project

The REAL Project began in 1995 in Sheffield, a city in the north of England, and brought together the university, the local education authority and many Sheffield schools to promote family literacy work with parents of pre-school children. From the outset the project had six aims:

1 To develop methods of working with parents to promote the literacy development of pre-school children (particularly those likely to have difficulties in the early years of school).
2 To meet some of the literacy and educational needs of the parents so involved.
3 To ensure the feasibility of methods developed.
4 To assess the effectiveness of the methods in improving children's literacy development at school entry and afterwards.
5 To disseminate effective methods to practitioners and to equip them with new skills.
6 To inform policy-makers about the effectiveness and implications of new practices

Structure of the REAL Project

The REAL Project had two phases. In the first phase (1995–96), early years educators working in schools and young children's centres across the city collaborated with Cathy Nutbrown and Peter Hannon to develop a range of methods for working with parents.

Taking as starting points those methods already being used in schools and centres and the ideas already developed by members of the project team, together they created a 'bank' of new methods and resources designed to address the literacy needs of parents and pre-school children (Weinberger et al., 1990; Nutbrown et al., 1996; Nutbrown and Hannon, 1997). Working groups focused on different strands of pre-school literacy and different target populations to devise and evaluate literacy activities involving parents and children.

This chapter explains how the most promising methods developed in Phase 1 were used in Phase 2 to develop an 18-month 'long duration, low intensity' early literacy programme of work with families. Based on the ORIM framework, the programme had five main components: home visits by programme teachers; provision of literacy resources (particularly books); centre-based group activities; special events (e.g. group library visits); postal communication between teacher and child. The core of the programme was similar at all schools but was shaped by local community circumstances and teachers' styles. A total of 88 families from those ten schools, plus one other school specifically chosen for its bilingual population (eight families working with each teacher) participated in the programme. Teachers were funded for release one half-day per week to work with the families in their group. Adult learning opportunities for parents were also developed. We thought carefully about the appropriate form of adult education to be incorporated into the programme: it had to be voluntary in the sense that, whether or not they participated for themselves, parents could be involved in the child-focused part of the programme. We offered two opportunities to all parents in the programme: (1) information, advice and support to access local adult education from various providers, and (2) a course devised on the REAL programme and accredited by the Open College Network. We tried to make these opportunities as relevant and attractive as possible to families, and details of work specifically for adults are also discussed in Chapter 5.

Teachers from the programme schools participated in a specially devised professional development programme which included five days at the start of the project followed by monthly twilight meetings during term time. (The teacher working at the bilingual school was experienced in her own right and had other links with the university team, so participated in the twilight meetings but not the initial five days.) It was of crucial importance that the teachers who made up the project team felt equipped and confident to develop and implement the programme with families. Issues of professional development and the particular experiences of the REAL Project teachers are outlined in Chapter 6; further perspectives of the teachers are discussed in Chapter 8.

The project took place at a time, 1995–99, of considerable strain and difficulty for education in Sheffield as elsewhere in the country. As Chapters 1 and 2 have shown, early education and literacy teaching were at the forefront of educational policy change.

An experimental design

Phase two of the REAL Project family literacy programme included a randomised control trail (RCT) design. The main reason for using an RCT design is that this was the way to identify any benefits that occurred in children's literacy scores as a result of the programme. Details of this aspect of the REAL evaluation are in Chapter 11.

Originally, a sample of 176 families with 3-year-olds had been drawn at random from the waiting lists of 11 schools in areas of social and economic disadvantage in the city. All schools were in areas (electoral wards) above the national median on the government's index of multiple deprivation and five were in the most deprived 2% of such areas nationally. At each of the 11 schools, 16 children aged around three-and-a-half were drawn at random from pre-school waiting lists (virtually all families in the areas were on such lists). All but nine families were white monolingual. All families agreed to participate in a university research study on the understanding that half of them, selected entirely at random, would be invited to join a pre-school family literacy programme with the remainder serving as a control group. The literacy skills of all children were assessed before and after the programme. There were eight children in each school in each group. Both groups of families cooperated fully in the study and programme take-up was very high. Attrition in the two groups over the 18-month period of the programme was less than 10%. Two families from the programme group and three from the control group were lost to the study.

The ORIM framework

The project used the ORIM framework (Figure 3.1), which arose out of earlier work to develop literacy work with parents (Hannon, 1995; Hannon et al., 1991) and, in so doing, to facilitate changes in the thinking and practice of teachers and other early childhood educators. Understanding this framework is essential for understanding the project. Chapters 3, 4 and 5 discuss the ideas on which it is based and work which emerged from its use.

The ORIM framework distinguishes various strands of early literacy (environmental print, books, early writing and key aspects of oral language). These are not the only strands that can be unpicked within literacy but, as will be seen later, they are a useful focus. The framework also identifies four key roles for parents whereby they can provide *Opportunities, Recognition, Interaction* and a *Model* of literacy for each strand of early literacy.

As Chapter 4 will show, this framework has provided a basis for schools and centres systematically to plan practical work with parents which supports and extends their literacy role with their children. Work can be focused in different cells of the framework; for example, focusing on work with parents on providing opportunities for early writing, to ensure that all important aspects of early literacy are the focus of attention and action at different times.

Family literacy

The REAL Project was a family literacy initiative which saw parents' and children's literacy as inextricably linked and where adults should have opportunities to develop their literacy and learning as well as that of their children. But the project was more inclusive than the model of family literacy being promoted, at the time, by some US and UK initiatives referred to in Chapter 2, where programmes were restricted to families whose parents accepted adult literacy tuition. As Part III will show, the project was

Strands of Early Literacy Development

	Environmental Print	Books	Early Writing	Oral Language
Opportunities				
Recognition				
Interaction				
Model				

(left axis label: **Parents can Provide**)

Figure 3.1   The ORIM framework

successful in reaching children in disadvantaged communities, regardless of whether their parents were deemed to have literacy difficulties, regardless of whether parents agreed that they had such difficulties and regardless of whether they wished to do anything about them. Though an element of the programme was designed and offered specifically to parents to support their own learning, parent participation in adult literacy tuition was not a precondition for families being involved in the REAL Project and this is important in understanding not only the development and content of the programme that was offered, but also its guiding ethos and value base.

Before moving on to demonstrate the use of the framework in practice, it is important to examine the four chosen strands of early literacy development and the four key roles that parents can play.

Four strands of early literacy development

When developing family literacy work it can often be helpful to distinguish between different strands of literacy:

● environmental print
● books
● early writing
● oral language (storytelling, phonological awareness, talk about literacy).

Many other strands of literacy could be considered here, including: techno- and multimedia literacy, but the above four strands are important elements in children's literacy development.

Figure 3.2 shows how four main strands under discussion here could be further unpicked, illuminating the wide range of literacy experiences that could be encountered by young children, especially in the home environment.

Environmental print

The 'roots of literacy' have their beginnings in the early experiences children encounter before school (Goodman, 1980). These roots include a growing awareness of the forms and functions of print. Children begin to notice what written language looks like and how it is used in everyday life. When such 'roots' are nourished, especially at home in the very early years, children have a good start in school literacy. Goodman wrote of the almost imperceptible way in which early awareness of print can develop in young children:

> I believe that the development of knowledge about print embedded in environmental settings is the beginning of reading development, which in most cases goes unnoticed.
>
> (Goodman, 1986, p.7)

In societies where print abounds, there is no shortage of examples. Commercial print of all kinds can be found on clothing, buildings, packaging, household equipment and so on. It may be temporary and ever-changing as with electronic billboards and digital screens on shopping centres, cars and transport depots (bus and rail stations and airports, for example). Apart from the remotest, most rural and uncommercialised locations, it is true to say that print in young children's worlds is inescapable. Print, such as that found on household packaging and shop signs, is meaningful to young children and has a place in their reading development as children draw meaning from familiar symbols in their environment (Goodman et al., 1978; Hiebert, 1981). In fact, it has been suggested that reading begins the moment young children become aware of environmental print (Smith, 1976) and many children develop a sense of such print awareness long before going to school (Burke, 1982; Goodman, 1980). As Goodman puts it:

> There is no question that there are many cueing systems which support and constrain the embedded print; colour, size, shape, pictorial cues, each in a system of its own, but to the child developing print awareness, a key discovery is that the print communicates a message when a child is asked how he knows the box contains 'lego' and he points to the print.
>
> (Goodman, 1980, p.8)

Goodhall (1984) found that, though 4-year-olds knew that print carried information, they were often inaccurate in their interpretations of that meaning because the strategies they applied to the task of interpreting environmental print were different. The children in her study used the context to 'guess' the words and labels shown to them. For example, many children in England could recognise 'Weetabix' on a cereal packet but might not recognise the handwritten word 'weetabix' when the contextual clues of colour, font and

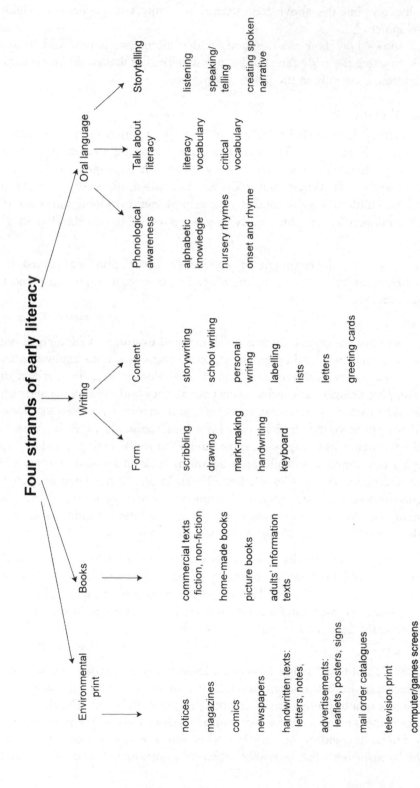

Figure 3.2 Four strands of Early Literacy Development

packaging were not given. Another study of children's approaches to interpreting environmental print (Jones and Hendrickson, 1970) suggested that children often recognise the form of a logo and interpret its meaning, but do not necessarily actually 'read' the print. Studies such as these raise a number of questions about what children are doing when they interpret environmental print. Are they *reading*? How useful is work on environmental print in programmes to support early literacy development? How does it help children to become literate?

Environmental print can stimulate talk about literacy as children ask questions such as 'What does that say'? It also prompts children, at times, to pick out and identify from signs some letters that are familiar to them, perhaps in their own name. Environmental print can stimulate some children to write and children often imitate the writing they see, such as notices or notes left for others.

Environmental print has a place in early literacy development and for most children this kind of reading material is part of their daily experience from birth. As Hall notes, print is part of the everyday relationships in young children's lives: 'Children, from birth, are witnesses to both the existence of print and the relationship between print and people' (Hall, 1987, p.42)

Books

Access to books, especially good-quality books, both children's fiction and non-fiction material, is essential if children are to build a good foundation of reading in their early years. Of course, the definition of a 'good book' is always open to debate, but in the REAL Project criteria for selecting books included, as a minimum, that books should be attractive, well illustrated and non-discriminatory. The books were chosen with great care to maximise the potential that each book had for use by families. The quality of illustration or the overall quality of the story and look of a book are matters for personal judgements but if children are introduced to books produced using the very best techniques in children's publishing, they are more likely to want to use them, want to turn the pages, to look at the pictures and listen to the story and to return to the book later.

Children absorb messages very quickly, both positive and negative, and so the literature offered to children and taken into homes needs to be selected so that it offers positive images of all members of society, of a variety of cultures and of both male and female. The first encounter with a particular book is important, and the cover, the feel, size, shape as well as content make a difference to whether children and parents are attracted to read it or not.

As well as the presentation and the illustrations, the text itself is very important. The best books are written with poetic and memorable turns of phrase and absorbing story lines. 'Well written' can mean many things, but Meek's (1982) idea of the 'intertextuality' and 'multiconsciousness' of books is a useful one to explore. By this, she refers to books that contain more than one thing, perhaps more than one story. She gives the example of a now old children's book, *Rosie's Walk*, by Pat Hutchins (1977), where the words tell a very simple story of a hen going for a walk around a farmyard. It is only in the illustrations that the tale of a fox stalking the hen is told. There is no reference to the fox in the text but the presence of the fox is fundamental to the excitement of the story and the potential the story holds for talk between adult and child. Waterland's (1992) idea of the 'multilayered text' continues this notion of there being more to the book than the words on the page.

All of these things contribute to the readability of the book: that which makes it possible to get to the end without being bored, to read a book again and again, to be unable to put it down until it is finished. Another factor that sustains interest in a book and contributes to the readability is the content in the actual story-line. What is the book about? Can children relate it to their own lives and everyday experiences? Does it provoke feelings and thoughts related to them and does it extend knowledge? All these elements come together in books that foster the development of children as readers who enjoy books and in the process learn to read and gain further knowledge about the world and themselves. Meek (1982) argued that reading books and stories together is a fundamental of reading:

> In the early stages of helping children to learn anything, the adult has to do a great deal. You can see this clearly as children learn to talk, when, right from the start, the learner takes part in real conversations – even by making noises in response to something said to him [sic]. Gradually the nature of the sharing changes and becomes more a matter of taking turns. So with reading and writing. A mother looking at a picture book with a four-year-old who is telling her a story about it is doing something essentially the same as a university tutor discussing a text with a student.
>
> (Meek, 1992, p.12)

If books are introduced to babies, the book is a particular kind of tool for interaction, like a rattle or a soft toy, but with the added dimension of language. If books contain words, the same pattern and rhythm exchanged between parent and baby is repeated each time the book is shared. The youngest baby can enjoy the rhythmic 'Once upon a bicycle so they say . . .' in Ahlberg's *Jolly postman* (1986) or the simple repetition of a pop-up book like *Peek-a-boo* (Claverie and Price, 1993). There is much to be said about what makes a good book and why (Nutbrown, 1999b) and there are various perspectives on children's literature and what they 'should' be given to read. As Styles *et al.* (1992, p.9) write:

> Examining relationships between children, adults and reading involves peeling off some of those assumptions (about how and why children ought to read). It may well mean calling into question some long-held beliefs about what reading is; the increasing importance attached to picture books and media education challenges the view that children's fiction means 'books'. More questions emerge about what is in a text and what readers bring to texts. And these questions lead to some serious thinking about power as well as responsibility, as adults negotiate with children about reading.

In recent years there has been a growth of literature for children based on the popular culture of the time. Books related to children's television programmes and films abound and numerous related comics for children are available in most newsagents. Marsh (2000) has argued that literacy related to children's popular culture should be valued and children's use of text in comics, film and TV-related story books, television and other multimedia literacies should be a part of children's literacy repertoires. In the REAL Project, where such literacy was found in families, the project team built on those existing practices. The introduction of books which were not available at the corner shop or in the newsagents or supermarket was then a way of extending the literacy opportunities available to families. Weinberger (1996) carried out a study of children's home literacy experiences and the roles of their parents. The following extract comes from her book *Literacy goes to school.*

> Children need to be given the widest opportunities to choose from texts that have been thoughtfully produced. To extend children's reading repertoires and give them the best chance of finding reading enriching and stimulating. There are many children who have access to these experiences through a choice of reading material at home. But some children do not have these opportunities, and it is for these children in particular that early childhood educators need to provide the very best reading resources, and have methods of exploring with parents ways that a variety of texts may be used by children at home.
>
> Nicholas Tucker, who has written extensively about books for children, reminds us that any book or piece of writing that is meaningful for a particular child at a particular time will enrich them and become part of their journey towards becoming more literate. In his words, we need to:
>
> > 'remember that less meritorious forms of writing can always have good effects should they happen to respond to their readers' particular needs at the time' (Tucker, 1993, p.116)

Elaine Moss (1977) illustrates this with a story of her adopted daughter's affection for a cheaply produced, and in her eyes, expendable book, which contrasted with the 'great classic picture books' that she thought were much more suitable. What she came to realise was that the story's content about the little kitten that was taken in and cared for had a deep significance for her daughter who, in turn had been taken in and looked after by her new family. She concluded that the book, although 'artistically worthless . . . hack-written and poorly illustrated', was very important for her child because its emotional content was right. It is worth bearing this story in mind before jumping to dismiss texts which do not readily conform to our ideas of what suitable reading material looks like.

Many of the books with which children are most familiar in their early years at home are actually different from the types of books they meet in nursery and school. What this difference in the settings of home and school implies is that those people who work with young children need to be aware of the children's early reading experiences at home, including information about the books which children know best, and their favourite books. It is therefore important to help children identify lessons from texts they know through talking with them about what they have already come to understand, instead of starting totally afresh in school. This helps the transition from home to school literacy for the less confident and less experienced children, and gives early childhood educators deeper insights into the literacy competencies with which children come to school.

(Weinberger, 1996, pp.125–6)

There is plenty to consider when thinking about the quality of reading material for young children. One thing the REAL Project attempted to do in loaning books to families was to bridge any potential divide between 'home' books and 'school' books in order to maximise children's repertoire and enhance the potential for future literacy achievement.

Early writing

Since the 1980s increasing attention has been paid to the development of young children's writing. Research into children's early mark-making (Goodman, 1980; Harste *et al.*, 1984; Ross and Brondy, 1987; Ferreiro and Teberosky, 1989) began to challenge the traditional belief that children could not and should not write until they went to school. As more and more was understood about 'emergent' or 'developmental' writing, teachers in the early years began to watch what children were doing and incorporate provision and support for such writing behaviours and interests into the pre-school curriculum. Ferreiro and Teberosky's (1989) work focused on the hypotheses about writing which children generated for themselves as they tried to understand writing rules and conventions. In their study of Spanish-speaking children they found that many children expected written strings of letters to 'mean' something and strings of letters for people's names were expected to be proportionate to the size (or age) of the person concerned, rather than the length of the name. Notes from their research report recorded that:

> David thinks that the written representation 'papa' is longer than the one for David Bernardo Mendez (his own complete name) . . . a girl who has just turned five . . . says 'Write my name. But you have to make it longer because yesterday was my birthday.'

(Ferreiro and Teberosky, 1989, pp.180–4)

Gregg's writing in Figure 3.3 was done when he was four years and one month old. It illustrates Ferreiro and Teberosky's research into this hypothesis. While the strings for 'my dad' and 'my mum' both contain nine characters, Gregg has made the first look bigger. Ferreiro and Teberosky (1989) summarise children's writing activity in relation to the hypothesis that a bigger object must have a bigger word:

> They do use greater numbers of graphic characters, larger characters, or longer graphic strings if the object is bigger, longer, older, or if a greater number of objects are referred to.

(Ferreiro and Teberosky, 1989, p.184)

They also argue from their data that writing is not copying an external model. The children in their study explored various ideas and hypotheses about writing – writing they argue, doesn't depend on graphic skill (their ability to make letters look conventional) but on the level of conceptualisation about writing – that is, the set of hypotheses they have explored for the purpose of understanding writing.

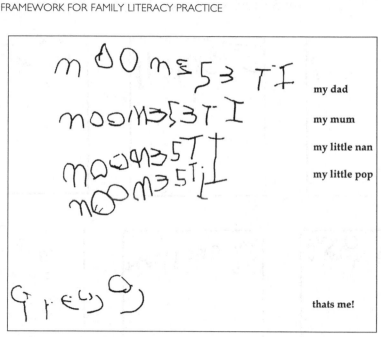

my dad

my mum

my little nan

my little pop

thats me!

Figure 3.3 Gregg's writing

To be effective in supporting young children's literacy development, teachers and parents need to understand what helps children to write, what forms their early writing might take and how writing develops. In Figure 3.4 the pattern of writing development is shown, from early marks to a more conventional and understandable message. Equipped with this knowledge, adults can tailor their interactions and support in ways which match developmental stages rather than battling against them.

Ross and Brondy (1987) suggested that in order to progress successfully in reading young children must come to understand that speech can be written down. Goodman (1980) discussed children's approaches to the development of a concept of directionality, approaches to letter formation and spelling strategies. She suggested that, early on, children who understand that there are 'correct' ways to spell words will ask adults how to spell. But some children have sufficient confidence and knowledge of letter sounds and blends to generate their own spelling rules. Hence, for example, 'house' is written HOWS, 'picture' as PICHER, 'girl' and GRL; as children use what they know to forge the words they wish to use.

Harste *et al.* (1984) considered children's readiness to take risks with literacy, seeing 'risk-taking' as a central process of written language. They suggest that 3- and 4-year-olds who take risks with writing and spelling make better language learners. Nutbrown (1997) has suggested that children engage in three processes as they make sense of writing: *observation* – they see people writing and using writing; *interaction* – they are involved in writing exchanges with adult models as part of real, everyday tasks; *representation* – they make their own graphic marks which gradually become more conventional in appearance as their skills develop and knowledge about writing increases. Some researchers have studied the writing of their own children (Payton, 1984; Baghban, 1984;

Figure 3.4   Stages of writing

Schickedanz, 1990; Bissex, 1980). This has resulted in a small number of case studies which has proved a useful source of material to examine the fine detail of children's early literacy achievements and patterns of learning.

Recent developments in the UK have resulted in a clear focus on early progress in literacy and numeracy and, though the 'performance' teaching of the literacy hour may have given way, to a greater or lesser degree, to a more learner-focused pedagogy, the introduction of the Foundation Stage ensures that literacy and numeracy remain centre stage in the early years curriculum though educators are urged to include play in their teaching and learning strategies (QCA, 2000).

Some children develop their sense of purpose through their early years by writing and being part of family writing experiences – writing birthday cards, lists, notes for other members of their family. Such experiences should support children's writing achievement in group and school settings throughout the Foundation Stage and beyond. For many children, home and school literacy can be different. Writing may be purposeful at home and less so at school, or there may be little writing at home and much more at school. Wray *et al.* (1989) noted that:

> Everyday in every school, teachers who have mastered the conventions of writing exhort their pupils who haven't, to write and to write for no apparent reason. All they know is, the more they write the better they become at it, so eventually the practice becomes an end in itself.

Much writing at school is done 'because it is' whereas writing at home, in 'real life', occurs when there is a need to communicate, remember and create.

Goodman (1980) suggested that children who understand early on that there are correct, conventional ways of spelling words will ask adults 'how do you spell . . .' and some children who have more literacy confidence and knowledge of letter sounds and blends will generate their own spellings without inhibition. Similarly, Harste *et al.* (1984) see 3- and 4-year-olds who are 'risk-takers' as better language learners. The balancing act for parents and early years educators is to help children 'have a go' and use adults to help them learn conventions and rules as appropriate.

Oral language (phonological awareness, storytelling, talk about literacy)

Three aspects of oral language appear to be key to children's literacy learning and development: storytelling, phonological awareness and talk about literacy. Until relatively recently, work with parents on these aspects of oral language in order to influence literacy was new ground, with little reported work on what has been done with parents on oral language that contributes to literacy development. On the other hand, it has long been recognised that oral language is the foundation of written language, it being more difficult to learn to read and write if you can't speak or understand speech. It seems to be the case, however, that even though the importance of oral language has been implicit in language development, it has not always been clear which aspects of oral language can be influenced by work with parents in their children's early years.

As Chapter 2 discussed, earlier work with parents focused largely on written language, but research suggests that a wider perspective is important. It is research which shows the importance of certain aspects of oral language (notably phonological awareness, storytelling and talk about literacy) that has influenced this change, leading to the suggestion that rather than trying to change fundamental aspects of language use, it is more effective and feasible to focus on these specific aspects of oral language. The remainder of this section summarises some of the key research.

Phonological awareness

During the 1980s researchers at Oxford University helped to pinpoint the importance of phonological awareness in children's literacy development (Goswami and Bryant, 1990; Maclean *et al.*, 1987). Written language is usually a way of representing speech, or the sounds we use in speech. Therefore, using written language usually presupposes some knowledge of the sound structure of oral language. The question is, what kind of knowledge of sound structure is most useful in early literacy development? Knowing the sounds that the 26 letters of the English alphabet supposedly 'make' is not all that helpful to young children, partly because they are so inconsistent. For example, 'c' next to 'h' as in 'ch' in 'chair' sounds quite different from the 'c' next to 'a' as in 'cat'. And it does not help much to know that the letter 'N' can represent the sound 'nuh' if such a sound is not heard in some words – as in 'string'.

Linguists break oral language down into 'phonemes' – with a supposed 44 in the English language (but regional accents, personal pronunciation variations and other factors challenge this 'absolute'). It seems that phonemic awareness is helpful in reading and spelling; however, phonemes are often difficult to spot and phonemic awareness seems to be something which people acquire as a result of becoming literate rather than something which, once acquired, helps us to become literate. Goswami and Bryant (1990) suggested that the important thing for children to be aware of is what they call *onset* and *rime* in spoken words, 'onset' being the beginning sound and 'rime' being the end sound of a word. Words like 'stroke', 'stripe', 'strum', strip' share the same onset and so they are said to alliterate. Words such as 'wing', 'thing' 'ring', 'bring' share the same rime and can be said to rhyme. Goswami and Bryant (1990) present substantial evidence from their studies of pre-school children which suggests that children who are aware of onset and rime find learning to read easier. They show how pre-school tests of this kind of phonological awareness predict reading attainment later; and how pre-school 'training' to help children detect onset and rime can boost later reading attainment.

One way in which children can become aware that words have different parts and that some share endings and/or beginnings is through nursery rhymes which repeat words with the same onsets and/or rhymes. Maclean *et al.* (1987) found that pre-school children's knowledge of nursery rhymes predicted later reading success in school. The obvious implication here is that encouraging parents and young children to share nursery rhymes at home could support children's early literacy development. An implication for family literacy programmes involving parents with young children is that this information should be shared with parents along with books, tapes and video recordings of rhymes being said or sung so that children experience a broad repertoire.

Storytelling and talk about literacy

Wells' (1987) longitudinal study suggested that the best predictor of children's reading attainment in school was a measure of what he termed 'knowledge of literacy' at school entry. This simple test identified how many letters of the alphabet a child could name or 'sound' alongside Marie Clay's 'Concepts about Print' test (Clay, 1972), which assessed whether children could distinguish print from pictures, knew what a word was, could pick out a sentence, and so on. Children's scores on this composite measure of written language were a much better guide to school literacy achievement than measures of oral language development. Other simple measures of literacy (such as whether a child can name a favourite book; Weinberger, 1996) have also been found to be powerful predictors of later reading achievement. This, of course, does not mean that we can improve school literacy attainment by, for example, teaching pre-school children to name letters, distinguish print from pictures, identify capital letters, and so on. It is much more likely that this kind of literacy knowledge at school entry is acquired as a result of other important things happening in the pre-school years. Wells' study of children's language in the home identified key experiences. These were: listening to a story told; other sharing of picture books; drawing and colouring and early writing. Foremost of all of these activities was listening to stories read aloud, which stood out above all the others as being related to the 'knowledge of literacy' measure and later test scores. Wells suggested that the reason for this centred on the various benefits children gain from listening to stories: experience of a genre later encountered in written form; extension of experience and vocabulary; increased conversation with adults; children's own 'inner storying' validated; experience of language use to create worlds; insight into 'storying' as a means of understanding.

Other work by Meek (1982) and Bruner (1987) has emphasised the importance of story in thinking and in literacy development. The challenge for any family literacy programme is how to support parents in telling and sharing stories at home.

The view of literacy taken in the REAL Project is not that school literacy can be improved just by teaching pre-school children letter names, how to distinguish print, words, and so on. It is clearly much more than that. However, it is worth considering how children can be introduced to these things in meaningful and unpressurised contexts. Written language can form an important part of the lives of pre-school children, with some noticing a great deal of print around them and some aware that the adults around them use print a great deal in their everyday lives. It is therefore quite natural for children in these situations to be curious about print, to ask questions and, from time to time, to want to talk about the print they see – just as they do about other things that are of interest to them. Children's vocabularies grow at an astonishing rate in the pre-school years and some of the new words they acquire could well be words which relate to literacy. Clay's (1972) 'Concepts about Print' test was designed to explore children's understanding of some such words, such as 'writing', 'word', 'sentence', but there are many other literacy-related terms that children might acquire and a family literacy programme could develop ways of helping parents support the acquisition of such terms by their children.

This section has briefly outlined key studies and issues that influence our thinking in the development of key aspects of oral language: phonological awareness, storytelling and talk about literacy. Such a clear focus on aspects of oral language in relation to literacy rather than on oral language in general can give focus to literacy work with families.

Four key roles for parents in their children's early literacy development

As we have seen in Chapter 2 (and as research has demonstrated), the idea that families can have powerful influences on children's early literacy development is well established (Douglas, 1964; Davie *et al.*, 1972; Wedge and Prosser, 1973; Newson and Newson, 1977; Nutbrown, 1999b; Weinberger, 1996). Hannon (1995) suggested that there are four main ways in which parents can help their children's literacy development (Figure 3.5), by providing *Opportunities, Recognition, Interaction* and a *Model* for their children of early literacy. This section lists the kinds of actions that parents might engage in, in order to fulfil these four roles.

Opportunities

In the early years parents can provide vital learning opportunities for their children's literacy development by:

- resourcing children's drawing and writing activities
- encouraging their socio-dramatic play

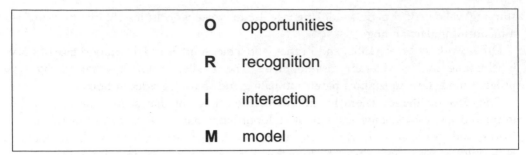

Figure 3.5   Four main ways in which parents can help their children's literacy development

- exposing them to, and helping them interpret, environmental print
- exposing them to nursery rhymes and other word-play rhymes or songs which aid speech segmentation and phonological awareness
- ensuring that story books and other written materials are available with time and space to use them
- enabling children to participate in visits, trips or holidays which provide further opportunities to talk, read and write.

Recognition

It is important that parents are aware of, and can identify, early milestones in development as well as the achievement of clear stages in literacy learning. Parents can provide unique encouragement for children if they show recognition, their value, appreciation and understanding, of children's early literacy achievements by, for example:

- praising children when they 'read' a book
- putting their writing or drawing on show (on the fridge, kitchen wall, etc.)
- telling others (granny, auntie, etc.) what the child has done or achieved.

Interaction

Children need their parents to spend time with them, supporting, explaining, endorsing and challenging them to move on from what they know about literacy to do more. An important part of such interaction is:

- the sharing of real-life literacy tasks where children can make a meaningful contribution; for example: adding their name or mark to a birthday card; helping to write a shopping list; helping to find particular items in the shops; turning the pages of a book while a parent reads.

Through such interactions parents will enable their children to progress from what they can do now with help to becoming more independent in the future.

Other forms of interaction include:

- showing children how to do something
- deliberately teaching a child something – for example, how to write his/her name

- playing word/letter/sound games
- participating in socio-dramatic play.

Models

Parents can act as powerful models of users of literacy if and when children see them using literacy themselves in everyday life. For example:

- reading a newspaper or magazine
- doing crosswords
- writing notes or shopping lists
- following a cooking recipe
- following instructions for assembling furniture or how to work a piece of equipment
- writing cheques
- filling in forms
- signing their name.

These four concepts and the specific actions attached to them form the key roles parents can play in enhancing their children's literacy development.

This chapter has explained the structure and rationale for the ORIM framework. Chapter 4 will demonstrate how this framework was used by project teachers working with families in the REAL Project to develop a family literacy programme.

4 Using the **ORIM** framework to develop a family literacy programme

Chapter summary
- Introduction
- Working with the ORIM framework to focus on parents' roles and strands of early literacy development
- Using ORIM over time – continuity and progression in family literacy work
- Summary discussion

Introduction

In Chapter 3 we explained how the ORIM framework could be built up from the four strands of literacy we identified as important in the early years: environmental print, books, early writing and key aspects of oral language, and four key roles that parents could play: providing opportunities, showing recognition, sharing interactions and being models of literacy users. In this chapter we show how the ORIM framework was used for planning and developing early literacy work with parents in a systematic way so that the REAL Project family literacy programme covered all cells in the framework over time. This section illustrates the kinds of work which can be done with families in each cell of the ORIM framework. Extracts from teacher's notes on their work with families are used to show what actually happened in families' homes and communities. In the final section an account of family literacy work with one family shows how it can be developed over time and how the ORIM framework can be used to track continuity and ensure gradual progression in family literacy work.

Working with the **ORIM** framework to focus on parents' roles and strands of early literacy development

Figure 4.1 (the ORIM framework) shows a matrix which combines the strands of literacy with the roles of parents already discussed in Chapter 3. Each cell refers to an area where work can be developed with families to help parents enhance or develop their support for their children's literacy. Throughout this section the ORIM symbol will be used to indicate which particular aspect or aspects of literacy are under discussion, the shaded cells being those under consideration. Reference to Figure 4.1 will show, for example, that this cell represents interaction around early writing.

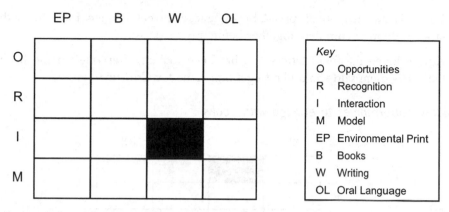

Figure 4.1   The ORIM framework – the focus here is on interaction around early writing

In each cell it is possible to ask: 'What can a family literacy programme do here to support parents?' or 'What can parents do to help improve children's experiences in this area of literacy?'. The examples given in this section are taken from teachers' notes of home visits and group meetings and illustrate some of the experiences which parents, teachers and children shared during the REAL Project.

Opportunities for developing the four strands of literacy

Providing opportunities to engage with environmental print

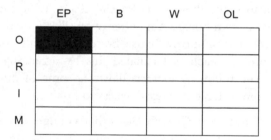

Much environmental print is free, and so the important factor here is to provide children with a range of experiences which bring them more obviously into contact with such print. The following examples from teachers' home visit notes show how a camera, household packaging and some commercially made foam letters for playing with in the bath can provide opportunities for children to engage with the print around them.

> We took a walk around the neighbourhood with a camera – finding letters of her name in the street signs – next visit – I took two sets of the photos and we used them to make a name label for the child's bedroom and I left the rest for the family to make a 'letter' snap game to play together.

> Her mum had collected empty packets as I had requested in my letter sent last week; cornflakes, crisps, etc. We started a scrap book of words and logos that

Louise knows: twix, beef spread, bread, crackers, weetabix, etc. I left this as the task for them to complete together before my next visit.

Adrian loved the foam letters and has been making everyone's name in the bath. His mum said she'd like to get him some for Christmas.

Providing opportunities to engage with books

	EP	B	W	OL
O		■		
R				
I				
M				

One of the most obvious ways to enhance children's opportunities to engage with books is to increase their availability through loan schemes. The REAL Project teachers loaned books from their collection and also encouraged families to visit their local library. Some, though not many, were library users before the start of the project, but most were introduced to their community library for the first time. The community library service was extremely helpful, with local librarians sometimes opening the library out of hours for a private group visit and others offering a specially planned workshop or story session. The librarians helped to make these visits 'special' – involving the children in making things and choosing their own books. A number of families joined the library as a result of these visits and continued to borrow books. Some parents also bought books for their children, and some project teachers facilitated this by arranging visits to a specialist children's bookshop. The following extracts illustrate some of the opportunities which were created for children to have increased access to books.

> Charlotte and I shared *Dear Zoo* with Demi (her younger sister). 'She loved it'. Her mum said 'We've joined the library now. You can get five books out. Demi's got some too.' Charlotte showed me her books – they were very excited about their library books which were obviously something they felt pleased and proud to have.

> Angela and her mum have been back to the library several times.

> Karen and the family were regular users of the local library and already mum had a clear idea of the sort of books Karen liked. At the moment she was interested in novelty and pop-up books, quite short story books, but with flaps to lift, etc., which helped to keep her interested in the story. Karen's mum said that she soon becomes bored if the story is too long.

> His grandma will bring him along to the library workshop as mum is on a course. We always spend the end of the visit looking at new books and he chose which to borrow.

Alan and his mum are continuing to visit Manor Library. Alan had finished a family book and nearly finished an alphabet book – his older sister had helped.

They visited the library again but had forgotten the ticket so they spent some time there reading stories. They are going next week.

Providing opportunities to engage with writing

	EP	B	W	OL
O			■	
R				
I				
M				

At the start of the project families were given a writing pack which included pencils, pens, paper, a glue stick, a notebook and envelopes, thus ensuring that all families had materials for the children to write with. Most families kept the pack in a place which was easily accessible to the children – a few had worries about children writing on the walls or furniture so preferred to give it to the children when they themselves had time to sit with them and ensure that there was no unwanted writing in inappropriate places! Many families added to this writing pack as the project developed and the project team introduced additional materials as appropriate. Opportunities for writing take the form of space, time and materials. The following examples show how simple such opportunities can be, but though simple, they are essential if any further writing development is to take place.

Mum provided Greg a small table to work on.

Both mum and dad provide him with writing equipment and table to write. They write cards together, e.g. for Fathers' Day.

Mum has set up a ring binder with lots of paper in for Regan to draw and write. She is using this a lot. They also have their own pencils and bags to put them in.

Providing opportunities to engage with oral language

	EP	B	W	OL
O				■
R				
I				
M				

Table 4.1   Ideas to help parents provide more oral language opportunities

Opportunities to develop phonological awareness	Lend nursery rhyme and poem tapes Make a rhyme tape with the parents and children Lend rhyme books Send a postcard with a rhyme on it, ask the parent to help the child to learn it before you next meet
Opportunities to develop storytelling	Ask a storyteller to run a workshop Run storytelling workshops yourself Provide story tapes Go to the story times at local libraries Provide puppets, props and 'story kits' so that children and parents can make up stories together Emphasise that young children like the simplest of stories and are often interested in stories which are about real life such as those that begin 'When I was a little girl', etc.
Opportunities to develop talk about literacy	Create times when adults and children talk about books and writing, using the vocabulary which supports this: title, illustration, author, etc.

One of the most important factors in creating opportunities for children to engage in oral language is the opportunity to share talk and play with language with adults. If we take the three aspects of oral language discussed in Chapter 3 (phonological awareness, storytelling, and talk about literacy), we can identify a number of ways of creating opportunities. Central to this is building up parents' knowledge of the importance of oral language; in many cases 'providing opportunities' in the REAL Project meant reminding parents of (or introducing them to) nursery rhymes. Table 4.1 lists some of the ideas that teachers on the REAL Project developed and shared with families.

Extracts from teachers' home visit notes show how these and other ideas were developed in practice.

> We are gradually building up book of rhymes. I left three this week, and more will be added next week at the library workshop session and on next home visit. I have asked her mum if she will continue with the rhymes after the story, perhaps at night, or at anytime Lydia wants to use the props we made together. She already knew 'Baa Baa Black Sheep' and 'Two Little Birds'.

> Alan continues to use his cassette recorder (bought as a birthday present after he borrowed the project cassette player). He enjoys listening to story tapes and nursery rhymes.

> It took Bridget a few minutes to overcome her shyness but then she loved singing into the tape and playing it back. I asked mum to begin a nursery rhyme scrapbook.

> Taped Lydia singing some nursery rhymes – favourites.

> Ready for new scrapbook/glue. Had letters and nursery rhymes ready to stick in the scrapbook.

Has kept all nursery rhyme props and continues to use them.

Mum and dad had collected all typed sheets of rhymes and put them into a separate file. Says them aloud regularly with brother. Has been playing with snap and domino game left on last visit, colour/number and name snap games.

Continue to collect more nursery rhymes for his file. These are included in regular bedtime routine. Also chatted to mum about Shirley Hughes pack and using book terms title, author, etc. Mum said she'd already done some of this as Caitlin had initiated it herself (we've been doing it in nursery).

Talk to mum about importance of nursery rhymes.

Storytelling. Lynn saw the tape recorder and was desperate to use the microphone. She did one song ('Two little dicky birds') and two nursery rhymes ('Humpty Dumpty' and 'Jack and Jill') which we played back (she joined in). We then did a story using props which Lynn enjoyed. She took the props and I told the story. We then listened to 'Goldilocks' on the tape recorder.

Parents have bought a video with nursery rhymes and songs on it.

Nursery rhymes posted to Fay during the holiday were in the folder and two additional rhymes. Older sister had helped. Fay could say nursery rhymes with some prompting.

Mum said that Lee enjoyed receiving nursery rhymes in the holidays – 'he knows some'.

We also recorded some nursery rhymes and listened to tape of *Where the Wild Things Are.*

New things stuck into scrapbook, e.g. my postcard from Safari Park with caption. Alphabet with accompanying picture alongside. All drawn by mum! She kept saying they weren't very good, but they were excellent.

Singing nursery rhymes (especially in the bath).

Showing recognition around the four strands of literacy

Showing recognition of children's use of environmental print

	EP	B	W	OL
O				
R	■			
I				
M				

In order to be able to 'recognise' an achievement, parents need to know something of developmental milestones and literacy behaviours that 'count'. In environmental print, parents may become interested in the logos and signs their children can recall and identify. Parents showing 'recognition' of any such achievement can be supported by leaving a bookmark, sticker, or even a computer-generated 'certificate' for the parent to award to the child for something they have done in literacy. Children may enjoy getting something special to put in their scrapbooks, and there is a role here for parents. The certificate or bookmark can be given for literacy achievements which parents think are important. They complete and sign the certificate and give it to their child. Next time you meet, talk about their reasons for the awards. Some project teachers also used the 'environmental print jigsaw' (Figure 4.2) with parents to help raise their awareness of children's achievements in recognising environmental print.

> At one visit Louise's mother told me: 'We've finished the scrapbook. She recognises a lot. Shall I keep the record sheet and add to it? She is learning new ones all the time.' Mum showed me the part-completed environmental print jigsaw which she had used to record what Louise knew about it and said to Louise, 'Show Diane what you have done.'
>
> Mum had filled in some of the environmental print jigsaw, ticking Greg's achievements and adding others.
>
> Playing a game of environmental print snap made from household packaging, his mum turned to him and said: 'You really know these now don't you! That's so brill!'
>
> We were out in the car and he suddenly shouted, 'That's a BMW bus mum.' Greg's mum showed me the environmental print jigsaw that she had filled in. We then read Greg's environmental print scrapbook together.

Showing recognition of children's use of books

Having an appreciation of 'what counts' as early reading can help parents to identify the achievements of their young children as they use books. The development with the 'book jigsaw' (Figure 4.3) was used by project teachers with individual parents and with some groups to highlight the many small steps which children take in learning to read. Each of these pieces contributes to developing literacy, and when parents shade in the jigsaw they can see what their children can do and which aspects they might wish to spend time

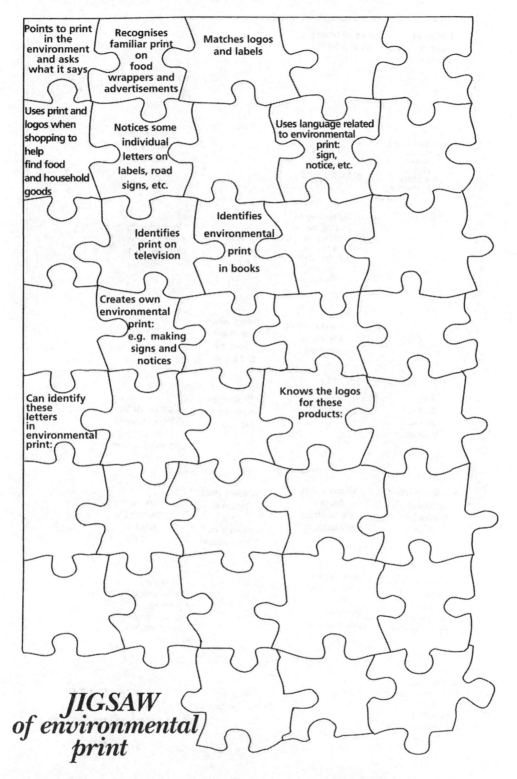

Figure 4.2   Jigsaw of environmental print (Nutbrown and Hannon, 1997)

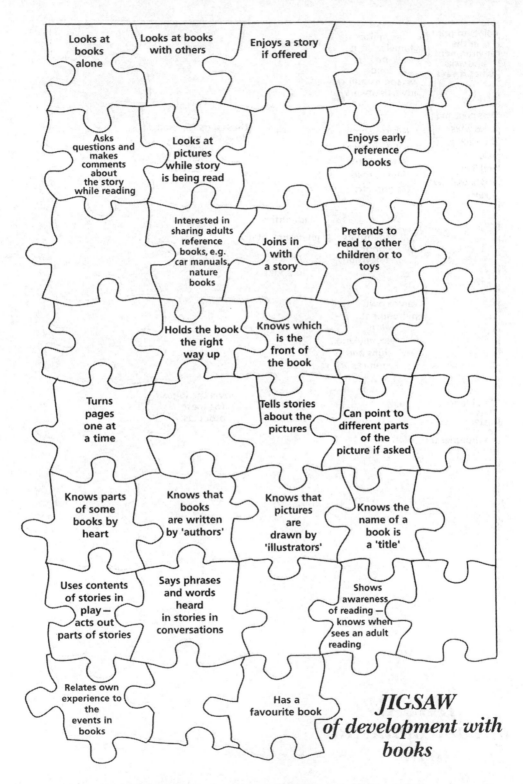

Figure 4.3   Jigsaw of development with books (Nutbrown and Hannon, 1997)

on to help their children further. The blank spaces in the jigsaw mean that parents can also add things which their children do with books which they think are important. The following examples show ways in which teachers and parents worked together to enhance parents' recognition of their children's use of books.

'He knows them all by heart now, I think.'

'He'll be your friend for life now you have read him those stories. He'll listen all day. We went to my mother-in-law's yesterday. Dave said "The children are quiet." I said "Because your dad is reading them a story – that's why!" When Mrs Hayes came he wanted her to read the book she brought. He wouldn't let her leave until she'd read it all.'

'He's obviously taken more in than I thought.'

Mum is very pleased with Michael's developing competence on their PC. He is using it for a variety of reading activities, word and picture matching, etc.

Mum spoke at length about Byron's enjoyment of *But Martin*, commenting on how he joined in and predicted the next page. I feel that she shows more recognition since she came to the group meeting on books and my discussion of what parents can do – we talked about recognition then.

His mum said that she felt Alan 'had come on a lot more than our Alex'. She was aware she had spent more time reading with him and providing pens, pencils paper, etc.

Showing recognition of children's use of writing

	EP	B	W	OL
O				
R			███	
I				
M				

Once parents are aware that young children's writing develops over time and as a result of opportunities and interaction with them, they are in a position to show recognition of their children's efforts, achievements and milestones. Some parents pointed out to project teachers and others just what their children could do. Parents also asked project teachers for help in identifying the developmental level of their children's writing or assessing their progress – often wanting assurance that what their children were doing was appropriate for their age. Asking parents to save and date examples of their children's writing is a good way of building up a collection over time which parents, children and teachers can look back on to identify changes and progression. Some teachers also used the jigsaw of early writing development (Figure 4.4). The following examples illustrate parents' recognition of early writing development.

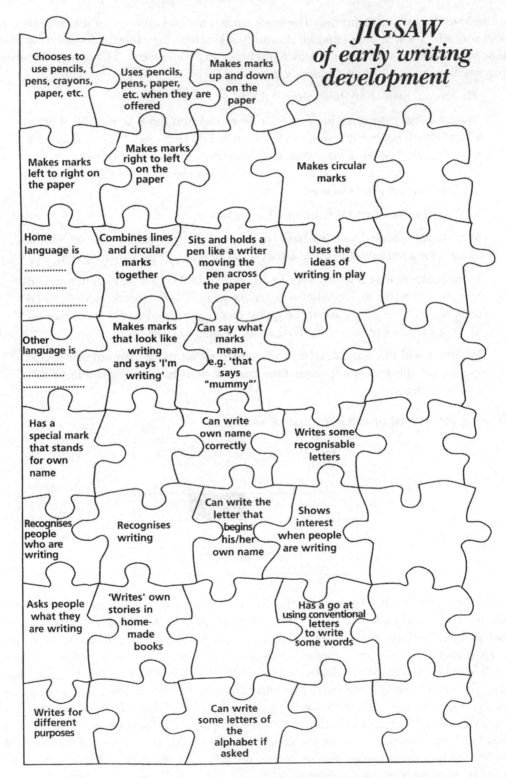

Figure 4.4   Jigsaw of early writing development (Nutbrown and Hannon, 1997)

'He is getting good at writing his name now.'

Patrick's mother asked 'When do children usually write their name? Emily could write hers at 3, but Patrick isn't interested.' A few months later she told me 'Patrick wrote his own name on a birthday card to his friend Callum the other day. It was so good I wanted to keep the card and send another one but Patrick wouldn't let me. He wanted to post it straight away.' She added, 'We have started spending time together doing some words when Carla is in bed. He is getting really good at writing his name. Some of his letters are very recognisable now, if I say it's for you I can get him to do anything! I buy them all a comic each week. Patrick has done some writing in his. It's really good. Look, you can read it, can't you?'

Greg has been practising writing his name. 'He's now doing recognisable letters' said mum. 'He's suddenly very interested.'

'He's getting very good at writing his name.' 'You're very good at 'e's'.

Mum said 'Should she be writing her name by now? I think Demi could at her age. All she does is write little circles. I've tried showing her but she's not bothered. I've done dot to dot letters but she can't do it. I taught Demi with capitals. I thought I'd get it right this time and use lower case, but she's still not ready.'

'She always does circles – is that normal? Do all children do that?'

Shared with mum examples of children's writing development. Mum sequenced them in correct order. 'That's definitely Jodie's stage, so that's about a year. Our Jade does "o"s and "c"s all the time so she's doing right for her age.' Mum shared this with dad when he phoned during the visit.

I showed some examples of children's writing to Charlotte's mum who was pleased to see examples like Charlotte's. Charlotte's dad had been keen to see the stages of children's writing development and he was 'Pleased to see she was doing all right.'

'Claire is really good at writing her name now. It is really clear and recognisable.'

Alice's mum was pleased that she had started writing her name from memory rather than just copying.

Mum says he is constantly writing his name. 'A year ago he wouldn't even pick up a pencil. Now his attitude is so different he just wants to do it.' Keith is working with mum/dad alongside Daniel who is just 3. Mum said dad was doing more at night with him because she (mum) had to go out to work at tea time.

Showing recognition of children's use of oral language

	EP	B	W	OL
O				
R				■
I				
M				

As with other aspects of literacy, to show recognition of children's achievements in aspects of oral language, parents need to know what the developmental milestones are and which behaviours, skills and understanding are important. Table 4.2 lists some of the ideas teachers on the REAL Project developed and shared with families. The extracts from teachers' home visit notes show how such ideas were developed in practice, what parents learned about oral language and how they then commented on children's progression and achievement.

Table 4.2   Ideas for helping parents to show further recognition of their children's oral language development and achievements

Enhancing recognition of phonological awareness	Talking together and listening to children share rhymes Do the 'phonological awareness' bit of the Language for Literacy jigsaw (Appendix 4.1)* Lend rhyme books Send a postcard with a rhyme on it, ask the parent to help the child to learn it before you next meet
Enhancing recognition of storytelling	Talking together and listening to children tell their stories Do the 'storytelling' bit of the Language for Literacy jigsaw (Appendix 4.1)* Tape children telling their stories
Enhancing recognition of talk about literacy	Talking together and listening to children's thoughts and opinions about books and writing Do the 'Literacy word web' (Appendix 4.1)*

*Available at www.sagepub.co.uk/nutbrown_appendix.pdf

From the teachers' notes:

> Sanjay had completed his environmental print scrapbook and had written his name on the front. Sanjay read all the logos with extreme confidence and his mother told me: 'He knows all his letters, can say them all.'

> Mum said that Lee enjoyed receiving nursery rhymes in the holidays – 'he knows some'.

> Angela's mother noticed that she is recognising the letters of the alphabet.

He is getting good at writing his name now.

Also he has nursery rhymes in plastic wallets in a blue file and dad observed him singing each one to himself as he turned the pages, 'and he sang the right one on the page' (picture clues!)

I taped Lydia singing some of her favourite nursery rhymes – her mum said they would play it to granny when they visited.

She had also begun a nursery rhyme scrapbook and she said Bridget recognised a lot of the nursery rhymes from the picture clues.

His mum commented how much Andrew remembers about literacy talk. 'He talks about front covers, back covers, barcodes and titles. He knows which way to hold the book and where to start reading.'

Interaction around the four strands of literacy

Everyone in the REAL Project was very conscious of the role that teachers can play in directly fostering children's literacy achievement, but the project wanted to capitalise on the key role that parents could play and emphasise that it is parents' day-to-day interactions that can really support children's literacy development. Different things appealed to different families but the following are some strategies for involving parents more directly in literacy work with their children.

- Leaving something half-completed – a poster, a snap game, a shopping list, a card to write and post – for the parent to finish with the child later.
- Using alphabet snap (or some other game) and sharing out the pieces to all in the room – assuming that everyone will join in.
- During a making activity – telling the child to ask adults to help.
- Being clear about the parents' role – talking directly to them – 'It is valuable for her if you join in'. 'When you do this with her it helps with . . .'
- Remaining aware of how much parents may learn from the models provided by project teachers – the feeling of being watched may be uncomfortable – but can also be very effective in demonstrating strategies. (Parents may be watching the teachers as well as their child's reactions and achievements.)
- Using group meetings to discuss parents' roles in their children's literacy.
- Planning outings which parents can repeat later themselves, including things to do which encourage interaction.
- Asking parents to watch for specific things – for example: 'While I'm reading this book to James – will you watch him and see how many times he joins in/points to the pictures/finishes the rhymes/etc.'

Parents' interactions with their children were crucial. They could do far more than the project team could do on their visits. The following examples show how parents interacted with their children around each of the four strands of literacy. Many are very 'ordinary' exchanges, but these are powerful ways of sharing literacy in families and so enhancing children's literacy development.

Enhancing interaction around environmental print

	EP	B	W	OL
O				
R				
I	████			
M				

Environmental print is often free and easily obtainable. Indeed, for many who receive large amounts of unwanted 'junk mail' there is often too much! But in this area many items of household items and waste packaging can be useful. The following ideas were used by project teachers to help parents enhance their interactions with their children around environmental print.

- Making logo scrapbooks appeals to some families, with both parents and children contributing to the collection.
- Written communication seems to have potential – it inevitably prompts interaction between parents and child both in receiving and in responding. Where parents and children read the print on the card or letter together, this can be really good value for money.
- Letters cut from magazines and newspapers can be used to make a label showing the child's name – for sticking on their door – or scrapbook.
- Making logo pairs from household products and food can be an enjoyable activity. Many parents have enjoyed playing a snap game or memory game with them. Further interaction continues when some parents help their child find more pairs of logos to add to the game before the teacher next visits.
- Play 'Kim's' game with environmental print cards: 'What have I taken away?'
- Folded paper can be used to start off making an alphabet book or frieze for a bedroom – using cut-out letters from newspapers and magazines.

Many of the above activities involve cutting print from newspapers, magazines and household packaging. It is important to remember that items made at home and for use at home can be less 'polished' than those made for use with many children in the nursery. An environmental print snap game can simply be the cut-out logos – no need to back on card or cover with tacky back – and then it can be used instantly.

One teacher wrote in her home visit notes: 'I left the environmental print jigsaw for Louise to do with her parents and also some ABC cutters and dough. I suggested that they might cut out the letters making Louise's full name.'

Reviewing what parents and children have been doing together between visits from the teacher showed the kinds of interactions parents and children shared. Project teachers recorded the following notes on parents' interactions with their children around environmental print:

Louise's mum said: 'We enjoyed using the dough and cutters but the dough became dried up so we threw it out. I hope you don't mind! Louise used it ever such a lot.'

Sanjay's mum helped him find the letters of his name in a newspaper and cut them out. I introduced the environmental print jigsaw and we (mum and I) filled in all the words and logos that Sanjay recognises already.

We all played environmental print games. Mark loved them. His mum encouraged him to identify the logos he knew. He recognised quite a lot. M came out to the car with me and read numbers on the number plate and asked what the letters were. His mum told him the ones he wasn't sure about.

Bridget likes going to town on the bus with mum/gran so we talked generally about environmental print around us and how she could look at labels on tins and packets of her favourite food, or foods she eats regularly. She likes to play shops, 'counters', etc. They are continuing a collection of environmental print, and they have made a game where her mum hides a word (cut from a magazine or logo) and asks her to find a matching word which may be hidden in another room.

Jonnie and his family have been collecting food labels, looking at different types of print in the environment.

Andrew has been making a scrapbook collection of wrappers, labels, and included several photographs of his summer holiday on the beach, helicopter and bumper cars, so we wrote captions underneath.

The spider we made at the library workshop session was hanging from the fireplace and other props were in evidence. We went through the rhymes we had sung and mum said he was saying them.

Sanjay's mum showed him how to use the magnetic letters.

Enhancing interaction around books

	EP	B	W	OL
O				
R				
I		██		
M				

Sharing books together is clearly key to enhancing children's knowledge and love of reading. In the following examples, we can see how many of the families incorporated book sharing into their daily lives.

Louise and mum read 'Old McDonald had a farm'.

Mum commented that Daniel (younger brother 2 yrs 10 mths) and Keith were now in a routine of bath at 6pm and then half an hour of activities (left from the project) and reading. Daniel wanted to join the library to be like Keith so whatever mum did with Keith she was making a conscious effort to do with Daniel.

Alan and mum are continuing to visit Manor Library. Alan had finished family book and nearly finished alphabet book – older sister had helped.

Greg and mum read the book and then filled in the book review together, mum asking Greg what he liked about the book and writing it down.

Mrs B has difficulty reading. She proudly told me that Curtis looked at the pictures and because there wasn't much writing, 'made up wonderful stories'.

Reading book at bedtime – mum and dad take turns.

His dad enjoyed reading Keith's favourite book to him at bedtime.

Enhancing interaction around writing

	EP	B	W	OL
O				
R				
I			███	
M				

Writing together, whether to make a book, add a greeting to a card, or make a shopping list, is part of the important interaction around writing which helps children to practise their skills and learn the usefulness and power of writing. The following examples show the variety of writing interactions which took place in families.

Her mum was keen to show me their scrapbook. Suzy had done more face pictures and mum has started to put scraps of writing and some examples of environmental print, etc. in too. Dad's birthday card which Suzy had written was also pasted in.

Bridget has been spending a lot of time writing and had made a lovely book with her dad about a family visit to the seaside.

Alice had a lot of lists in her folder that mum had encouraged her to do, with pictures on the lists for the shopping where Alice had tried to draw apples and bananas. Mum had also spent some time doing writing patterns and Alice had coloured these in.

We decided to write a letter to Father Christmas. Suzy and her mum cut out a picture and together we wrote the letter. We chatted about all the work they've done together over the last 18 months. Mum completed the writing jigsaw again (she had done it at the workshop but other things could be added now).

Mark had been doing lots of drawing and writing with his dad. There was also the most complex game which they had drawn on paper which covered the whole of the top of the coffee table.

Mum has written a wonderful 'Waggy dog' story and Felicity has drawn pictures to go with it. Mum and Felicity are now very interested in reading stories together.

Enhancing interaction around oral language

	EP	B	W	OL
O				
R				
I				■
M				

Interaction around oral language is really about sharing language – so there's lots of talking here. The following strategies were used by the project team to enhance interaction around oral language and support parents in this aspect of early literacy development.

- Using a 'Rhyme sack' to encourage parents to share a nursery rhyme – allocating roles – 'Will you help Sally find the things out of the sack while I say the rhyme?'
- Writing to the family reminding them of the date of your next visit – giving a clue about the nursery rhyme character who will come with you.
- Making simple nursery rhyme puppets using materials that parents are likely to have at home.
- Finding all the letters of the alphabet, sticking the letters on card (cornflake packets, etc.) and cutting them out will provide a set of alphabet letters – magazine covers and newspaper headlines make a good size for this activity.
- Including rhyme books in the loan collection.
- Asking parents if they can remember any playground rhymes from their school days.
- Including some wordless books for loan which encourage storytelling rather than reading.
- Taking some story props or small-world toys on a home visit and making up a story.
- Asking parents to tell 'true' stories about everyday things – going to the shops, losing keys . . .
- Taking a 'story bag' which contains an interesting object which can spark off a story.
- Talking about storytelling strategies with parents.
- Reminding parents to use appropriate vocabulary (cover, author, page, illustration, etc.) if they are reading or writing with their children, suggesting that they make a point of reading the 'title' and the name of the 'author'.

The following examples show how parents shared interactions with their children which supported the development of children's phonological awareness, storytelling and knowledge of literacy language.

> I made a new resource bag for Adrian, focusing on storytelling using *Gingerbread man* (one of his favourite stories). We looked through it together. It has two versions of the story; finger puppets, Ladybird colouring book of story (with short text extracts on top of each page) and duplo man, woman, horse, cow and fox. We also made a larger gingerbread puppet to put fingers through for Adrian to use. Mum made one with Leon too.

> They enjoyed playing alphabet snap. It has been well used and the box was torn with use!

> She has started singing nursery rhymes at bedtime (following mum's encouragement). She now sings 'Humpty Dumpty', 'Jack and Jill' and 'Hickory Dickory' every night.

> As a lead into our planned library workshop sessions, I wanted to focus on nursery rhymes. So the card sent out set the scene by asking them to fill in the missing words of the rhyme. On the visit I took along three photocopied sheets of rhymes to make into a book and appropriate activities. 1 2 3 4 5 – card fish, stuck with sequins, piece of dowelling and string for rod. 2 little birds – kitchen-roll middles, felts to decorate and tissue for wings; baa baa black sheep – felt pieces/string for three bags of wool, cut out numbers 1, 2, 3 and left felt for parents to complete the rhyme.

> Alan and mum went to the library group visit and have been back since. 'Alan likes to choose his own books.' After using REAL tape recorder, mum bought Alan one for his birthday. He played nursery rhymes tape and sang along. Mum has noticed that 'he's wanting to write more letters now'.

> They are maintaining the scrapbook and adding new nursery rhymes to it after each visit.

> Watched nursery rhymes video and then used finger puppets as a prompt for Alan to tell the rhymes.

> I began the ABC scrapbook with Sanjay and his mother. He found cutting difficult and his mum seemed perturbed by glue so I suggested that they draw pictures of Sanjay under 'S', mummy under 'm', and daddy under 'd'. We started this during the visit; Sanjay wrote his name too. The next visit, the ABC book was complete but pictures for a few letters were missing. Mum had written words to match the pictures.

> Took card, paper and letters to make a large poster of his name. James particularly liked using the scissors and was proficient at this. The next time I went they had used paints, felt tips and printing to make James' name.

Adult models of users of the four strands of literacy

Being a model of a literacy user means being aware of how and when you use literacy and making a point of letting children see you doing it. It is difficult for parents to read books (or even newspapers or magazines) when they have young children and many report that they wait until the children are in bed before sinking into a chair with something to read. But it is important for children's literacy development to see their close adults using written language. Programmes can encourage parents to make a point of using literacy in front of their children: reading a recipe, the television guide, instructions for a toy or piece of equipment, car maintenance manual, writing greeting card or jotting down a note. The following examples of 'being a model' show what happened in the REAL Project.

Providing models of users of environmental print

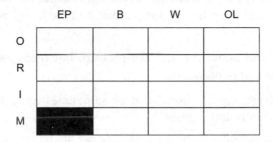

Expert users of environmental print often absorb the messages from print in their surroundings without anyone knowing they are doing so. Therefore, being a model of environmental print sometimes requires a little more thought than, say, modelling being a reader. Sometimes it's necessary to say, for example, 'I'm just reading this notice to see what time the shop opens' or 'I'm keeping a look out to see what number is on the bus – we need number 97'. They may also be seen reading print on the TV, computer, in TV magazines, the newspaper, looking up a number in a telephone directory, looking through a mail-order shopping catalogue. The following examples show how parents made clear to their children, their use of print in their neighbourhoods and homes.

> On the train Adrian's mum said 'We're getting near – there's the sign for Meadowhall'.

> I heard her mum tell her 'Wait – there's a sale on. Let me read it to see when'.

> Mark's dad showed him the numbers on the petrol pump – 'that tells me how much it will cost'.

Providing models of users of books

Even though many parents say that they don't read for their own pleasure or relaxation in front of their young children, there may be many occasions when children see adults reading. They may borrow their own book from the library when they take their children, a way of modelling use of books which, once drawn to their attention, parents

	EP	B	W	OL
O				
R				
I				
M		■		

can make a point of doing in front of their children so that children see that parents read too.

Helen's dad is attending a 'Basic English' course at the local community school; he is dyslexic and reading aloud to Helen each night has helped him such a lot with his own fluency and confidence in reading, because he was reading words which he could read fluently and the fact that he read aloud was helping him, too.

Mum does not read books for her own pleasure but reads lots of magazines, does puzzles and competitions, etc.

'I read to her every night – her dad does sometimes now. Then I hear her "reading" to her dolls and teddies.'

James' mum said she likes reading books that she enjoys, because her pleasure 'spills over' to James.

Mum also talked about reading for herself. She doesn't like to read books; they take too long, but she does read magazines.

Providing models of users of writing

	EP	B	W	OL
O				
R				
I				
M			■	

This is about letting children see adults writing for everyday purposes: to take a message, jot down a list, write a greeting card, write a cheque, complete a form. When children see adults write, they are often stimulated to 'pretend' to do the same so seeing adults write for a variety of purposes is important.

When they were writing together his mum said 'Write your name on the bottom so we know it's yours'. 'Like this . . .' and showed him how – he watched her intently.

Mark had written a number of shopping lists when mum had been writing hers.

Mum translated Sanjay's Persian to English and he watched her filling in the form.

Providing models of users of oral language

	EP	B	W	OL
O				
R				
I				
M				■

There are several ways in which parents can consciously model their use of the key aspects of oral language which support early literacy development. There is inevitable overlap between 'modelling' and the other three aspects of a parent's role and in oral language particularly this overlap is apparent. The important thing is that children witness their parents' use of oral language – sometimes this will also involve parental interaction with their children and opening up opportunities for them at the same time. Table 4.3 gives some of the ideas used in the REAL Project.

Table 4.3   Ideas for helping parents make a point of being a model of oral language users

Modelling phonological awareness	Initiate the saying/singing of rhymes and jingles Suggest playing I Spy type games Singing modern songs that rhyme and alliterate
Modelling storytelling	Initiate storytelling Make up stories following the child's ideas for beginning and characters Tell true stories Point out models of literacy users in books and on TV: 'He's reading', 'She's writing a letter'
Modelling talk about literacy	Parents themselves use 'language for literacy' in front of the children Do the 'Literacy word web' (Appendix 4.1)* with parents to remind them of all the words which can be used to discuss literacy Encourage parents to do a book review with their children as a tool for discussion of the book Use magnetic letters on the fridge, talk about them and the words they make. Talk about possible words or letters when doing a crossword

*Available at www.sagepub.co.uk/nutbrown_appendix.pdf

Parents developed these and their own ideas to support their children's development in this area. As the teachers' notes show, they also became more aware of the models family members (often unwittingly) provided for the children.

> Twinkle star made at workshop was in bedroom. Mum said whenever she saw it she said the rhyme.

> We do them all the time – they're fun – and jingles from the TV – I say – Let's sing. . . . And so we do!

> She sees me doing the word puzzles now and then – I don't feel bad about it occasionally because I know she can learn something too!

> Her nan is always telling little stories about what happened at the Lunch Club – or in the post office.

So what does a home visit look like?

So far we have seen what has been done in various cells of the ORIM framework. Of course, not all work is discretely focused in one cell; usually activities span several cells, and often teachers covered several cells during a visit, as the following two extracts from teachers' notes show.

> Took storytelling resource bag for Caitlin. We looked at everything together and I explained to mum the idea behind it. Mum commented that Caitlin enjoys telling stories and already knows the Goldilocks story. Went on to use salt trays and chalkboards to model handwriting skills for mum. Talked about importance of developing movements, etc., for writing not always copying adult writing. Mum seemed keen to attend writing workshop so must arrange it for early September. Finish by reading some books left previously and choosing new books to borrow. Caitlin again looked for logos. Mum said they now use more talk about book's title, front, back, author, etc. When I write down books borrowed, Caitlin usually likes to write too. Today she held the books and read the title while she wrote it for me. Mum commented that Caitlin often does this at home. She looks at labels on bottles, packets and writes it down. Caitlin loved teapot book and sang/read rhyme many times as she looked at it. Mum said how much Caitlin enjoyed *Dinosaur Roar*, it's her favourite book so far. I suggested they try the library during the holidays when mum said although Caitlin had lots of books she still liked to read new ones. Mum said she might go. Mum talked to me about having been to college to do adult literacy and maths courses some years ago. Said she'd enjoyed them. It came into the conversation as I was leaving when mum commented, 'with all this to do it's like homework again!', referring to items I'd left for them to do in the holidays.

During this home visit the teacher carried out some planned activities around storytelling, writing, books and talk about literacy. She was careful to explain what was done and why to Caitlin's mother. Through discussion the teacher learned that the mother continued and extended activities between home visits. All aspects of ORIM were reported in these notes for each of the strands of literacy on which we are focusing. What is also clear is the child's enjoyment of what happened and the beneficial influence they have.

> We decided to write a letter to Father Christmas. Suzy and her mum cut out a picture and together we wrote the letter. We chatted about all the work they've done together over the last 18 months. Mum completed the writing jigsaw again (had done it at workshop but lost it). Reported how much Suzy loved *Brown Bear* book, can read it all on her own. Mum planning to buy it for her for Christmas. Showed mum ISBN number and copied it down for her (didn't know you could order books this way). Have joined the library and wants to join Emily too (only 8 months old). They showed me the books they'd borrowed, also got 'Kipper' video to follow up, having read the story. Mum feels Suzy has got a lot from the project. I talked again about the Open College accreditation and said I could help her to do the portfolio. Mum is still thinking about it but I left her the handbook to look through (it would be a great confidence boost for mum). Mum had been talking to nannan about the writing workshop. Wants to continue borrowing books and resource bags for now and I've promised to call and see them after school sometime after Christmas. Mum keen to show me scrapbook. Suzy had done more face pictures and mum has started to put scraps of writing etc. in too. Dad's birthday card, which Suzy had written. Has also started environmental print matching game. Before I left they gave me two presents and a card as it was my last home visit. Mum got quite emotional about it, as did I, says it won't be the same after Christmas: 'It'll seem strange you not visiting'.

This account of a final home visit shows how, together, the parent and teacher reflected on what they had achieved over 18 months. A positive relationship had clearly grown between them and there is a sense of future continuity.

Sometime after the project ended one teacher wrote this account of her home visiting experience:

> It was with apprehension that I approached the house and rang the doorbell. I told myself this was just another home visit; I had after all visited scores of families at home as part of our school's policy of home-visits to children just before they started school. This time, however, it was different. This visit was to be the first of many; it marked the beginning of a long relationship between myself and the family. Although the REAL Project professional development course had provided an excellent introduction to family literacy work, nothing could quite prepare me for this moment! How would I be received? Would they still want to participate? What would they think of the project?
>
> Mrs R greeted me with a smile; she'd been expecting me. Sally was waiting for me too, with her younger sister Kira who watched every move I made in silence. Sally was very shy, although the situation became more relaxed when I showed her my bear puppet, Polly, who helped her to choose some books to share together from my box. As time passed, we all became more relaxed. Mrs R and I chatted and she commented that she didn't really know what to do with

Sally in terms of reading and writing, as she thought that children did not start literacy activities until they went to nursery or school. Later on, however, she showed me a Father's Day card from Sally and her sister Kira in which both children had made their marks. Clearly, there were literacy activities taking place in this home; like most of the others, it was going to be a case of raising parents' awareness of the literacy activities they were already engaging in and extending these practices. It was important to build on the existing literacy practices in each home; what worked for one family might not be appropriate for another.

On subsequent visits we were all more relaxed; Sally had overcome her shyness and her attention and motivation increased. She clearly enjoyed my visits and the activities I planned for each visit. Visits were planned to give similar weight to each of the four strands of literacy; environmental print, books, writing and oral language. In planning, thought was also given to the opportunities, recognition, interaction and models (ORIM) that parents could provide. For example, in environmental print, we collected logos from food packaging that Sally recognised and stuck them onto paper; this became a simple book that she could read. We also played 'snap' with cards made from food packaging. Using resources such as packaging that were easily and cheaply available showed parents that many everyday items could be put to good use with a little imagination and initiative.

Work around books focused on choosing appropriate titles, sharing books with children (discussing illustrations and content, predicting what might happen, using book language such as title, author and publisher) and looking at different genres. In Sally's home, books were shared with increasing amounts of interaction, whether it was myself or her mum sharing them with her. Families were encouraged to borrow from a large selection of REAL Project books at each visit.

Writing activities done as part of home visits were those that illustrated the purposes of writing. Writing birthday cards, Christmas cards, shopping lists and clues for a treasure hunt were just some of the activities I engaged in with the children and their families. On one occasion I told Sally that Polly the bear puppet was not well and asked her to start to make a get well card with me for Sally and her mum to complete and post after I'd gone. Sally drew on the front of the card and began to write inside. At this stage, her playwriting consisted of some of the letters from her name in random order. On seeing this, her mother exclaimed 'Sally, what are you doing?' She then turned to me and said anxiously, 'She's writing her name all jumbled up!' I explained that Sally was in fact 'pretend writing' using the letters she knew: those from her name. Sally's mum seemed relieved and commented, 'You see, I wouldn't know any of this if you didn't come!'

There were three areas of oral language that were covered in the REAL Project; phonological awareness, storytelling and talk about literacy. For the first of these, typical activities included singing nursery rhymes, reciting rhymes onto a tape recorder then playing them back, and making nursery rhyme character puppets using materials such as paper plates, socks and paper bags. Sally was quite reserved on visits that focused on phonological awareness, although her mother reported that she confidently sung the rhymes with the puppets after I'd gone, and that they had made puppets for other nursery rhyme characters. Activities for storytelling included making up stories about family members or toys and retelling traditional stories using props. Finally, talk about literacy consisted of activities to develop children's literacy vocabulary – to use the language of literacy (by introducing them to terms such as letter, full stop, author, write, read, etc.). It also included activities to enhance alphabetic knowledge, such as alphabet snap and alphabet jigsaws.

Although I felt my visits to Sally and the other children on the project benefited the children, I was conscious of the fact that the main aim of the project was for parents to carry on and extend the activities I started. It is unlikely that there would have been any measurable gains in the project children's literacy development had parents not been aware of the importance of their roles and continued with the literacy activities between visits. I worked with Sally and her family over an 18-month period and feel very privileged to have witnessed some of the most important stages of her early literacy development. Sally's mother told me she was very glad she agreed to take part in the REAL Project; that it had influenced the things she did with Sally. The REAL Project acknowledged that parents are children's first and most important teachers, helping them to build on existing literacy practices and recognise their achievements.

My experiences in working with these families were almost all positive; parents wanted to help their children and were keen to implement new strategies and activities. I learned so much from the families I worked with; their enthusiasm, imagination and receptiveness to new ideas were an inspiration. I feel that home visiting was the key to the success of the REAL Project and could benefit many other families in the future.

Family literacy can involve siblings and fathers as well as mothers

Reflecting on the teachers' notes of work with families, we identified not only the literacy events described in this chapter but two additional, important themes which are worth commenting on. Families were all engaged in some literacy at home. Mothers were active, but the involvement of siblings and of fathers is also worth noting.

Involvement of siblings

Of the 88 families involved in the programme, 79 children had siblings. Though the project targeted only one child in each family, many siblings were also included in two main ways: in the activities with the programme teacher and parent during home visits, and in programme-initiated activities with their parent(s) between visits. Additionally, older siblings sometimes helped younger children who were involved in the project by engaging in literacy activities with them (often in activities the programme teacher had left). The following examples give a flavour of the kinds of things siblings became involved in during home visits:

Involving younger siblings during home visits

Keith was writing a letter to Father Christmas decorated with stamped Christmas pictures. His mum commented that he was doing more writing and wanting to do it. We made a Christmas cracker, including joke, chocolate, etc. Keith's 2½-year-old brother joined in with all the activities and his mum said he was picking up a lot of things because he was trying to copy Keith (listening to stories with him and making the things during the visits).

I spoke with Adrian's mum during a review meeting. She told me that Adrian enjoyed using the resource pack, particularly the chalkboard. He had used paintbrushes outside to write on floor and house walls and had used the salt tray. His younger brother Leon really enjoyed it and made lots of patterns.

And between visits siblings were involved too:

Mum has been helping Justin with matching colours and she commented that Bradley (2-year-old younger brother) was remembering them as well. 'I was doing it with Justin and Bradley was only watching.'

Regan's little sister has used the magnetic letters and board more than Regan!

Adrian's mum ... talked about drawing lots of pictures during the school holidays and writing with him and his younger sister Chloe. She said if she wants some peace and quiet she sits and reads to them! Adrian loves books and remembers stories well.

Sally enjoyed 'Grandad Pot' which she borrowed last time. She has started singing nursery rhymes with her mum and little sister Kira especially in the bath.

Older siblings' involvement with programme children between visits

Omar (older brother) and Hansa (older sister) sing nursery rhymes with him.

Travis, Shannon's brother, helps him with his writing and reads to him.

Kristopher (Dean's older brother) had been reading the story to him every day. Dean still enjoyed it. His mum had also read it to him. He was very proud that he had a 'book bag' like his older brother has from school.

Mum said that she hadn't had time to do anything with Philip because of moving, but his older sister Eve has been reading to him occasionally.

Her 7-year-old sister said: 'I write her name and she watches, then she can do it.'

Her mum said Lynn had loved the alphabet snap game. She had played it with mum, dad, grandad and older sister Sara. Sara had also been talking about the letters with Lynn, holding them up and telling her what each letter was.

Katie (12-year-old sister) has begun taking Michael to the library regularly.

Ruksana (8-year-old sister) writes what he asks her to write. They play school. Sometimes he's the teacher. Sometimes she shows him how to write Urdu when she's writing it.

Rebecca (his elder sister) has helped Ralph to make 'three bags full' and he has been singing the rhyme and many others. Mum is very pleased that his confidence in singing rhymes is developing and thinks Rachel has helped this.

Involvement of fathers

At the end of the programme, all families were interviewed. Seven fathers (8.8%) were present at these interviews with the mothers; no fathers were interviewed alone. When asked who helps their child most with reading and writing, 66% said the mother helped most, while 29% said both mother and father helped about the same. The remaining 5% said another relative helped most, usually a grandparent or older sibling.

Teachers' notes of home visits tell an interesting story about fathers' involvement. Parents (nearly always mothers) were asked, during each visit, what they had done between visits. The teachers never directly asked what fathers had been doing between visits; they simply recorded their own work with families and noted what parents told them, so all the accounts of fathers' involvement were volunteered, rather than prompted. It is possible therefore, that the amount of literacy between fathers and children going on in homes is, if anything, under-reported. Sixty-four percent of families reported some literacy activity between fathers and their children between visits. At least 14% of fathers had been at home during at least one home visit and 9% of fathers attended at least one group event.

Teachers' notes give a flavour of the kinds of literacy activities which fathers shared with their children. One mother commented that her partner 'Was always too embarrassed to sing, and things, before' but since the family had been involved in the programme she said 'he does a lot more with them'. Examples show that there are many ways in which children can share the four strands of literacy with their fathers:

Environmental print.
They have completed the environmental print book. We read it together. Some of the packaging was cut out with his dad.

Books.
She shared *Jasper's beanstalk* with her dad while I was visiting. Her mum said: 'Dad read it to her because he reads her bedtime stories.'

Writing.
Suzy's mum told me that her dad often writes with Suzy; he's been teaching her the alphabet and numbers. There's evidence of this in one of the writing books mum showed me. Suzy's dad had been writing a few sentences and Suzy had written hers underneath. Mum commented that he sits and helps Suzy a lot.

Oral language.

Phonological awareness

Dad singing nursery rhymes with Keith, last line of 'Baa baa black sheep' to 'One for the little boy who lives down Bramall Lane' (dad is ardent Sheff Utd fan). This we recorded on the tape.

Justin and his family are continuing with scrapbook work, including mum drawing pictures for Justin on the nursery rhyme sheets. Dad has made up a rhyme about the Teletubbies to the nursery rhyme tune of 'Two little dicky birds' – changing the names of the birds to two of the characters in Teletubbies. He had written it in the scrapbook.

He sings along with dad and his 50s and 60s songs.

Mum said they would practise nursery rhymes in the car. Dad makes his own words up she says. He changes the words to fit in with situation.

Talk about literacy

On holiday they've been drawing letters in the sand with their dad.

Storytelling

We talked about storytelling. She says she sometimes makes up stories but usually prefers to read them. She told me that Adrian's dad makes stories up more than her.

The following examples show how fathers covered all four roles in the ORIM framework:

Opportunities.

Dad has bought her an old diary from work which she's enjoying writing in.

Recognition.

Mum reported how impressed Adrian's dad is with how much he knows about books.

Dad was there and was very pleased that over the summer Craig has learnt to write his name.

Julian wrote a Christmas list at nursery and later that evening he recalled the list to his daddy.

He has nursery rhymes in plastic wallets in a blue file and dad observed him singing each one to himself as he turned the pages, 'and he sang the right one on the page'!

Dad had framed the 2 cards I had sent.

Interaction.

'Dad reads a story every night before they go to bed. Even when he comes home from work he's on the floor reading to them.

I ask if they want to borrow a game. We played alphabet snap which he wanted to borrow. Mum says that dad will enjoy playing it with him 'but Michael will have to let him win!'

They have been playing alphabet snap a lot. Sally loves it. Mum says it has really helped her with recognising letters and says she's going to get some. Sally has played a lot with dad.

Model.

His dad sits and reads car magazines with Jethro.

He's been making more photo-books of their holidays with dad – photographs with captions underneath.

Nancy had written a Mothers' Day card with her dad.

Michael continues to enjoy his computer. Dad has loaded a number of early reading programmes for him.

Using ORIM over time: continuity and progression in family literacy work

So far this chapter has explained how work can be planned and developed to focus on particular cells of the ORIM framework. In reality however, though the focus might be on a particular cell, there is inevitable (and desirable) overlap between cells. We have seen how many family members can be involved and have said that the ORIM framework is useful in ensuring that, over time, all aspects of early literacy development and all four parent roles that we have identified can be focused on. In this section we have reproduced the notes of one of the teachers, Anne Stafford, who visited Robbie. The notes give her account of work with Robbie and his family over 18 months. The project lasted 78 weeks (including various school holidays when there were no visits). The first visit took place in week one.

Visit 1: Focus on getting acquainted with the family and books

FAMILY: ROBBIE WEEK 1

The first home visit.

Focus on a planned aspect of literacy and parent's role

Robbie enjoyed receiving card addressed to him. He recognised his name when mum gave it to him to open and they read it together. At first he couldn't understand why it was for him because it wasn't his birthday! Focus on interest created through box of books. Dear Zoo – novelty aspect of opening flaps and recognising animals. He asked a lot of questions related to this book. Talk about size, shape, etc.

Anticipate what parent might do following the visit

Robbie was very keen for her to read the books and while I was there mum said 'we will read them all again at bedtime'.

Books:

Hungry Caterpillar, Where's my teddy? Dear Zoo.

The aim of this first home visit was to get to know the family, discuss the project and begin a working relationship. In week 1, the teacher focused on choosing books from a selection and sharing the books together, activities which clearly put Robbie at his ease. She was careful not to put pressure on the family during this first visit, and simply suggested that they read the books together before the next visit. The teacher created *opportunities* between mother and child for environmental print by sending a letter confirming the date of the visit. This also provided an opportunity for *interaction* around environmental print (reading the letter together). There were also *opportunities* for the parents and child to read books together after the visit, using some books loaned. Robbie's mother, Wendy, expressed her intention to share the books together (*interaction*) after the teacher had left. Aspects of the ORIM framework covered in this visit have been shaded in.

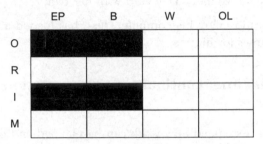

During the second visit, Anne discussed with Wendy what they had done since her first visit. Wendy recognised her son's enjoyment of one book in particular – they both enjoyed it so much they had read it repeatedly. The main focus for visit 2 was environmental print, and Anne left materials with the family so that the parents could provide *opportunities* for environmental print by collecting logos. She intended that the family would help Robbie's *recognition* of environmental print and *interact* with him in the process. Doing these activities together and showing how adults use environmental print, the parents also acted as *models* of expert users of environmental print.

Visit 2: Focus on environmental print

FAMILY: ROBBIE WEEK 3

Review what parents and child have been doing

Robbie and mum had read one of the books in particular over and over again – Where's my teddy? Robbie went through the book with me, pointing out important detail to himself on each page as we progressed. He asked questions. Mum was very keen and confidently expressed how they had both enjoyed the book and why, and she asked if they could keep it again, because she had enjoyed reading it to him. Mum said Robbie had been more interested in the books than the paper and writing materials.

Focus on a planned aspect of literacy and parent's role

Recognition of familiar logos, labels. Labels, wrappers taken from selection of foods, variety of writing forms and some with familiar picture to aid recognition, e.g. penguin on Penguin wrapper. Matched the wrappers which were alike. Robbie was able to recognise some of the wrappers. Took photograph to put inside Robbie's scrapbook.

Anticipate what parent might do following the visit
Making own collection from packets, foods, etc. which they use and are easily recognisable to Robbie. Scrapbook and sellotape left for them to assemble the collection along with any further cards, letters, writing from me. Reading books: it will be interesting to see on next visit if Robbie has spotted any more detail in illustrations.

Books:
Where's my teddy (request from Robbie's mum to keep this book) Where's Spot?

Aspects of the ORIM framework covered in visit 2 are shaded in dark grey while those covered in earlier visits are shown in pale grey.

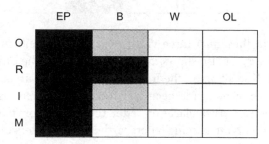

At the start of each visit, Anne reviewed what the family had been doing since the previous visit. Between the second and third visits, they had made collections of photographs and logos from environmental print, and so Anne used this opportunity to *model* writing. The main planned focus of the third visit was on writing; in this case a pretend passport for the child to take with him on holiday.

Visit 3: Focus on writing

FAMILY: ROBBIE WEEK 11

Review what parents and child have been doing
Making collection of wrappers, labels, and included several photographs of his summer holiday on the beach, helicopter and bumper cars, so we wrote captions underneath. Had not followed up on activities as they had been out quite a lot. He had cut out some animal pictures and Robbie had wanted to stick them in the scrapbook.

Focus on a planned aspect of literacy and parent's role
Made a passport (photocopied cover of passport – stuck onto thin card) and we wrote name, address, age, birthday, eye and hair colour and put it in his scrapbook. He asked if I would leave one for his brother. Mum said 'I'd never think of doing anything like that.' Took in magazines to cut out letters to make his name and his brother's name. Good use of scissors.

Anticipate what parent might do following the visit
Cutting out individual letters, mum suggested 'we could do the alphabet and make his friends' names and his family'. Did not want to part with 'Where's my Teddy' and they both read it together before I went. It struck me that mum was not self-conscious because I was there and she was reading aloud. It felt as if they were just the two of them together.

Books:
Teddy Robber, My first ABC, I want to see the moon.

All aspects of the ORIM framework around writing were covered on visit 3 and there was also some shared interaction around books.

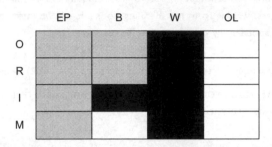

We can see how, in these first three visits, over half the cells in the framework have been visited in some way. It also shows that, as yet, work on the oral language strand has not been introduced. Reflecting on the framework and work already covered, Anne was able to identify oral language as the necessary focus of her next visit.

In visit 4, Anne focused particularly on letter recognition or 'talk about literacy'. She introduced activities involving naming letters, ordering the letters in the child's name and printing with sponge letters.

Visit 4: Focus on oral language – talk about literacy

FAMILY: ROBBIE WEEK 15

Review what parents and child have been doing
Wendy had very definite views on the books borrowed from before. She always said why Robbie liked them or why he disliked them. Continuation of collection from scrapbook, although mum did say because of work it wasn't always easy to do a lot of activities. She does, however, always read bedtime stories.

Focus on a planned aspect of literacy and parent's role
Involved Wendy in painting activity, printing with sponge letters, helping him to order letters in his name and make the right selection when choosing another letter to paint. Interesting comment made: 'He enjoys painting and printing with these a lot more than looking at an alphabet book.' Robbie had borrowed an alphabet book on my last visit, and was not interested in it at all. Mum became involved in follow-up making paper plate puppets: 'It's the ideas I need' she said.

Anticipate what parent might do following the visit
Continue to cut out letters rather than looking at them in a book, find them in magazines, catalogues. On my next visit I will take in dough and maybe some plasticene to leave so they can continue to cut out letter shapes.

Books:
Peace at last, Lifesize animal counting book, Can't you sleep little bear?

All aspects of the parent's role around language (talk about literacy) were covered in this visit. In addition, Anne noted Wendy's comments on Robbie's views of the books borrowed from the programme, showing her *recognition* of his opinions.

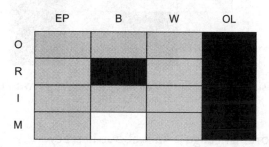

Anne worked her way quite systematically through the various strands of literacy; in visit 5 she focused on phonological awareness, in particular nursery rhymes. In this visit, she left an activity unfinished and asked that Wendy and Robbie complete it before the next visit. This strategy of leaving something to finish off proved to be an excellent way of promoting shared literacy *interaction* within the family between visits.

Visit 5: Focus on oral language – phonological awareness

FAMILY: ROBBIE WEEK 19

Review what parents and child have been doing
Did not see scrapbook today, but Wendy says books are read every night at bedtime. Older brother buys books from school book club – share together.

Focus on a planned aspect of literacy and parents' role
Activities linked to nursery rhymes – mum said 'You give me ideas with stuff like that'. 'Do you think of these things before you come?' 'I'd never have thought of doing that with him, look at the concentration on his face. He's so quiet and busy.' Prop to accompany rhyme. Sticking, cutting, matching 1 2 3 to 3 bags of wool. Left this rhyme unfinished and asked mum to complete if possible in time for my next visit.

Anticipate what parent might do following the visit
Completion of activity and to maintain rhymes by including them at bedtime after books have been read. Refer back to photocopied sheets of rhymes and say them regularly, with props as an aid to different 'audience'. Keep booklet of rhymes started so we can continue to add to them over time.

All four aspects of ORIM for phonological awareness were touched on in this visit. Aspects from other strands of literacy, particularly books, were also covered. As Anne had anticipated, the parents could refer to the sheets of nursery rhymes, thereby providing a *model* of reading.

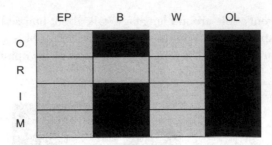

The sixth home visit continued the focus on oral language, with the emphasis on letter recognition.

Visit 6: Focus on oral language – talk about literacy

FAMILY: ROBBIE WEEK 25

Review what parents and child have been doing

Nursery rhymes and books borrowed. Wendy had bought some foam shape numbers for the bath. She made a point of telling me that the story 'Where's my Teddy?' had been read on one of the children's tea time TV programmes, and her partner said he recognised the story, and it sounded just like Wendy reading it to Robbie.

Focus on a planned aspect of literacy and parents' role

Alphabet books, stamps and stamp pad and matching letter to picture and finding magnetic letter to put on board. Wendy and Robbie made his name with magnetic letters and I left paper for Wendy to continue, suggesting cut out magazine pictures or drawings. Domino alphabet cards, we made the whole set as mum said 'We can play these with James when he comes home from school.' (James is older brother, aged 7). Taped James singing the alphabet.

Anticipate what parent might do following the visit

Continue playing with cards left – matching and recognising – playing together. Reading of books and continuation of learning nursery rhymes. Suggested Wendy could continue the idea of this game using numbers, colours, names of family instead of letters.

Books:

Gingerbread man, Brown bear, Owl babies.

In this visit, Anne reviewed some of the opportunities Wendy had been providing between visits; these included providing resources for number recognition and reading books together. Anne also left activities to reinforce letter recognition. Cells from the ORIM framework covered in this visit were:

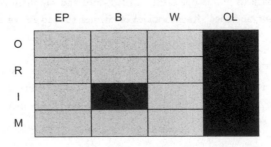

For visit 7 Anne planned more activities around letter recognition. Her notes show the parent's role in providing *opportunities* (buying an alphabet jigsaw) and *interaction* (playing games made on the last visit).

Visit 7: Focus on oral language – talk about literacy

FAMILY: ROBBIE WEEK 30

Review what parents and child have been doing

Wendy has bought an alphabet floor jigsaw. They have played the games they made previously with Robbie. Continues to say and sing nursery rhymes. Always enjoys receiving card before my visit, no one else allowed to open it.

Focus on a planned aspect of literacy and parent's role

Made jigsaw game with name and numbers. Talked about differences between letters and numbers, ready for workshop session on letters and numbers. Sorted letters and numbers using alphabet jigsaw number cards, letter tiles, etc.

Anticipate what parent might do following the visit

Continue with carpet tile game using letters and numbers, mum anticipates working with Robbie and older brother. Also singing rhymes which mum says he does regularly, quite unprompted, at anytime. I left another scrapbook.

Books:

Enormous turnip, One Snowy Night, Once upon a time.

In this visit, Anne left resources for the family to encourage *opportunities* around talk about literacy and Robbie's mother was keen to use the activities with both her children – clear examples of her *interaction* with them. Wendy also *recognised* Robbie's interest in nursery rhymes.

	EP	B	W	OL
O				■
R				■
I				■
M				

Notes on the eighth home visit highlight the enthusiasm of Robbie and his mother for the activities and the programme generally. At this point in the programme, Robbie's mother was in the habit of talking about what she and her son had been doing between visits, and Robbie's enjoyment of the literacy activities he did with his mother was obvious to Anne when she visited. She also noted that Robbie's mother seemed more confident in working with her child.

Visit 8: Focus on oral language – talk about literacy

FAMILY: ROBBIE WEEK 38

Review what parents and child have been doing

Wendy said they had continued to play domino games. I left another jigsaw (alphabet) but this replaced one they had borrowed earlier. Continuing to sing and say nursery rhymes. When I arrive we go straight into the kitchen and Robbie sits at the table, waiting and watching to see what comes out of my box. He really enjoys all practical activities and anticipates what we will be doing by all the materials we take out.

Focus on a planned aspect of literacy and parent's role

Made zig-zag book – letters of his name, cut out after drawing pictures to match letters. Left this to be completed. Made fishing game – cut out various sized/coloured fish, put on paper clip and caught them one by one with magnet. Played this using letters in his name and then he had to put them in order. Also numbers 0–10 which he had no problem with. Treasure hunt game – following instructions – played two games. Robbie and then Wendy had a lot of fun playing this. Mum said 'I bet we'll play this again when James comes home.'

Anticipate what parent might do following the visit

I left paper and clips for them to continue with this. Made suggestions for them to continue with fishing game using family names, words, matching pairs (two numbers or two letters the same). I noticed '5 speckled frogs' game we made at last workshop was pinned to the door. Wendy readily joins in with spirit of the game where a year ago she was much more self-conscious.

Books:

Not now Bernard, Brown Bear, You can't catch me!

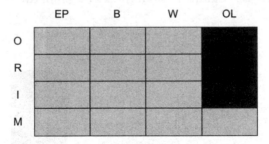

Visit 9 was the first to focus on storytelling. In her notes Anne highlights Wendy's developing capacity to act as a *model* for the child. Firstly, she referred to the mother's alphabet drawings (thereby modelling talk about literacy) and secondly she referred explicitly to the mother's questioning during a storytelling session. Anne mentioned again the parent's confidence in doing the activities she has suggested.

Visit 9: Focus on oral language – storytelling

FAMILY: ROBBIE WEEK 46

Review what parents and child have been doing

They've been singing nursery rhymes (especially in the bath). Playing domino snap game which I left last time. New things stuck into scrapbook, e.g. my postcard from Safari Park with caption added by Wendy. Alphabet with accompanying picture alongside. All drawn by mum! She kept saying they weren't very good, but they were excellent. Returned alphabet jigsaw they had borrowed.

Focus on a planned aspect of literacy and parent's role

Storytelling using puppets made during the session. One paper plate puppet and one sock puppet. I thought it may be easier to have two so they could have conversations between each other, then move on to storytelling. We initiated this by giving them names and mum and partner soon got into the voices and were quite confident about using different voices while I was there. Robbie is always willing to do things and really enjoys practical activities. He was busy playing and talking when I left, with puppet on each hand. Also cut out and labelled (mum interacting most of the time, in fact at one point we both spoke together to ask Robbie a question and I felt that mum was taking over that model role). Catalogue pictures for scrapbook, my bedroom, kitchen, etc.

Anticipate what parent might do following the visit

Storytelling with puppets. I will ask how it's going when I see them on the trip to the farm next week. Complete 'my house/rooms' with catalogue and captions and continue to include items in scrapbook from days out, etc. All practical things we have made are still in evidence, either in well-kept scrapbook or on kitchen door.

Books:

Lighthouse Keeper's Lunch, In the small, small pond, Going to sleep on the farm (in preparation for farm visit).

All four aspects of ORIM for the storytelling aspect of oral language were covered in this visit.

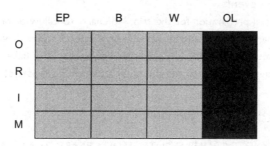

The following two events, a farm visit and a teddy bears' picnic, were organised as end-of-term events. Although neither had a specific literacy focus, both encouraged general interaction between parents and children and allowed REAL Project families to get to know one another. They were planned as fun outings for the families.

Group event 1: Farm visit

REAL PROJECT GROUP EVENT – VISIT TO A FARM WEEK 48

Parents and children participating:
Robbie and mum, Bridget and mum, Justin, Aaron, mum and dad, Keith, Alan and mum, Helen.

Number of parents attending:
5

Number of parents invited:
7

Any reasons why some did not attend?
Karen was coming with dad but received last-minute hospital appointment. Lydia and mum – domestic problems. Helen came with me – mum was ill!

What happened?
Minibus to the farm and return. We were shown around by one of the helpers. Allowed to touch, hold animals including chicks, horses, goats, rabbits, guinea pigs, ducklings, pigs and cows. We had our picnic in the garden. We had it all to ourselves – it was a glorious day and after lunch the children spent an hour playing with bat/balls and had the run of the large fenced garden. Picked fruit before returning.

How did it go?
A very low-cost, hassle-free but most enjoyable day. The weather helped to make it pleasant for both parents and children. They had the space to move around freely, see, touch the animals, to share some very basic activities, e.g. having a picnic, playing games together.

Comments from parents and children
The parents could enjoy the day because the children were safe. They were always just either looking or touching. The leader who showed us round commented on what a well-behaved and interested group they were. They all commented on how they had enjoyed the day. We ended up picking fruit before coming back on the bus. Children carrying baskets, parents filling them. Even when they got spilled there were no cross words.

Lessons for future events
There was not a lot of preparation for this trip. No charts to follow or pre-prepared sheets. The children and parents talked and shared things with each other. It was a lovely day to share and enjoy something they may not see or do very often. They talked together and with each other, with their own children and the other children. Took lots of photographs.

Group event 2: Teddy bears' picnic

REAL PROJECT GROUP EVENT – TEDDY BEARS' PICNIC WEEK 51

Parents and children participating:
Aaron, Justin, mum and dad; Helen and mum; Bridget and mum; Keith, Alan and mum; Karen; Robbie and mum.

Number of parents attending:
6

Number of parents invited:

7

Any reasons why some did not attend?

Karen's parents could not attend so Karen stayed with me.

What happened?

After morning nursery at 11:20 we gathered to make sandwiches and prepare picnic. Parents and children helped to put out biscuits, crisps, make juice, etc. Played with their own children and the other children.

How did it go?

Luckily we had a fine day again and we were able to eat outside with bears and then play with the bats, balls and footballs afterwards.

Comments from parents and children

A wonderful card and present from one of the families that summed up the whole year, and all the work that has been done. It really made my day! It was home-made and mum had written on behalf of the family and the children had written in it also – ORIM to perfection!

Lessons for future events

It was not a very literacy-focused event; it was just a pleasant afternoon, where parents and children could share something simple and enjoyable together.

The main activity of visit 10 was particularly novel and involved writing on a T-shirt. The aim was to provide an original writing opportunity for the family but a secondary objective was to draw their attention to an aspect of environmental print that is sometimes overlooked.

Visit 10: Focus on writing/environmental print

FAMILY: ROBBIE WEEK 65

Review what parents and child have been doing

Wendy said Robbie had been really interested in numbers and letters. Playing alphabet game and number dominoes. Enjoyed 'Lighthouse Keeper's Lunch', especially Robbie. Completed 'house' book; cutting and labelling appropriate pictures for different rooms. Two letters during holidays sent to home including holiday postcard were stuck in the scrapbook. They brought back a number poster for each child for their bedrooms and are looking out for a reasonably priced alphabet poster to accompany it. The number poster displayed number, the written word and actual number and appropriate number of objects with caption, e.g. 5 green frogs.

Focus on a planned aspect of literacy and parent's role

Writing/drawing activity using T-shirt marker pens. I had asked beforehand if Wendy could find an old white or light coloured T-shirt. We talked about what to put on front, agreed on Robbie's name, and a drawing of himself. I took in some stencils to add further picture designs. I asked Wendy to discuss with Robbie something for the back of the T-shirt, he suggested his age and other numbers, so I left that part of the job for her to continue. Took a photo of Robbie in his T-shirt.

Anticipate what parent might do following the visit
Complete T-shirt design. Continue with scrapbook and saying/singing nursery rhymes. Robbie chose Monster book of ABC sounds. Mum said he was interested in alphabet books.

Books:
Monster book of ABC sounds, Jasper's Beanstalk, Don't put your finger in the Jelly

The notes of this visit demonstrate Robbie's development over time. On this occasion, his mother commented how much her son liked alphabet books and learning about letters and numbers (*recognition*). Earlier in the project, after visit 4 (week 15) however, she had specifically commented that Robbie did not like alphabet books.

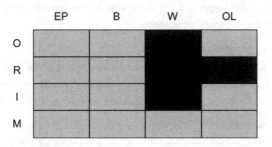

The following group event, attended by Robbie's mother, appeared to achieve its aim of raising parents' awareness about literacy, introducing them to the ORIM framework and increasing their confidence.

Group event 3: The REAL Project video

REAL PROJECT GROUP EVENT – A LOOK FOR WHAT WE HAVE ACHIEVED
PLUS MORE IDEAS WEEK 68

Parents participating:
Lesley, Margaret, Wendy, Nicola, Jane.

Number of parents attending:
5

Number of parents invited:
6

Any reasons why some did not attend?
Message from one parent who couldn't attend – family have moved away from the area. Lydia's mum, who I feel prefers home visits to group meetings.

What happened?
A consolidation of what has been happening and a boost of confidence to keep things moving until the children go into school. We watched the video because I felt the time was right for them to see it and realise that they had worked on the same lines as the people in the video. Constant comments throughout were 'We've done that', 'Oh I remember that story'.

How did it go?
I think I was justified in showing the video at this point; it wasn't new and daunting for them. It emphasised and reinforced all the good practice they have been doing. We talked openly

together, how they felt less self-conscious, embarrassed about reading aloud and with expression to the children.

Comments from parents and children

One mum said 'It will be easier now for me to help my younger son because I know what to do!' We talked a little bit about storytelling and how everyday things could be made into a story. Margaret said 'Every morning he wants me to tell him what I've dreamed about and I have to make it up' – Brilliant!

Lessons for future events

This was the first group event without children. It was worthwhile because I wanted to give them some praise, recognition and a belief that they were so important because they were the ones who carried on this work after I'd gone. I could provide ideas but they were implementing it day to day and I think they are beginning to realise the power they do have in regard to their children's development.

In the final home visit, they focused on writing and letter recognition, with a new activity – decorating biscuits with letters in icing. In her review of what the family had been doing between visits, Anne commented on this mother's increasing initiative when engaging in literacy activities with her son.

Visit 11: Focus on writing and oral language – talk about literacy

FAMILY: ROBBIE WEEK 70

Review what parents and child have been doing

A lot of work has been going on since the last visit. The books we made at the group event for the children to draw and write in have proved quite popular. Several pieces of writing in it, along with felt puppets and a bonfire where mum said 'I was sharpening the crayons and I thought the shavings would look good as wood on the fire. I was quite impressed with myself!' Nursery rhyme work, alphabet and numbers.

Focus on a planned aspect of literacy and parent's role

Alphabet biscuits, decorating plain biscuits with icing and making letters on each one. Initially the letters of their own name using small round sweets as decoration. We used magnetic letters to make name, wrote it also with marker pen and then made the letters with sweets on top. Robbie wanted to make more for the letters in his brother's name. We also recorded some nursery rhymes and listened to tape of 'Where the Wild Things' are.

Anticipate what parent might do following the visit

Most families have not really been too bothered about the story tapes. They haven't chosen them, so we have usually listened together. But Robbie's mum and I said the narrative on this tape was much too quick, not giving enough time to look at the pictures properly and no indication when to turn the page. Also the music was a definite distraction. Left some sequencing pictures to complete and order. Continuing with story book.

Books:

Fur, Arthur, But Martin

Aspects of the parent's role from three strands of literacy were covered in this visit are as shown:

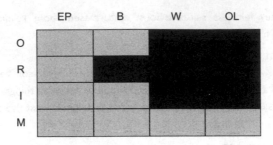

The ORIM framework has been gradually covered as visits have progressed so that over time all aspects of the parent's role have been addressed in relation to each of the strands of literacy.

Another group event was held to emphasise the importance of storytelling in young children's language and literacy development, and how stories can be told using everyday events as a basis.

Group event 4: Storytelling

REAL PROJECT GROUP EVENTS – STORYTELLING WEEK 73

Focus of the event:
Storytelling

Parents and children participating:
Wendy, Debbie, Jane, Lesley

Number of parents attending:
4

Number of parents invited:
7

Any reasons why some did not attend?
No messages were received.

What happened?
Talked about storytelling; how easily everyday stories could be made up; they could be long, short or 'to be continued' stories. They could be told anytime, anywhere and may sometimes use language, for example, 'scary', 'frightened', more extended vocabulary.

How did it go?
I think some parents were already doing this but had maybe not realised the importance of the 'just happened to think it up' story.

Comments from parents and children
Positive comments about children listening to stories, about when they were babies and the favourite stories which they like to hear over and over again. Also quote from one mum: 'he likes me to tell him what I've been dreaming about – he asks me every morning'.

Lessons for future events
We went on to talk about 'accreditation' for the Open College.

The final group event had two purposes: to provide parents with more strategies for telling stories and to inform the parents about the Open College Network accreditation. Robbie's mother was one of those who went on to achieve this qualification.

REAL PROJECT GROUP EVENTS – OPEN COLLEGE NETWORK (OCN) ACCREDITATION WEEK 77

Focus of the event:
Accreditation meeting with Margaret and the parents.

Parents and children participating:
Wendy, Nicola, Jane, Margaret

Number of parents attending:
4

Number of parents invited:
7

Any reasons why some did not attend?
Messages from two parents unable to attend. But one of these would like to be involved in accreditation.

What happened?
Talked generally about compiling a portfolio and went through what may be required. Came to conclusion that it might be what has to be left out because so much has been collected over 18 months.

How did it go?
We decided in the new year to come together as a group and compile one together and then ask Margaret to come to a meeting and look at what we had selected.

Comments from parents and children
We know we have photographic evidence and tape recordings and work I have saved from group meetings on various areas. One mum said it would be nice to see other people's ideas because we will also have done something different.

Lessons for future events
We decided to take things one step at a time, firstly compiling the evidence and as we do it, maybe the areas covered and what we were trying to achieve when, for example, we made snap or domino games.

Summary discussion

We have used the notes of one teacher to illustrate one family's involvement in a family literacy programme. This has conveyed the work with the family over time and gives a sense of development and of the relationships between the teacher and the family. We can see how over time, one teacher planned for continuity and progression, using the ORIM framework to prepare interesting and relevant activities on all four strands of literacy development in the framework and which addressed four aspects of parent's roles. The accounts of work with Robbie and his family show how much went on and it becomes clear how much literacy is going on in the family.

This family's continuing commitment to family literacy is evident, as is their willingness to participate in literacy activities between visits (in spite of other pressures such as time constraints due to work). The family clearly valued the programme; this is evident in the way that postcards from the teacher were displayed and literacy resources made in earlier visits were saved in a scrapbook. Importantly, the accounts show how Robbie's mother's confidence appeared to grow as she developed a positive working relationship with the teacher. It seems that she became increasingly comfortable with her role as her own child's teacher; over time she seemed more willing to give her opinion about the books and games the family borrowed.

Robbie's literacy development over time is clear. Robbie seemed interested in books from the first visit, in which he asked many questions about the books. But other aspects of his literacy development can be seen, for example, at the beginning of the programme Robbie was not keen on drawing and writing (see visit 2 – week 3) or reading alphabet books (see visit 3 – week 11). By the end of the programme, however, he had come to enjoy both of these; in visit 10 (week 65) he was reported to be 'really interested in letters and numbers' and clearly enjoyed writing on the T-shirt and decorating biscuits.

Using the ORIM framework, Robbie's programme teacher worked with his family to plan and develop a family literacy programme which: built on what existed; developed from one visit to the next; created a relationship through which the mother developed her own role; and supported Robbie's literacy development through a flexible programme of continuity and progression.

5 Opportunities for parents as adult learners

Chapter summary
- Introduction
- Taking adult learning seriously: implications for practice
- Developing an accredited course for parents
- Reflections on adult learning: parents' voices

Introduction

In the context of the REAL Project, parents worked with a programme teacher and their own child, most often at home and sometimes in small groups. As explained in Chapters 3 and 4, the project sought to make a difference to children's literacy by enhancing the roles of parents in providing literacy opportunities, recognising their children's literacy achievements, interacting with their children around literacy and being a model of a literacy user themselves. In addition, it was important to provide opportunities for further adult learning for parents who wanted them. It was also necessary to think carefully about the ways in which adult learners are different from young children and how parents' learning might be best supported. In this chapter we first outline our position in relation to adult learning. Second we explain how we developed an accredited course for parents, enabling those who wished to gain recognition for the work they had done with their children. The chapter concludes with the perspectives of one project teacher who supported a small group of parents as they worked to gain accreditation and four parents who reflect on their experiences.

Taking adult learning seriously: implications for practice

Working with parents to promote young children's literacy means recognising that parents are learners too. In this section we consider: how adult learning is different from children's learning; parents as experts on their own children; parents having views on school literacy; parents' views on helping their own children's literacy development; the possible needs of bilingual parents; and the goals for adult education to which early literacy programmes should aspire.

Adult learning is different

Although there are many fundamental similarities between the ways adults and children learn, there are also some important differences. Adults bring more prior knowledge to a topic and adult educators therefore have to be even more willing to listen and learn. Adults are likely to be much more aware of their reasons for wanting to learn something – or not wanting to learn it. Simply 'pleasing' the teacher or other people will not matter as much to them as it does to children. They are likely to be impatient with activities which do not meet their goals.

Most young children have a positive attitude to learning new things. However, some adults may have had difficult experiences, perhaps in their own schooling, which have left them feeling that they are incapable of learning in an educational institution context. They may feel that they are doomed to failure or that too much contact with teachers and schools will eventually make them angry, frustrated or anxious.

The implication for teachers of young children is that they need to pause and rethink their educational values and approaches when they plan work with parents.

Parents are experts on their own children

No professional outside the family can ever expect to know children as well as their parents do. Professionals may sometimes have a different kind of knowledge, or different ways of looking at things, but that does not imply that they know best.

The implication for practice is that professionals should think carefully before challenging parents' views about their children.

Parents have views on school literacy

All of us have views about reading and writing at school. Some parents may have wholly positive memories of their own experiences while others may have wholly negative recollections. For many, there will be a mix of views and some parents may puzzle over the 'latest' trend in teaching methods. Whatever their views, they are bound to influence parents' experience of early literacy education for their own children.

The implication for practice is that, at some point in a programme, it may be helpful to explore with parents what are their views of literacy and how that affects their role.

Parents have views about their role in helping their children's literacy development

Many parents are confident about their ability to help their children's general development but some have anxieties in the area of literacy. Anxieties may be at a very broad level (for example, an expectation that their child 'may find it difficult – as hard as I did') or they may be very specific (for example, about whether it is correct to use upper case or lower case letters in writing with children). As well as anxieties, parents may have convictions about how best to help their children. Some parents' initial views about how they can best help their children may well differ from the views of many teachers and literacy programmes. The point of a family literacy programme should be to offer parents options for how they can help, not to impose particular methods.

The implication for practice is to remember that in seeking to offer a different perspective on early literacy we should respect existing views.

Bilingual parents may have different learning needs

Parents may not be literate in, or may not speak, the language in which their children are expected to become literate at school, but it is a mistake to focus on what parents do not know or to jump to conclusions about their aspirations for their families. Bilingual or multilingual families have many resources to support their children's literacy development.

One must also think about the educational experiences of some bilingual families. Parents may have experienced educational systems in countries where very different teaching methods are used in comparison to those used in the UK to teach their young children. They may have different assumptions about the role of school, the roles of teachers, the operation of schools and the purpose of schooling. For parents who grew up and were educated in the same system as their children, their experiences as bilingual students in schools may have been good or bad. Whatever their experiences, it will almost certainly have been different from that of many monolingual professionals teaching their children or implementing early literacy education programmes.

The implication for practice is that good early literacy education programmes should begin by listening to families.

What goal for adult education should an early literacy education programme have?

Adult education – in the sense of engaging in deliberate, aided learning experiences – can take so many different forms according to the needs, circumstances and aspirations of the learners that it would be a serious mistake to try to cater for all needs within the confines of family literacy programmes. Such programmes may stimulate adults' desire for educational experiences but in our view the priority must be to open doors for adults rather than try to accommodate the whole range of demands.

The implication for practice is that professionals need to know what is available in their locality and how to help adults gain access to it.

The REAL Project developed two main adult learning routes for parents. First, details of locally based adult education classes run and funded by the local authority were sent to all parents with the offer of support from project teachers to find out more, visit the learning centres, meet learning mentors and enrol if they wished to. Second, an opportunity in the form of an accredited programme through the Open College Network,[1] the Raising Achievement in Early Literacy, was offered to parents and could be followed by them by completing a portfolio of the work done with their children at home and during REAL Project groups sessions.

Developing an accredited course for parents

Seeking to accredit parents' learning forces us to face the issue of respectful assessment of adults' learning. The question for the REAL Project was how to accredit the work parents do within a framework of understanding and supporting their children's literacy. There were many questions to be addressed here – questions that have to be faced by any programme with similar aims.

Who does the assessing?

Is it appropriate for members of the project team, who have spent a year developing a relationship with parents on the basis of partnership in children's learning, suddenly to turn into assessors of parents' learning? What kind of relationship might develop between the assessor and the assessed? Is it appropriate that a parent–teacher partnership turns to discussing the level of achievement at which a parent is performing? Should such a partnership move into a relationship of assessor and assessed?

What is assessed?

How might accreditation of parents' learning assess what is done in everyday literacy and avoid the pitfalls of contriving 'products' or situations for the purposes of assessment (thus undermining any earlier emphasis on everyday, real-life literacy)?

What is the assessment for?

Nutbrown (1997) identified three basic purposes for assessment: for teaching, for management (identifying effectiveness) and for research. But accreditation of parents' learning – coming at the end of their learning experience – goes further. It is for the purposes of recognition, of validation of learning and achievement, or for future qualification.

Finding a respectful way of assessing adults' achievements – in the context of their roles as parents who have chosen to work with teachers to find more ways of supporting their children's literacy development – was an important challenge for the REAL Project. It was important to ensure that assessment of parents' work was achieved in a way which enhanced, and did not detract from, parents' existing positive views of their roles and relationships with their children and with programme teachers. After much deliberation, accreditation through the Open College Network was developed (and funded through the local education authority) for any parent who wished to take up this opportunity. Details were sent to all parents in the form of a letter, parents' names were handwritten and letters were personally signed. The invitation came, not from the teachers who had worked with the parents, but from the project directors who they had met occasionally. With the letter was a brief leaflet explaining something of what was involved. No pressure was put on parents to take up this initiative; project teachers offered to talk about what was involved with parents if they so wished.

One of the project teachers, Anne Stafford, moved into a new role when the project ended, with a brief to develop learning opportunities for parents within the school. Reflecting, in her journal, on her role with parents who worked for accreditation of their work and learning, she wrote:

> The project parents who completed accreditation with the Open College Network were recognised for the work they had done with their children by each producing an individual portfolio, and receiving their own certificates from David Blunkett (then Secretary of State for Education). Four of the eight parents who worked with me on the REAL Project remain, some six years later, as my core ambassadors in school, recruiting other parents. They are my PR team and have continued their own lifelong learning by accessing a range of courses. They now expect

from me, and I have to deliver. The relationship of trust and understanding, even seven years on, is alive and well and now impacting on engaging other parents to support their children in the same way. It has opened up opportunities and possibilities for parents in school and we have tried to help parents overcome some of their personal barriers to learning – they now have more choices.

A few weeks ago, a parent who I worked with on the REAL Project whose child was then in Y5 in school, began another school initiative on a paired reading course. From those early beginnings when the children were three years old, our school continues in the belief that we have to work with the parents to effect this change. That 'can do' message runs through the fabric of our school; how important that message becomes in raising standards and expectations in their own children. This raising of self-esteem, this increased confidence in themselves and in their own achievements is a powerful model for their children. Nurturing parents' expectations of themselves helps them to expect more for and of their own children, because we are continually against an 'it'll do for them' attitude that can so often prevail.

What began as visits to homes half a day each week over a period of time has rolled out and led to the creation of a whole new approach to parents' learning and to parents' roles in school and in their children's learning – now embedded in the school's vision and philosophy. In the midst of all the uncertainty, the challenging community and the upheaval many of our families face in their lives, the school is now a constant and reliable factor.

There will always be the difficult task of maintaining and consolidating existing opportunities for parents while striving to give parents and their children the choices and opportunities they need to succeed, as a family. There is always work to do to bring new families on board and all this happens within the reality of the culture of a deprived community, with some 'hard to reach' parents who at times find it impossible to build a productive relationship with a school. But in spite of all this, there is enthusiasm and energy and vision for that handful of parents who began working with me seven years ago which have had a positive and lasting effect on other parents in our school.

Reflections on adult learning: parents' voices

A minority, nine parents (all women) out of 88 families, took up the adult education component of the programme – but those who did valued it, and it is to some of these parents that we turn now. The parents who successfully achieved OCN accreditation each have their individual accounts of that experience. The last words in this chapter on creating opportunities for parents as adult learners consist of the personal stories of four of those parents.

Jane's story

I enjoyed going to the presentation to get my certificate and to see how much effort everybody had put into the work. I found the writing-up hard at times to put it all into words, everything we wanted to say about the project. It was easier to write about what Bethany and I had done together because we had made so many things!

I liked working together in a group at school when we put the files together we knew which bits fitted into which sections and it felt good to be recognised for all the hard work we had done.

We've still got Beth's project in a box in the loft. We saved it all and when we moved a few weeks ago we looked through it all again and Beth said 'Remember when we did the house book we even put our wallpaper on the front cover!'

I wanted to help Beth and it was nice to be involved in a group and meet other mums. The portfolio was something I achieved for me at the end of it all. When I start something I want to see it through to the end, even writing it up when Beth had gone to bed. I felt really proud to be part of a team effort and especially when we went to meet David Blunkett.

Lesley's story

When I wrote everything down it helped me to see how much easier it would be to help my younger child because I understood much better what I was doing and why I was doing it. I knew I had to give up my time and make time to do the written work and at times it wasn't easy with a very young baby and three other children. I did the writing in between feeds and when the other children had gone to bed.

It made me realise that children come to learn things when they are ready and not when we think they should be ready and that helped me with my youngest child because I had done the work with Katie. I put a lot of work into the files but I did it for 'me'. I think we were helping our children to learn in a better and easier way and because of it I now feel more confident in my job as a dinner lady. I feel confident to read a big group of reception children a story because I know how to read it and keep them interested.

Wendy's story

When I had done all the written work for the file it made me feel guilty I had not done all this with my older child because I now understood why I was doing this work and how it could have helped him as he went through school. I did the project with my child but the work we did on our files was my achievement. Jools learnt and I had learnt, we both got so much out of it. It was good to work together, a group of mums from Parson Cross who had a lot of things in common about wanting to help our kids. We weren't sure if we were up to that sort of writing but Anne Stafford would tell us 'you can do it', and when somebody believes you can do it then it gives you confidence to have a go. We worked together to sort it out then we went away to write our story.

Nicola's story

Writing up all the work made me realise how much I had really done with both my children and in some ways I felt my younger child who was always present on the visits benefited just as much as my older child who was a project child. Even though we were working on our own files we never felt we were on our own because we could always come up to school and talk to each other if we weren't sure about something. It was a real team effort and we were all really pleased with everyone's success. There was always so much support from each other; I did a lot of my writing quite late at night when they had gone to bed and even though it was quite late at times when I finished I never felt like giving up.

Note

1 The Open College Network is an accrediting body which supports the accreditation and assessments of adults in South Yorkshire who follow programmes developed through its validation.

6 Professional development for family literacy work

Chapter summary
- Introduction
- Professional development for family literacy workers: rationale and aims
- Designing a professional development programme for family literacy workers
- Time for professional development in family literacy
- Is professional development essential?
- Implications for future professional development programmes for experienced early years teachers

Introduction

In this chapter we argue that those who undertake work with parents on early literacy development or run a family literacy programme need to be supported through properly designed professional development. Drawing on the REAL Project as an evaluated example of such a research-oriented professional development programme (with examples of practical sessions and consideration of the time which might be allocated to such a programme), the chapter considers how a professional development programme can be designed. The chapter includes the perspectives of practitioners who have experienced such a programme, thus showing how such work might be evaluated to ascertain its usefulness and potential. Finally, the implications for development and provision of professional development to support high-quality family literacy programmes for parents and their young children are considered.

Professional development for family literacy workers: rationale and aims

The notion that teachers need specific and planned opportunities to equip them for direct work with parents is not new. Nutbrown *et al.* (1991) argued that for this role teachers needed professional development opportunities which included time and input to develop early literacy programmes for parents in their schools and local communities. This argument was taken up by Hannon *et al.* (1997), who accepted that adult learning is different from young children's learning and argued that teachers working on family literacy programmes needed specific professional development in order to work with parents as adult learners as well as the parents of their children. In this chapter we draw on the experiences of teachers in the REAL Project who undertook professional development in preparation for their family literacy work.

The professional development programme for programme teachers in the REAL Project consisted of five full-day sessions (weekly with follow-up work and preparation) which teachers were funded to attend, and monthly after-school meetings, of two hours each, during term time (twilight sessions). Two further days of professional development took place: one at the halfway point of the programme and one at the end.

The aim of the professional development programme was to equip the teachers to carry out their family literacy work:

- with confidence
- with respect for individual families
- with an understanding of the family literacy context in which they were working.

To this end the professional development programme was designed to:

- help teachers to enhance their existing knowledge and current thinking on early literacy work with families
- offer new insights and knowledge from research
- encourage teachers to examine their attitudes towards working with parents
- help teachers to develop strategies for problem-solving so that the first response to a difficulty was to seek a solution rather than admit defeat
- provide the necessary knowledge to understand the adult learning needs of parents and develop appropriate approaches to such learning
- develop a sense of team membership and teamwork.

The monthly 'twilight' sessions throughout the project addressed emerging issues and provided opportunities for teachers to:

- share highlights and difficulties in their work
- address forthcoming needs
- plan future work
- collaborate on shared events
- compare experiences and feedback on families' responses
- share their own developing views of the programme
- support each other.

Such wide-ranging aims might seem rather ambitious, but as the remainder of this chapter will show, specifically designed and systematically delivered professional development across this broad curriculum offered enormous benefits to the teachers engaged in family literacy work. In the next section we look in more detail at the professional development programme designed for teachers who were about to work on the REAL Project, a family literacy programme with parents of pre-school age children.

Designing a professional development programme for family literacy workers

It gave me more knowledge about how young children learn, made me feel more confident about putting those ideas forward in front of other professionals and certainly within the school ... we were getting our 'pot of knowledge'.

Briefly, the 'pot of knowledge' referred to above contained four main ingredients:

- Theoretical aspects of: early literacy development; work with families; parents' roles in early literacy development; parents as adult learners.
- Practical work to support parents (through home visiting, group work and special events) in developing young children's early literacy development in: sharing books; early writing; using environmental print; developing phonological awareness, storytelling and talk about literacy.
- Current information and contact points in the neighbourhood to support parents' own learning needs: a specially designed accreditation programme with adult learning support; details of local adult education courses.
- Developing skills through teamwork to: solve problems; share difficulties; celebrate successes; develop work arising from family interests; record events; identify needs; work flexibly.

The content and processes of the professional development programme drew on a bank of ideas developed by Nutbrown and Hannon (1997) in order to equip teachers in the four areas listed above. Of vital importance, at the outset, was the five-day research-oriented programme which involved teachers in:

- reviewing research articles on aspects of early literacy development, work with parents and parents as adult learners
- examining their own attitudes towards parents and working with individual families in families' homes
- discussing the practical content of family literacy work
- solving problems and discussing practical issues which arose during the project – such as rescheduling visits; balancing their project role with classroom roles
- devising ways of planning and recording their work with parents.

Topics included:

- working with families
- theoretical understandings
- using the ORIM framework (Hannon and Nutbrown, 1997)
- work on four strands of literacy (environmental print, books, writing and aspects of oral language)
- developing the programme to fit families
- recording work with families
- journal writing.

Box 6.1 gives details of the programme and examples of some of the sessions.

Box 6.1 Programme outline

Day Focus

1
- The Family Literacy Project
- Working with families
- Theoretical understandings: early literacy development and adult learning
- The ORIM framework

2
- Working with families
- Using ORIM to develop work on environmental print
- Using ORIM to develop work on books

3
- Using ORIM to develop work on early writing
- Using ORIM to develop work on oral language

4
- Using books in the home
- Developing resources

5
- Developing the Family Literacy Programme with individual families
- Keeping records
- Getting the Family Literacy Programme under way
- Continuing support

Each day was planned to help family literacy workers to focus on specific themes. Box 6.2 shows the programme for Day 1.

Box 6.2 Preparing for early literacy work with families Day 1

9.00   *Introductions*
- Sharing backgrounds and experiences
- Becoming a team
- Journal writing 'Thoughts on beginning family literacy work'

10.30   *Coffee*

11.00   *The Family Literacy Programme and the ORIM framework*
- An outline of the programme
- Video outlining the ORIM framework
- Discussion

12.15   *Lunch*

1.00   *Theoretical understandings – early literacy and adult learning*
- A theoretical overview of early literacy development
- Home visiting and implications for ways of working with families
- Understanding parents as adult learners

2.30   *Tea*

2.45   *Working with families*
- ● Why do we want to work with families?
- ● What can parents do to support early literacy development?
- ● Examine our attitudes to parents
- ● Building on the strengths in families – 'Assets not deficits'

3.30   *Thinking about Day 1*
- ● 15 minutes reflective journal writing
- ● Close

The professional development programme included follow-up activities and preparation work for the next session, such as those given in Box 6.3.

Box 6.3 Follow-up for Day 1 and preparation for Day 2

- ● Reflect on the issues arising from Day 1 in your journal.
- ● Read the following parts on the manual provided: Section 1 (1.1, 1.2, 1.3, 1.4, 1.5, 1.6 and 1.7). These short pieces give theoretical information which supports the work covered throughout the day.
- ● Make notes in your journal on things that strike you as important to return to.

If you have time:

- ● Spend some time looking through Section 2.
- ● View the video again.

Each of the five days followed a similar format, with new ideas being introduced, issues being revisited and an attitude of problem-solving and building on strengths being developed. Many of the activities used in the programme drew on a specifically designed professional development manual (Nutbrown and Hannon, 1997) and a video (Nutbrown *et al.*, 1996). Figures 6.1, 6.2, 6.3, 6.4 are illustrative of the material used.

Though the professional development programme was highly structured, it remained informal. Issues were discussed within the group in a spirit of collective problem-solving and (at times) celebration which contributed to the development of the sense of teamwork. Journal writing was important in this literacy project and time for such writing was built into every professional development session, as was time for sharing journal entries as appropriate.

Time for professional development in family literacy

As we have seen, the professional development programme outlined here began with five full-day sessions. These were held on the same day each week for five consecutive weeks, allowing time in between for follow-up work and preparation. The monthly after-school meetings (of two hours each) during term time were also an important means of

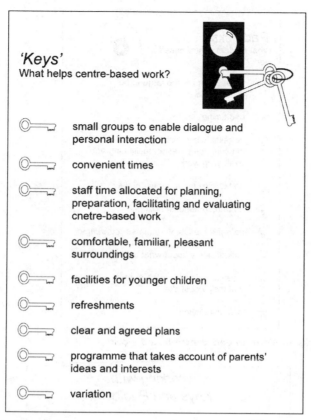

'Keys'
What helps centre-based work?

- small groups to enable dialogue and personal interaction
- convenient times
- staff time allocated for planning, preparation, facilitating and evaluating cnetre-based work
- comfortable, familiar, pleasant surroundings
- facilities for younger children
- refreshments
- clear and agreed plans
- programme that takes account of parents' ideas and interests
- variation

Figure 6.1   'Keys' – What helps centre-based work?

maintaining the team approach and keeping regular contact. These monthly meetings were key in sustaining the project team and provided opportunities for:

- Sharing of problems and difficulties. Some of the teachers were working in very difficult circumstances and needed recognition and support from the rest of the group.
- Conceptual development – together teachers and the project directors struggled to clarify their thinking about aspects of the project. For example, conceptualising parents' roles in the project prompted discussion of parents as 'spectators' or 'actors' or 'partners'.
- Journal writing – everyone on the team took a short time during each session to reflect on journal entries and write in them.
- Sharing ideas and successes in work with families.
- 'Catching up', 'checking in' and 'touching base'. The monthly early-evening meetings were key in the development and sustenance of a network of support for the project teachers.

One teacher commented: 'These meetings were indispensable.'

A further day of professional development at the halfway point of the family literacy programme was used to review work and ascertain further professional development

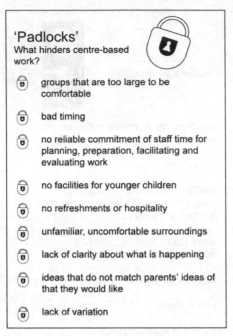

Figure 6.2   'Padlocks' – What hinders centre-based work?

Figure 6.3   Working with keys and padlocks

needs. A final de-briefing day was held when the family literacy work was complete. In total, this amounted to some 70 hours of dedicated professional development work, a considerable investment of time when viewed alongside the short (one- or two-day) policy-related training courses offered to teachers at the time (during the late 1990s) on

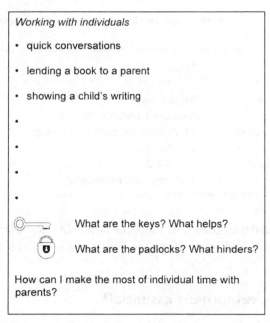

Figure 6.4 Working with individuals

themes such as baseline assessment of 4-year-olds, the National Literacy Strategy and the Code of Practice for Special Educational Needs (Nutbrown, 1999b).

For the teachers in this project the long duration of the family literacy programme was an important factor in building up relationships for work with parents. As one teacher commented:

> . . . it was the long-term commitment that was quite a big factor in it, because we were going in [to homes] very regularly and it was a long enough time for us to get that relationship up and running . . .

It seems that time was an important feature of the teachers' professional development programme, too; at the start and during the programme teachers valued the opportunity to meet, work, think and solve problems together:

> . . . It was not just the development programme at the beginning, it's also the support all the way through.

The teachers regarded their professional development programme as important, not just in developing the knowledge and skills which they valued so greatly, but also in building up mutual professional trust with one another. Table 6.1 shows how the time allocated to the programme was distributed pre-, during- and post-project.

This is not intended to be a formulaic recommendation (that is, that 70 hours of professional development are needed effectively to equip teachers to undertake family literacy work). Rather, the point here is about *purpose* and *planning*. That is to say that sufficient time should be allocated before, during and after a programme to meet the

Table 6.1   Time allocated to the programme pre-, during- and post-project

Phase	Sessions	Hours
Pre-project	five full-days (one day a week for five weeks)	30
During project	14 after-school 'twilight' meetings	28
During project	One full day	6
Post-project	One full day	6
Total	7 full days and 14 'twilight'	70

particular professional development needs of the family literacy workers and enable them to grow as professionals and to develop their continued work as a team.

Is professional development essential?

Unequivocally, all the teachers reported that a knowledge base which underpinned their skills was crucial and that their participation in a professional development programme which focused on theoretical aspects of early literacy development, parents as adult learners, and practicalities (like home visiting, group meetings) and solving difficulties was essential. When asked how important the professional development programme was to their family literacy work, they make comments such as those illustrated in Figure 6.5.

What permeates the responses in Figure 6.5 is the sense of teamwork and professional trust which developed within the team as part of the ongoing contact during the initial five-day programme and the monthly team meetings. The teachers felt that their enhanced theoretical knowledge and the opportunity to work and grow as a team contributed to the success for their family literacy work. All the teachers identified their involvement in a cohesive, trusting team as a positive and essential part of their family literacy work.

All the teachers considered their professional development programme to be essential to their family literacy work and a key factor in establishing and sustaining the quality of the work they did with families. As one teacher said:

> I think if you hadn't have done those five days you wouldn't have got the quality work out of it that you did. So I think it was really vital and certainly for me I thought it was excellent . . .

This evaluation of professional development suggests that 'quickie courses' are not enough for successful family literacy work which benefit workers as well as families. A one-day 'this is how you do it' session would not have satisfied the teachers working on this project because they would have not been afforded the opportunity to grow as a professionally supportive network who could rely on their own skills and knowledge in making decisions and on their colleagues for professional and personal support. Taking family literacy seriously, these teachers tell us, means taking teacher professional

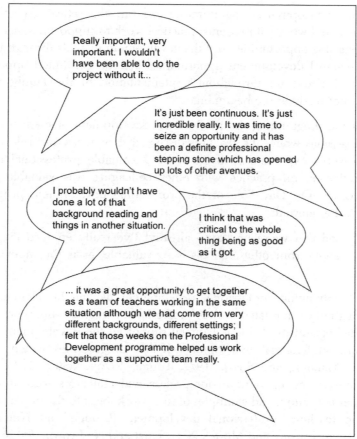

Figure 6.5   Teachers' comments on the importance of the professional development programme

development for family literacy work seriously too, and so enhances professional growth:

> I think the process was so gradual that I did do things differently, but a little bit like watching a child grow, you are not actually aware that they are growing, but you know they are growing and I think it was like that for me.

Implications for future professional development programmes for experienced early years teachers

The experience of working on a family literacy programme and receiving ongoing support for their work was a valuable professional development experience in itself. Viewed from the teachers' perspectives, there are three key implications for the design of future professional development programmes for teachers. Specifically, these are that:

● such work should be supported by sufficient time for continuing professional development for workers

- professional development programmes focus on: theoretical aspects of literacy development and work with parents; practical work to support parents; information on adult learning opportunities and the development of skills through teamwork
- such professional development opportunities include continued opportunities for learning and discussion throughout implementation of the family literacy programme – not solely at the beginning.

At the start of the programme, the professional development element was defined as those planned sessions where the teachers discussed their work and relevant research. However, the whole experience proved to be a valuable professional development experience. Reflection on practice with other colleagues was valuable in terms of developing practice. On Day Five of the professional development programme one teacher wrote in her journal:

> I'm a little sad that we're on day 5 already! I've really enjoyed the course: talking to people from other schools is so valuable, as is the input and the discussion.

The design of continuing professional development as 'taught' elements alongside teachers carrying out work related to their professional contexts is not new: for example, in the 1970s in England the Schools Council supported the development of two early years continuing professional development (CPD) programmes which ran over an academic year (Manning and Sharp, 1977; Tough, 1976). Neither is involvement in reflective action-research uncommon for professional educators who undertake CPD courses in higher education, and examples of such work attest to the impact of such CPD experiences on teachers' professional development (Clough and Nutbrown, 2001; Nutbrown, 2002; Armstrong and Moore, 2004; Hirst and Nutbrown, 2005). This level of professional development – the combination of the development of practice with reflective critique of academic papers – and the length of time devoted to it, is akin to some higher degree work (Hedge, 1996), including CPD programmes funded by the Teacher Training Agency and Higher Education Funding Council.

The teachers' reflections on their professional development for family literacy suggest that such an experience is essential for them and it proved to be a cornerstone of their ongoing network of support.

PART III

Evaluation and the Perspectives of Participants

The ideas put forward in Part II of this book were informed by research but the future development of family literacy requires continued research. Some of this needs to be theoretical to help us understand the context for family literacy practice but there is also a distinct need for good quality evaluation or evaluative research to help us understand what programmes are valuable in what contexts. In this part of the book we first (in Chapter 7) offer a view about evaluation – what it is, what it should accomplish and how findings from evaluation studies should be shared within the education community. We have tried to follow these principles in evaluating the REAL Project. This part of the book presents four different elements of our evaluation: studies of the value of the programme from the perspectives of practitioners, parents and children (Chapters 8, 9, 10) and a quantitative study of its value in influencing children's literacy development (Chapter 11).

7 The importance of evaluation

> *Chapter summary*
> ● Introduction
> ● Why evaluate?
> ● Writing
> ● An evaluation checklist
>   – Description of context
>   – Clarification of aims and desired outcomes
>   – Previous research
>   – Programme/initiative description
>   – Take-up
>   – Participation, stop-out and drop-out
>   – Implementation
>   – Quality of processes
>   – Participants' views
>   – Outcomes in activities
>   – Outcomes in literacy measures
> ● Further reading

Introduction

Our view of evaluation has been developed through a series of studies, several of which have been referred to in earlier chapters. Some key ideas about evaluation – what it is, what it should accomplish and how findings from evaluation studies should be shared within the education community – have been set forth at some length by Hannon (1995). In this chapter we summarise those ideas and show how they have influenced the design of the evaluation of the family literacy programme in the REAL Project.

The project took place at a time of increasing interest and activity in exploring new ways of promoting literacy learning in and out of school. Some initiatives took place within particular communities, areas or organisations. Others were national or were of clear national significance. Large-scale initiatives often had smaller ones nested within them. Whatever the scale and focus of an initiative, we argue that consideration should be given to evaluation and that the ideas to be outlined below are of general relevance.

Evaluation can take many forms. Individual practitioners, working with limited time and resources, cannot be reasonably expected to attempt to produce conclusive, documented evidence that what they are doing is successful. It might be enough to document what has been done and to collect participants' views about its value.

However, if the programme is a well-funded project that aspires to be of national or international significance, involving many learners and practitioners, there is an obligation to do more.

Why evaluate?

Without evaluation we are at the mercy of educational fashion and prejudice. If we try something new in family literacy we ought to evaluate it. Without evaluation of some kind we cannot be sure that we are accomplishing what we set out to do, and we cannot show other people (particularly those with responsibility for funding decisions) that what we are doing is valuable.

It is important to recognise that – as the term suggests – 'evaluation' is about *values*. Many values in early literacy education and family literacy are widely held. For instance, most people want children eventually to be competent readers, good spellers, to enjoy books, and so on; and family literacy workers want parents to be confident about their own capacities as teachers and learners. But problems arise when values conflict, or we want to give priority to one over another. For example, is it more important that parents follow what professionals regard as 'good practice' or that they get involved in their own way? Here the process of evaluation ought to involve making our values and priorities clear. The evaluation should reflect the values in our practice. There is no point, for example, in evaluating a programme by testing children's reading ability on standardised measures if what we really value is children's enjoyment of shared stories.

Another important point about evaluation is that it is about *choosing between options*. At the very least the options are to run a programme or to leave things as they are. If we are in a situation of genuinely having no options, it is probably a waste of effort to conduct an evaluation. Where there are options, say to repeat a programme or to change it in the light of what has been learned, an evaluation ought to try to compare what was done to some reasonable alternative. What else might children and parents have experienced? Would it have been any better? How else might we have spent our energies?

Writing

Writing is an essential part of evaluation. If time is short and the evaluation will have no audience other than the person who carries it out, it is still worth writing something – even if only a paragraph or two. The very act of writing about what we have done helps us to concentrate on it, distances us from the immediacy of action and enables us to reflect and learn from experience. Writing also opens up the possibility of sharing our experience with others at some point and reminding us at a later date of how we approached different aspects or challenges. Research and evaluation are a way of telling a story of what happened in a family literacy programme in terms which can enable others to judge its relevance and value for their situation. It should also tell that story in a systematic and inquiring manner, fulfilling as far as possible Laurence Stenhouse's definition of research as 'systematic enquiry made public' (Stenhouse, 1975). During the REAL Project, teachers and researchers wrote frequently (for example, in records of contacts with families, in reflections at the end of professional development sessions). Such writing was kept and has been referred to in this book. This book itself, and other publications from the project, are further attempts to use writing to learn from and communicate aspects of the project.

An evaluation checklist

Figure 7.1 is an evaluation checklist which suggests 11 points to consider in evaluating a family literacy initiative. It guided our approach and may be of interest to others contemplating an evaluation of a programme. We explain, below, what the 11 points meant to us.

EVALUATION CHECKLIST

Points to consider in an evaluation

1. Description of context
2. Clarification of aims and desired outcomes
3. Previous research
4. Programme/initiative description
5. Take-up
6. Participation, stop-out and drop-out
7. Implementation
8. Quality of processes
9. Participants' views
10. Outcomes in activities
11. Outcomes in literacy measures

Figure 7.1   Evaluation checklist

Describing the context

The first step in evaluating an initiative should be to describe the setting in which it takes place. It is impossible to reach a view about the value of some action without relating it to a particular context. Writing this down helps us identify assumptions underlying our practice and enables other people to work out the relevance of our experience for their situation. In this book we have tried to describe the context of the REAL Project in terms of the policy and research contexts in which it took place and we provide details of the families with whom we worked.

Stating aims and objectives

Undertaking an evaluation requires clearly stated aims for an initiative. What are the desired outcomes? The first objective ought then to be to find out how far the stated aims have been met. (There may be scope for finding out about other things, too, but that should not be at the expense of the central task.) In the REAL Project we had six main aims that were stated in Chapter 3.

Building on previous research

All family literacy initiatives, however unique or innovative, are related to other earlier work and to previously reported evaluations in some way. It is important to acknowledge and build upon the work which has informed and stimulated new initiatives and to give readers of a report a sense of how this evaluation adds to what is already known in a field. Therefore some part of the evaluation effort should go into finding out and summarising previous work. This we have done in Chapter 2.

Programme/initiative description

In any evaluation it is important to give an outline of the programme under evaluation, what frameworks and processes were used. The important point here is to give enough information for a reader of the evaluation report to be able to grasp the nature of the programme at the outset of the work and to make it possible to identify the relationship between what was planned and what actually happened. A detailed description of the family literacy programme in the REAL Project was given in Chapter 4 and further information as needed in other chapters.

Take-up

It is too often assumed that evaluation of literacy programmes can be based solely on participants' test scores but this can be inappropriate. There are some preliminary points to be considered, the first of which is take-up. How many of those invited to participate in a programme actually take up the invitation? If the proportion is very low, that suggests at once that the programme may have limited value. If it is high, further questions can be asked. Details of take-up of the REAL family literacy programme are given in Chapter 9.

Participation, stop-out and drop-out

Those who participate in a programme may not stay with it. Hence it is important to monitor participation and drop-out. (Stop-out – leaving and then returning to a programme – is important too.) It takes thought and record-keeping to document this but the effort is worthwhile for something can then be learned about the value of an initiative from how families 'vote with their feet'. Reasons for drop-out, for example, may reveal that the programme was something that mattered to a family but that circumstances made it impossible for them to continue. These points are covered in Chapter 9.

Implementation

The implementation of a programme is crucial. How it works in practice can be significantly different from what was planned. Information about what was done, the materials and strategies that were used, what it cost in terms of staff time, the knock-on effects, and so on, can be very helpful in reaching a view about the value of an initiative. Diary notes, observations, interviews, photographs and examples of work are some of the sources of information which can contribute to this part of an evaluation. These issues are addressed in several chapters.

Quality of processes

An evaluation can explore the quality of processes in an initiative and associated programmes. This can be a challenge. Every initiative has processes of some kind. These can occur, for example, in the provision of opportunities for parents' learning, in parent–child talk about environmental print, in conversation in a parents' group, or in a teacher professional development course. It is often worth reflecting on the quality of what goes on. We do not have to be very sophisticated to reach conclusions. For example, if, in a parent group, only one or two ever contribute to the discussion or, in classroom writing, pupils are restricted to a single genre, there are grounds for questioning whether the process is as valuable as was hoped. These issues are addressed in several of the following chapters.

Participants' views

Ultimately, initiatives are much more than abstract ideas, plans or documents. They are about people doing things together. The participants can include parents, other family members, teachers and other professionals as well as children. Therefore it makes sense to seek participants' views. The conventional ways of doing this are through interviews, questionnaires and noting conversations. Much depends on the resources (time, money) available for the evaluation but, even when time and money are short, some way can usually be found to check on participants' views. Chapter 8 concerns teachers' views of the REAL programme and Chapter 9, the parents' views. Chapter 10 reports our attempt to explore the children's views.

Outcomes in activities

The main question that an evaluation ought to answer is whether or not the initiative has secured the desired outcomes. This takes us back to the aims. Outcomes could be activities, such as the number of families making frequent use of the community library as well as changes in early literacy development, such as children's knowledge of environmental print. Chapters 8, 9 and 10 all concern such outcomes – as seen from the perspectives of teachers, parents and children.

Outcomes in literacy measures

Is there a case for using tests to measure outcomes in literacy development? The answer is 'yes' but only if three things can be satisfactorily addressed. First, tests are not a substitute for the other components of evaluation already discussed in this chapter. The second consideration is the nature and quality of tests. These need to be valid and to reflect the initiative aims. It can be difficult to find tests which meet these criteria, especially for young children (Nutbrown, 1997). Third, the test scores of learners in an initiative have to be compared to something – on their own they are meaningless. There are many possible comparisons – to pre-programme scores, to national norms, to a control group – but each has pitfalls. If test scores are to be used, evaluators must be very confident that they know what these pitfalls are, and how to avoid them, before allowing the initiative to be judged on the basis of test data (Hannon, 1995). In the REAL Project we went to some trouble to develop appropriate measures and to make valid comparisons within a randomised control trial design (Hannon et al., 2005). An outline of that design and the key findings is given in Chapter 11.

Having explained what we see as essential elements of evaluation, the next chapters will focus on evaluating the perspectives of practitioners and parents on their involvement in the REAL Project and of children's views of family literacy. Their views are followed by a brief report of the outcomes of the project as shown by measures of children's literacy development.

Further reading

The ideas in this chapter are set out at greater length in Chapters 8, 9 and 10 of the following book:

Hannon, P. (1995) *Literacy, home and school.* London: Falmer Press.

For further reading on measures of early literacy development, see:

Nutbrown, C. (1997) *Recognising early literacy development: Assessing children's achievements.* London: Paul Chapman Publishing.

8 Teachers' experiences of family literacy

Chapter summary
- Introduction
- Involving teachers in family literacy evaluation
- National policy and the research context
- A multi-method approach to eliciting teachers' views on their experience
- What conditions support teachers' family literacy work?
  - Time
  - Relationships
  - Home visiting
  - Teachers' attitudes, knowledge and skills
- How useful is the ORIM framework in developing family literacy work?
- Lessons from teachers on developing successful family literacy work

---

Introduction

As we have seen in Part I of this book, the scope and nature of early childhood education have broadened with recent policy developments, and early childhood teachers are increasingly involved in non-traditional roles in new developments and initiatives. Such is the case, too, with family literacy programmes, with many early childhood educators becoming involved in a variety of family literacy programme delivery (Brooks *et al.*, 1996; Cairney and Munsie, 1995; Hannon and Nutbrown, 1997, 2001). Although family literacy programmes have been researched and their impact evaluated, one issue that has largely been ignored is the experience of the early childhood teachers. It is not addressed, for example, by Brooks *et al.* (1996), Dickinson (1994) or Wolfendale and Topping (1996), while Hannon (2000a) has noted that the absence of discussion on the topic is problematic.

This chapter describes a multi-method approach to eliciting teachers' views and reports the experiences and perspectives on family literacy work of the teachers who developed and worked on the programme with parents and their young children.

It shows how teachers emphasised the importance of dedicated time to work with families; the creating of positive relationships with families; and the usefulness of the ORIM framework for developing literacy work with families.

Involving teachers in family literacy evaluation

Research into family literacy practices of parents, children and others have been widely reported (Heath, 1983; Teale, 1986; Taylor and Dorsey-Gaines, 1988; Weinberger, 1996; Barton and Hamilton, 1998; Hirst, 1998, 2001) and several family literacy programmes have been documented and evaluated (Dickinson, 1994; Cairney and Munsie, 1995; Hannon, 1995; Morrow, 1995; Wolfendale and Topping, 1996; Hannon and Nutbrown, 1997). Experienced pre-school teachers with skills and knowledge for work with children and for promoting early literacy development are not normally trained to work with adults. Little is known of the perspectives of teachers working on family literacy programmes. Some evaluations report the perspectives of adult literacy workers on programme outcomes for children and parents (Brooks *et al.*, 1997) but the impact of working on such programmes on the family literacy workers is rarely discussed. This chapter looks at the experiences of ten teachers in terms of what, from their perspective, made family literacy work successfully for families and what they gained themselves from undertaking such work.

National policy and the research context

Chapters 1 and 2 discussed the policy contexts in which the REAL Project took place. The teachers who participated in the project were working 'against the grain' of the current mainstream experience. While in their classrooms teacher autonomy was increasingly being eroded by policy decisions which impacted on curriculum and on pedagogy, their family literacy work had the potential to be the opposite. In their 'out-of-classroom' roles, the teachers were more autonomous, developing new ideas and methods of working with individual families and, effectively, creating fresh approaches to home-literacy curriculum and pedagogy. In their family literacy roles, they could work outside prescribed curriculum and timetables and in a research-oriented climate which included support, resources, time and continuing professional development and which encouraged ongoing reflection, critique and evaluation.

As we have seen, the REAL Project that provided the setting for this study of teachers' perspectives involved parents and pre-school children from 80 families and ten early years teachers. The additional school with a group of eight bilingual families was also part of the project but the family literacy worker with this group was part of the university team and not a practising teacher, hence she was not included in this part of the study. The programme, developed and implemented by teachers at ten schools, was 'long duration' (18 months) and 'low intensity' (contact every three to four weeks). Work with families was based on the ORIM framework (discussed in Chapters 3 and 4) which helped teachers to plan, develop and evaluate literacy by promoting four strands of early literacy development (writing, reading and rhyming at home with family members and greater awareness of environmental print) and four roles of parents (providing opportunities for literacy; showing recognition of children's literacy achievements; sharing literacy interactions; and being a model of a literacy user).

As outlined earlier, the programme had five components: home visits by project teachers; provision of literacy resources (particularly books); centre-based group activities; special events (for example, group visits to a local library, visits to a shopping mall); and postal communication between the child and the project teacher.

A multi-method approach to eliciting teachers' views on their experience

Given the national context for the family literacy work as set out in Chapters 1 and 2, the nature of the family literacy programme (Chapters 3 and 4) and the professional development programme for teachers (Chapter 6), it was important that our evaluation investigated teachers' perspectives on the following questions:

1   What conditions support teachers' family literacy work?
2   How useful is a conceptual framework in developing family literacy work?
3   What is the role of professional development in supporting teachers' family literacy work?

Chapter 6 has already discussed question 3 so the remainder of this chapter will focus on the first two questions.

It was important to learn from the teachers how future work might be developed in the light of their experience and to elicit any negative (as well as positive) responses. Table 8.1 shows the five main methods used to determine teachers' views. The multi-method approach was adopted to maximise the potential for eliciting comprehensive pictures of the programme from the teachers' viewpoints. All data (and earlier drafts of this chapter) were viewed and commented on by the teachers so that misinterpretations could be corrected and new insights developed. Teachers participated readily in these data-gathering exercises. Some reported that they felt more comfortable with the one-to-one telephone interviews than when they carried out peer interviewing with a tape recorder. Teachers also felt that they had ample and varied opportunities to express their views on the programme, and to talk about 'lowlights' as well as 'highlights'. They confirmed that they were not reluctant to talk about the things they found difficult as well as those elements they saw as successful.

These methods generated ten written responses to peer interviews; five transcribed taped peer conversations; ten individual telephone interviews; and ten written responses to the postcard question.

Data from methods 1, 2, 3 and 4 in Table 8.1 were analysed, first discretely and secondly in combination, to identify themes which were widely shared across teachers in the group. Documentation data (method 5) were drawn on further to illuminate issues which emerged from analysis of previous data sets. Analysis identified several views which were salient in the data collected from different sources and were widely shared. The remainder of this chapter will focus on these in so far as they illuminate our two research questions:

1   What conditions support teachers' family literacy work?
2   How useful is a conceptual framework in developing family literacy work?

Table 8.1   Five main methods used to determine teachers' views

Methods	Description
1 Self-paired peer interview using pre-prepared interview schedule	Teachers interviewed each other in self-selected pairs, using an interview schedule. They made notes of their responses on the schedule. Responses were collated and returned to the teachers for checking, amendment and clarification.
2 Pre-paired peer discussion with stimulus document and questions	The collated data (from interview 1 above) and a series of additional questions were the stimulus for the taped peer discussions. Teachers discussed a range of questions and issues with each other (in pre-allocated pairs, using different pairings from those in interview 1). These discussions were recorded on tape. Tapes were transcribed and returned to teachers for checking, amendment and clarification.
3 Individual telephone interview	Teachers were interviewed, by the first author, individually (by telephone) using a pre-prepared schedule as an *aide-mémoire*. Taped interviews were transcribed and returned to the interviewees for checking, amendment and clarification.
4 Single question postcard	A postcard was sent to the teachers bearing a single question (additional to those covered in the above interviews) which asked for an anonymous written response. All teachers responded.
5 Documentation	<ul><li>occasional notes sent by the teachers to the project team</li><li>conversations with the project team during the programme</li><li>notes from team meetings</li><li>teachers' jottings on programme record sheets</li></ul>

What conditions support teachers' family literacy work?

All ten teachers greatly valued the opportunity to work with a small group of parents over a period of 18 months and they found it changed their thinking about their work with all parents. One teacher said:

> It really made me refocus on what family agendas are, which was in some ways quite separate to school agendas, and I think it made me more open about home situations.

The conditions which supported this work were, teachers said: time, home visiting and flexibility, all of which contributed to the development of positive relationships between teachers and families.

Time
The long duration of the programme (18 months) was both an advantage and a disadvantage. Funded release from classroom work was essential; without this the

teachers would never have been able to participate. The lifespan of the project was identified as one of the crucial factors in the development of successful relationships:

> . . . it was the length of the time we were able to work with the parents so you didn't feel you needed to rush things which you often do on a lot of projects that are ten weeks long and you feel you have to leap straight into it.

> . . . the parents, as time went on, they got more and more into it and in the end, they were quite sad to finish it. Certainly a lot of them were, I think they would have liked it to have carried on . . .

However, the duration of the project also created some difficulties for teachers in their classroom and management roles:

> You come straight back to the nursery. Straight back to all the problems you've got there.

> For a full-time teacher with all the extra responsibilities, management roles, everything else, that [family literacy work] is an added pressure.

> The workload in school doesn't diminish when you're out. There's a concern about the staff you leave behind.

> I think what I would definitely try and do again is not have that dual role of being in charge of the nursery and doing this. It's difficult.

One teacher who worked part time – and had no difficulties in fulfilling her dual roles said:

> It worked well, I worked on the programme when I was not teaching so there was no 'cover' involved.

Relationships

A clear finding, and one where all ten teachers were unanimous, was that teachers need dedicated time to focus on work with families. All teachers felt that having dedicated time helped them to develop a flexible, responsive programme through home visiting. Central to their work, all the teachers said, were positive relationships with families. Typical comments included:

> I think relationships were the key factor, that was the bedrock of it really.

> We had to build good relationships with them and trust, most important those two things.

Home visiting

All of the teachers interviewed were unequivocal in highlighting relationships as a fundamental feature in their experience of family literacy work. Similarly, everyone interviewed identified the practice of home visiting as essential.

> Home visiting was **the** factor.

> I think the successful part was the home visiting part of it; I don't think it would
> have been successful if it would have meant having parents coming into school
> for meetings, not for my group anyway.

Working in families' own homes seemed to help teachers to develop the kinds of
relationships with parents they had said were important. The teachers were clear about
conditions which made it possible for them to engage in such work: dedicated time in
order to sustain work with families, and a flexible working attitude which made it possible
to fit in with families' lives.

> I think it's the consistency. They liked the fact that they knew you were coming
> and it was the same person coming in, and you built up a sort of trust.

> I had to be really flexible and non-judgmental about anything.

Teachers' attitudes, knowledge and skills

Teachers had a clear sense of what they brought to the collaboration with parents – the
attitudes, knowledge and skills which they judged to be crucial for such work. They
presented a consistent message about: the importance of a positive attitude towards
parents' roles in early literacy development; having time to do the work; professional
development to support their increasing knowledge of literacy development; skills to
work alongside parents in parents' own homes; teamwork and networking as factors
contributing to their own increased professional confidence.

The teachers conveyed attitudes of respectful, non-judgemental responsiveness towards
the families they worked with. Phrases like – 'starting where families are', 'Taking on
board what families want to do', 'Handing it over to them . . .' permeate the data.

How useful is the ORIM framework in developing family literacy work?

Chapter 3 explained the theoretical underpinnings of the conceptual framework, ORIM
(Nutbrown and Hannon, 1997) which was central to planning and developing the REAL
Project programme. Chapter 4 showed how the ORIM framework can be covered, over
time, with families. But how useful did the ORIM framework prove to be to the teachers
as they worked with it, over time?

All the teachers said that they used the ORIM framework to plan their family literacy
work. The framework had been evaluated previously in a survey of teachers in 24
schools, with the majority finding it useful for planning and evaluating early literacy work
with parents (Hannon and Nutbrown, 1997). That evaluation focused on using the ORIM
framework to plan and develop work with *groups* of parents. In the evaluation of ten
teachers running the REAL Project programme, the focus was most often oriented
towards *individual* families. It was important therefore, to investigate the usefulness to
teachers of the ORIM framework for planning individual family literacy work.

All teachers said that they used ORIM to plan their work, and also to reflect (after
home visits) on what happened.

Table 8.2 Teachers' three main uses of the ORIM framework

Teacher	1. A planning tool to ensure range of coverage (before the event)	2. A reflective and analytical tool for checking family literacy coverage (after the event)	3. A central and essential component of the family literacy programme which informed all programme planning
1	✓		✓
2	✓		
3	✓		
4	✓		
5		✓	✓
6	✓		✓
7	✓		✓
8		✓	✓
9	✓		
10	✓		

I used ORIM a lot at first – I was worried that I wouldn't get through all the cells.

At first I continually referred to ORIM, but as time went on I used it more to check that I hadn't missed anything out.

I got a bit confused sometimes as to whether an activity was 'opportunities' or 'interaction'. And I got muddled about 'models' – was I the model or the mother? That sort of thing – we talked a lot about ORIM and once I started using it as a 'servant' rather than a 'master' – and not a 'blueprint to be slavishly followed' – I found it really useful.

I think I used ORIM quite naturally – as part of my thinking – as the project went on.

Table 8.2 shows how the teachers' use of the ORIM framework fell into three categories:

1 as a planning tool to ensure range of coverage (before the event)
2 as a reflective/analytical tool for checking family literacy coverage (after the event)
3 as a central and essential component of the family literacy programme which informed all programme development.

Two teachers said they used it mainly as a reflective device for checking that they had covered the main elements of parents' roles and strands of literacy but they also felt it was central and essential to programme development. Eight teachers said they used it mainly as a tool to aid their forward planning and four of those also felt it was central and essential. Six teachers said that they considered the ORIM framework as a central and essential component of the programme but used it also to either check work done or plan family literacy work. Six of the ten teachers gave two key uses for ORIM; the remaining four used it as a planning tool.

This analysis suggests that the teachers found ORIM to be an effective aid to family literacy work. Further analysis of teachers' home visit notes indicates that all teachers used the ORIM framework on a regular basis to identify work done and anticipate future work with parents. The teachers became less conscious of using the ORIM framework as they developed their work over time, the framework perhaps becoming more intrinsic and less overt in their thinking.

Lessons from teachers on developing successful family literacy work

As Chapter 6 has shown, the teachers in this study felt supported and confident in their family literacy work as a result of their professional development experiences which added, not only to their knowledge and skills, but also to their network of support. Reflecting on their experiences with families, they have stated unequivocally that they needed time to carry out such work properly but that time alone did not solve all the difficulties they encountered. They also spoke clearly about giving such work time to develop and emphasised the importance of developing work over time, without rushing, and working at the pace each family found right for them. It is time, they told us, that was needed to foster the positive and trusting relationships which so obviously were crucial to sustained involvement with families. The flexibility of their work, due to the emphasis on home visiting, meant that the programme could be fitted to families, rather than families fitting into a 'one size fits all' programme. Work could build on everyday literacy in families' homes and the individual nature of the work was identified by the teachers as an important part of it.

What stands out too, are the respectful attitudes towards parents which all the teachers held and the ways in which they shared their knowledge and skills about early literacy with parents which built upon what existed in families rather than seeking to impose a different view which might undermine parents' roles and confidence.

This chapter ends with a personal account from Judith Butler , one of the teachers in this study who reflected some years later on her involvement in family literacy work:[1]

> Staggering under the weight of two large bags loaded with carefully chosen books, Play dough and writing materials, the unexpected greeting from the small pyjama-clad figure peering out from between his mum's legs as she opened the front door was more than a little disconcerting. 'Go away!' said Steven. 'I don't want you!'

> Working with the Sheffield Raising Early Achievement in Literacy project, I was funded to spend one day every fortnight for 18 months with eight families. I focused mainly on home visits, but also held group workshops for the parents and special events for parents and children. This long-term, low-intensity and essentially practical work was intended to support adult family members in activities to promote literacy in very young children.

> Steven's reaction to my arrival at his front door was not typical. But perhaps he expressed the anxiety that others – parents and children – felt to some degree. The families had all agreed to take part in the project without really knowing quite what it would involve.

I think much the same applied to the project teachers. I well remember the training day when after intense discussions about theory and philosophy, someone was bold enough to ask, 'But what exactly are we going to do?' In fact, the work was linked to strands of early literacy development, including books, early writing, oracy and the 'environmental print' children see all around them in shops, adverts and road signs. Each home visit or group activity would focus on one aspect. Books were key, and choosing one or two to borrow became a feature of each home visit.

I found that only one of the families used the local library regularly, and there were very few books for young children other than well-chewed board 'baby books' in evidence.

In most homes, I did not see newspapers or other adult reading, although there were often comics and annuals for the older siblings. Even so, the mothers – and one grandmother – who joined in the visits responded enthusiastically, and many of the earlier visits focused on looking through the books and responding to the children's eager comments: 'Read it now!' or, 'Read another one!'.

Steven did let me through the door, but for several weeks his visits consisted of reading a story, having a drink and a biscuit, and choosing a book to borrow. Then he would say: 'You can go now.'

In group meetings, adults talked about what makes a good book, shared ideas for linking pictures to text and encouraging prediction and recall. We were welcomed at the local library and at Christmas the project funded a book token for each child. So, off we went to Waterstone's. It was a first-time visit to a bookshop for all but one family. 'Can they get the books out? Won't they mind?' No, they didn't mind. Indeed, the staff respected the children as customers and showered them with balloons and bookmarks.

Searching out environmental print also provided lots of fun for all the family. On home visits and group outings, emptying kitchen cupboards or walking to and from the shopping centre, revealed unexpected print awareness.

Adults were frequently astonished at the children's ability to identify logos on breakfast cereal packaging or the shop signs of fast-food outlets. Mums and children made scrapbooks and card games of labels and logos they recognised. Some included football emblems, and one child collected the letterheads of the companies his parents worked for.

On another occasion we all spent a happy summer's day at a farm, following a photographic trail to 'find the signs'. And our Christmas bookshop visit included following some rhyming clues to find the signs along the way. Setting up these activities was time-consuming but extremely worthwhile, as they enabled adults and children to work collaboratively in a relaxed setting.

Many of the children's early writing experiences took place on home visits. These centred on providing opportunities – materials, space and time – as well as the recognition of the stages of writing development, the modelling of writing by adults, and children and adults working together. But letters between the project teacher and children were the most powerful tool for bringing the children to an awareness of the reasons for writing.

Spotty Dog, a toy which I took with me on home visits, wrote to the children and got a wide range of replies. He always included a stamped envelope with his letters. Holiday postcards and diaries were also motivating. Adults became increasingly confident in encouraging and then scribing the children's spoken language.

With the help of this variety of approaches, the programme of work developed over 18 months until the children were ready to start in reception class. This was low-intensity work, but it became part of all our lives. Perhaps the culmination of the project came when three of the project mothers received accreditation from the Open College for portfolios of work done with their children, and all the parents and children received certificates and congratulations from David Blunkett (who was then Secretary of State for Education).

The children I worked with on the REAL Project are now in Year 5. I have been privileged to be able to follow their progress and maintain contact with their families through the years, and I am humbled by the openness, trust and commitment they showed.

I am convinced that the ways of working with families developed in the project, particularly the building of supportive and non-judgemental relationships, can and should be the basis of educational practice in the foundation stage and beyond.

Note

1   This extract was originally published in the *Times Educational Supplement*, 13 February 2004.

9 Parents' experiences and views of a family literacy programme

> ## Chapter summary
> - Introduction
> - Did parents participate in a family literacy programme, and to what extent?
> - How did parents evaluate the programme?
>   - Parents' views of the programme
>   - Parents' views of programme outcomes
> - What changes, if any, did the programme make to parents' family literacy practices?
> - Implications of parents' perspectives for the design and development of family literacy programmes
>   - Building on existing relationships and familiarity
>   - Offering a programme at the right time
>   - A non-stigmatising programme
>   - A highly flexible approach

Introduction

This chapter examines the REAL Project family literacy programme from the perspective of the parents involved in it. This is important because, despite their involvement being crucial to the success of any programme, relatively few studies of programmes to date have sought parents' views. Drawing on interviews with parents at the beginning and end of the programme and home visit records, the chapter asks three questions:

1 Would parents take up the invitation to participate in a family literacy programme, and to what extent?
2 What were parents' views of the programme?
3 What changes, if any, would the programme make to parents' family literacy practices?

Five main sources of data were used to respond to these questions: family characteristics (educational and occupational level, poverty, size of families, ethnicity, language and existing literacy practices); how parents responded behaviourally to both child and adult aspects of the programme (rates of take-up, participation, drop-out and numbers of visits, group meetings and special events in which they participated); observations made by teachers during the programme (group meeting and home visit records documenting how parents responded to the programme plus some of their comments); teachers' ratings of families' participation; parents' comments made to independent interviewers at the end of the programme and how their responses compared to those of other parents never involved in a programme.

Did parents take up the invitation to participate in a family literacy programme, and to what extent?

Chapter 7 discussed the importance of considering take-up rates when evaluating family literacy programmes; such factors have been overlooked in some evaluations, perhaps because gauging them can be problematic. For example, take-up is sometimes treated in terms of whether or not places are filled on a programme, or whether families in programmes are from the target population (St. Pierre *et al.*, 1995; Brooks *et al.*, 1996), although this tells us nothing about what proportion of the target group takes up the programme. The restrictive nature of some programmes, specifically whether parents must undertake an adult education component, is likely to affect take-up rates. Even Start programmes in the USA experienced 'difficulties in the recruitment, retention, attendance and motivation of families' (St. Pierre *et al.*, 1995, p.86), while in Britain an evaluation of one ALBSU – Adult Literacy Basic Skills Unit – initiative also reported recruitment difficulties (Poulson *et al.*, 1997).

The actual participation of those families who take up family literacy programmes is also an area of interest for researchers, since programme success or otherwise will inevitably depend on the extent of participation. Researchers have devised a variety of methods of gauging parents' participation: records of the frequency of parent–child reading sessions (Hannon and Jackson, 1987; Whitehurst *et al.*, 1994), asking parents to rate books they had shared with their children as part of a programme (Whitehurst *et al.*, 1994); records and reports from professionals involved in delivering programmes (Pfannenstiel and Seltzer, 1989); and parent report (Hebbeler and Gerlach-Downie, 2002).

Factors such as take-up and rates of participation are crucial in evaluating programmes, because take-up figures can tell us if parents find the *idea* of involvement in a programme useful and participation rates indicate whether parents stay with the programme and develop the ideas offered through it. Our first research question was about whether parents would accept the invitation to participate in the programme and, having done so, would they stay involved?

Take-up

There was maximum take-up. All parents who were chosen at random to participate in the programme took up the invitation to take part. (Details of characteristics of families who took part in the programme and control groups are in Table 9.1.) This is more positive than previous studies might have led us to expect (St. Pierre *et al.*, 1995; Poulson *et al.*, 1997). When asked why they decided to take part the majority (almost two-thirds) said it was because they wanted to help the child, for example: 'I thought if it would help

Table 9.1   Family characteristics

	Programme group N=85 %	Control group N=73 %
Family structure		
Number of adults in household:		
1	12	21
2	86	78
3 or more	2	1
Number of children at home:		
1	9	12
2	58	45
3	20	29
4 or more	13	14
Mother's educational level		
No qualifications	41	38
Some qualifications	42	38
(CSEs, GCSEs, 'O' Levels, level 1 NVQ or equivalent)		
Five or more CSEs, GCSEs, 'O' Levels or equivalent	12	21
'A' Levels or equivalent	4	3
Higher-level qualifications	1	0
Mother's occupational level		
1 Higher managerial and professional	3	0
2 Lower managerial and professional	5	8
3 Intermediate occupations	12	17
4 Small employers and own account workers	0	1
5 Lower supervisory and technical occupations	7	1
6 Semi-routine occupations	34	36
7 Routine occupations	19	19
8 Never worked and long-term unemployed	20	17
Father's occupational level		
1 Higher managerial and professional	7	6
2 Lower managerial and professional	12	8
3 Intermediate occupations	5	1
4 Small employers and own account workers	13	14
5 Lower supervisory and technical occupations	12	8
6 Semi-routine occupations	35	33
7 Routine occupations	6	4
8 Never worked and long-term unemployed	2	6
No data (details not given, usually because father does not live at the home)	8	20

Bridget, I'd like to be part of it' and 'I grabbed at the chance to take part and I'm really glad I did.'

Participation

It is one thing for parents to accept the invitation to get involved in a family literacy programme, but continued participation is quite another matter. As was argued in Chapter 7, the level of participation is another important factor in judging the level of involvement of a programme. In order to evaluate the extent to which families had participated in the programme, we asked programme teachers to develop a collectively agreed scale of involvement and then to rate families' involvement on this scale of 1–5 as shown in Box 9.1.

Box 9.1 Parental participation rating scale

5   Participated regularly – clear and continuing indications of activity between contacts

4   Participated regularly – intermittently active between contacts

3   Participated regularly – but virtually no indication of activity between contacts

2   Participated minimally or irregularly – very little work focused on literacy

1   'Stopped out' for one or more periods but did not withdraw from programme

---

Figure 9.1 shows the number of families participating at the different levels, with 92% of families participating 'regularly' (at level 3 or higher) and 45% involved at the highest possible level of participation. The majority of families kept regular and active involvement in the programme, an opposite finding to that of some other studies (e.g. Hebbeler and Gerlach-Downie, 2002).

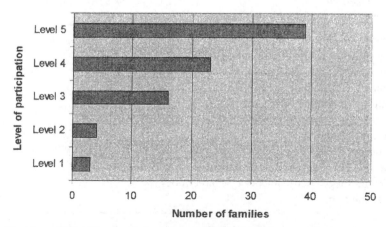

Figure 9.1   Number of families participating at different levels according to programme teachers' judgements (N = 85)

So what did this participation look like? Chapter 4 has already shown the kinds of activities which families shared, covering all cells of the ORIM framework, but the following details give a sense of the levels of activity. Over the duration of the programme 921 home visits were made by 11 teachers, most families having about ten visits. Over 2,300 book loans were recorded, just over 25 per family. Most parents (86%) attended at least one centre-based parents' meeting or family event; over half attended three or more such events.

Considering the long duration of the programme, it would be reasonable to expect that some families would leave it. However, attrition was extremely low. One family moved to another city and so was lost to the programme; another family 'disappeared' and contact was not possible. Three families 'stopped out' of the programme for periods of time, but returned when their home circumstances became more settled.

The majority of families in the REAL Project programme participated regularly and many participated fully. The following example, taken from a programme teacher's home visit records, describes how parents had followed up her previous home visit:

> Karen and her dad used the playdough we had used to make her name into a plaque. We had left it to go hard; dad had varnished it and stuck it on a piece of wood (already stained), put a cord at the back, and it was hanging on her bedroom door! She proudly showed it to me when I went in!

There were many similar examples, where families participated fully and almost always continued the activities left at the end of each home visit.

There were, too, a small number of parents who appeared to participate less regularly. Unsurprisingly, families that were experiencing domestic difficulties, such as splitting from a partner or neighbourhood harassment, were less likely to participate fully, as this programme teacher's home visit notes show:

> I'm struggling to keep this family going although mum obviously thinks the project is important. I tried to explain the importance of her involvement. I also spent a lot of time in general chat; mum rarely goes out. The scrapbook disappeared when the family went into the refuge; it has turned up with very little in it.

Some families had priorities other than the programme, such as a new baby or a house move, as these teachers reported in their home visit notes:

> Mum is expecting a baby and has not been well. She said she has not done anything towards literacy with Jack since my last visit.

> Justin and family moved house during the summer and mum has been completely absorbed in decorating. No evidence of literacy activities.

Often, families that were experiencing some kind of change or upheaval participated in the programme more fully and frequently when their lives became more settled. A small number of families who did not report domestic difficulties participated to a lesser extent, as one teacher's home visiting records show:

Mum asked me if I needed her there as she wanted to clean the bathroom!

In common with other family literacy programmes, while the REAL Project was aimed at parents and children, in practice the programme teachers reported that they most often worked with mothers and children on home visits and at meetings. In some families both mothers and fathers participated and many fathers were involved in literacy activities with their children between visits.

Within the family literacy programme, however, take-up of the parent accreditation component discussed in Chapter 5 was low, involving only nine parents (just over 10%). When compared to the take-up rate of the family literacy programme as a whole, this might seem a somewhat disappointing response. Most parents who did not take up the adult programme component gave reasons such as lack of time for not doing so; for example: 'It's a good idea, but if you've got to work, you've got to work!' Other reasons given included a lack of confidence or a lack of interest, for example: 'I'm not really into college work.' One said: 'I don't want credit for it; it's just what you do as a mum!'

However, as we have already seen in Chapter 5, the nine who took up the opportunity valued it highly. All thought it was worthwhile and made comments such as:

> We've all enjoyed what we've done, it didn't feel like 'work'. Time's really flown by!

The mothers enjoyed getting together as a group, discussing problems and offering support. Some found it challenging and made comments such as:

> At first I thought 'No way am I going to get this!' Eventually I thought 'I've done all this work . . .' It's the writing up that gets me, but with all of us doing it together I think it will be better.

Would so many families have agreed to participate if adult learning was a component for all from the start? We can only speculate as to how insistence on parents participating in adult education as a condition of involvement might have affected initial take-up and continued participation, but the available evidence suggests it would seriously have reduced take-up.

How did parents evaluate the programme?

Another key issue for practice and policy is how parents (as opposed to outside experts, professionals and policy-makers) view such programmes and what they think of what they have been invited to become involved in. Only a small amount of research has been done in this area (Brooks *et al.*, 1996; Hannon and Jackson, 1987; Hannon *et al.*, 1991; Hirst, 2001; Kirkpatrick, 2004), making it all the more important to seek parents' views.

After the programme ended, parents who participated in the programme and similar families who had never been in a family literacy programme (these we refer to as the REAL Project control group) were interviewed about their family literacy practices. They were asked questions relating to the ORIM framework about each of the four strands of literacy.

Parents' views of the programme

The aim was to find out parents' views of the programme itself; their thoughts on the home visiting, the programme teacher, the meetings, special events and the parent education component.

Parents were extremely positive about the programme. When asked what they thought about the REAL Project, 90% gave positive responses, and the remainder thought the programme was 'fine'. Even though interviewers tried to make it easy to say negative things, there were no negative remarks. Parents said:

> I've loved being able to spend quality time to do these things with him, like painting, drawing and playing games. It's just sort of opened my mind that there are things you can do with them apart from sitting watching videos.

> It's been a big help actually. I do think Alan has learned a lot. It makes parents aware of the things they can do with children, because to be honest, especially when you have your first child, you're a little bit unsure.

> I definitely think Julian's had an advantage, because it's shown us which direction to go into and it seems to have worked. It's given me that closer link with school and it makes Julian happy doing it. It feels like he's achieved something.

Only one of the respondents felt that the programme was too much like school. The remaining 84 parents made positive comments, such as: 'It was a nice little stepping stone between home and school', and: 'To me it was like helping her to learn, but not like learning in school.' Only one parent felt being in the programme was a pressure, but that was for understandable reasons: 'Because I was splitting from their dad, everything was hard then.'

Others made comments such as:

> It was sometimes a bit difficult with me working, but not a pressure. I enjoyed doing it.

Five parents identified difficulties. These included getting to meetings and the programme coinciding with the arrival of a new baby. Another identified the most difficult thing as:

> explaining to other parents why Zak was in the project and not their children. They wanted to be part of it. I told them names were pulled out of a hat.

A positive endorsement of the programme was that virtually all parents felt that it should be offered to other families.

Parents rated programme teachers very highly. When asked how they had found working with the programme teacher, parents' responses were all positive and ranged from 'fine' to 'brilliant', 'a friend', and 'very caring'. To the question 'What did you think about the project teacher visiting you at home?' parents gave a variety of responses, all generally positive, with half of all parents saying that they had enjoyed having the teacher visit them at home, and 46% saying it felt 'fine'. Some parents went on to qualify why they enjoyed the teacher visiting at home, for example, by adding that the child looked forward to the visits, or that they liked the fact that the visit was in their own home, or that the home visits had helped the family to develop a good relationship with the teacher. Smaller numbers of parents felt that the child had benefited from the one-to-one attention, or that the child was more settled in the home than elsewhere. The only slightly negative comments were that it was strange at first, although it soon became part of the routine. Three parents were glad that the programme teacher was somebody they already knew from school.

Those parents who had attended at least one meeting, visit or event (86%) were asked for their views and, again, the majority responded positively, with several making comments about the group meetings. About a quarter of parents said the meetings were enjoyable and that they had learned from them. One teacher's group meeting notes highlight how much some parents appreciated and enjoyed these meetings:

> Two parents told me the following day how much they'd enjoyed the meeting. They both felt they'd learned a lot – had not previously used book-words (title, author, etc.) while reading with their children, but are going to now!

Twenty-one per cent said they had enjoyed meeting the other families on the programme. Three parents had felt apprehensive before attending meetings and preferred home visits, while two parents said that attending group meetings was difficult because of work.

Parents thought the best things about the programme were benefits to the child. Eighteen per cent of parents said that the programme had helped to develop their children's awareness of how best to help their child and the same proportion mentioned specific programme ideas, activities or resources. Fourteen per cent said that home visiting was one of the best things about it; the convenience of having someone visit the home made it easier to participate. Twelve per cent liked the trips most of all and 8% most valued the individual attention given to the child by the programme teacher.

Two-thirds of all parents expressed disappointed that the programme was over and expressed sadness. Many spontaneously used the word 'sad' to express their feelings even though it had not been presented to them as part of the interview question. The home visit notes of one programme teacher convey the disappointment felt by one family at the end of the programme:

> Before I left, they gave me two presents and a card as it was my last home visit. Mum got quite emotional about it, as did I. She said 'It won't be the same after Christmas; it'll seem strange you not visiting.'

Eight per cent of parents would have liked the programme to continue into the reception class of primary school, making comments such as:

> I'd have liked it to carry on, even though the children are in school, with the parents meeting maybe once a month.

Seventeen per cent said they were content to move on, and made comments such as:

> She enjoyed it while it were happening, but school's ideal for her now.

Only two parents were relieved the programme was over, saying: 'It's probably a good thing for her now'; 'I'm relieved he's in school!'

Few parents made any negative comments about the programme. In fact, when they were asked what was the worst thing about the programme, over 80% replied '*nothing*'. Five said they remembered being embarrassed on an occasion when their child did not cooperate, and another five found it hard to fit the programme around work commitments or other difficult situations (such as health worries or domestic upset). Two said that having to get up early because of programme-related activities was the worst thing, while one felt that finding time to do the activities the programme teacher had left was difficult. Another did not enjoy completing book reviews with her child and one felt that messy activities, such as playdough and glue, were the worst thing.

Parents' views of programme outcomes

Having learned what the parents thought of the programme for themselves, we were interested to know how they felt the programme had helped their children.

All parents believed children had benefited from the programme, mentioning both global and specific benefits. Just under 25% of parents mentioned only global benefits, such as:

It's brought her on a lot.

I think it's helped her get ahead, she's more advanced than her classmates.

Within two months of starting the project he came on great.

The majority mentioned benefits such as an enhanced development of literacy generally (37%) and improvements in children's specific skills and knowledge in reading, writing or environmental print. They made comments like:

It's done him good. He's interested in books and wanting to read signs. He takes notice more.

One parent who felt that her child had benefited from the programme in terms of early literacy development said:

If every child in this country could have this level of attention, literacy levels could be raised.

Twenty-two per cent of parents had noticed an increased confidence in their children as a result of the programme, while around 13% said the programme had: helped to prepare their children for school; enabled their children to form good relationships, particularly with adults or teachers; enhanced their children's intellectual development, in particular their concentration and motivation to learn. They made comments such as:

I think it's given him a bit of experience before he started school of what to expect. I think it's given him a better start.

It gave him some individual time with his teacher so it made their relationship a bit closer, I think.

He has more confidence with other adults.

It's helped him with his memory.

It's made him more willing to learn.

Around 75% of parents felt that the programme had altered the things they did with their children. Many gave examples which can be viewed in relation to the ORIM framework and strands of literacy.

Comments regarding the *opportunities* they provided for their children, included:

We wouldn't have bought the videos and tapes.

I got more ideas of things to do, like writing in sand and salt and environmental print.

On *recognition* of the child's achievements, parents said:

Sometimes Diane [a programme teacher] used to leave me little leaflets, things to look out for. I used to consciously observe Louise then, whereas perhaps I wouldn't have done before.

On the way they *interacted* with their children:

Before I would have just opened a book. I probably wouldn't have prompted Jack as much as I do.

Now I know rhymes I can sing with the little one.

Parents did not talk specifically about altering their behaviour to provide a *model* of literacy for their children, but 40% said they had changed in relation to the literacy activities they did with their children. Most mentioned specific areas in relation to books or environmental print.

Of the 20% who said the programme had not affected what they did with their children, around 75% did not have younger children. These parents made comments like:

It's not really changed what I do, with them being older. If I'd had a little one, then yes.

For 16 parents the programme altered the things they did with their children even though they were older. These parents made comments such as:

Although they're older, I know how to talk to them, how to teach them.

It made me spend a lot more time with his older brother. I do a lot more reading with him; it's had a big impact.

Over two-thirds of parents felt that the programme had made a difference to them. Of these, 70% said they were more aware about how to help their children, while 10% said they had more confidence because they now felt they were doing the right thing with their children. One parent added: 'You don't have to have money to help your kids.'

Around 33% of parents felt that they would deal with teachers and school differently as a result of participating in the programme. Of these, six said that they had more confidence in dealing with teachers because of the good relationship they built up with the programme teacher. Others said that school seemed more approachable as a result of the programme. Of those who felt the programme would not affect the way they dealt with school, some said they already had a good relationship with teachers and school.

What changes, if any, did the programme make to family literacy practices?

So far we have only referred to interviews with programme-group parents (because certain questions could only be asked of parents in the programme). Now we turn to questions that were asked of the control group families as well as the programme group in order to see whether there were any differences.

Parents were interviewed at the end of the programme (as were parents in the control group). Analyses indicate a number of areas where the programme had a clear impact on family literacy:

Favourite books

The proportion of programme parents reporting their child had a favourite book was significantly higher than the control group. This is important, since having a favourite book in the pre-school period can be an indicator of children's later success in reading (Weinberger, 1996). As the only difference between the two groups was that one had undertaken a family literacy programme and one had not, it seems that participating in the programme positively influenced families' perceptions of books and reading.

Environmental print

Significantly more programme parents reported pointing out environmental print to their children than control-group parents.

Writing

High proportions of both programme and control parents recognised their children's achievements in writing, provided opportunities for writing and interacted with their child around writing. However, all programme-group parents reported provided a model of writing whereas almost 7% of the control group did not, a difference which was significant.

Oral language

The highest numbers of statistically significant differences between programme and control groups were found for the oral language strand of literacy (phonological awareness, storytelling and talk about literacy). Programme parents recognised their children's use of literacy language at a significantly greater rate than control-group parents. All programme parents recognised that their children knew some nursery

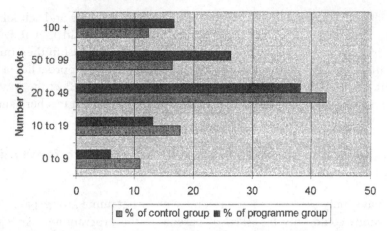

Figure 9.2   Number of books owned by programme and control groups (Programme group N = 85; Control group N = 73)

rhymes, whereas a small percentage of control parents said their children did not. Significantly more programme parents said that their children liked to be told stories and only half of all control parents asked their children to tell stories, whereas for the programme group this figure was over two-thirds.

The proportion of programme children owning more than 50 books was higher than those of the control group (Figure 9.2), something that fits with the programme parents' reports of providing more opportunities for literacy, by buying books.

Generally high proportions of both programme and non-programme parents said they read books and wrote with their children, but the programme seems to have made a difference to parents' roles in other areas of literacy. The programme seems to have had an impact here on parent participation in literacy activities that are perhaps less widely recognised by many parents. This includes oral language, but also in providing a model of writing, opportunities for environmental print and having a favourite book.

Implications of parents' perspectives for the design and development of family literacy programmes

So far, this chapter has illustrated the ways in which parents viewed their experiences of the family literacy programme. Such perspectives, we suggest, are key to the design and implementation of socio-culturally appropriate family literacy programmes in the future. The parents' views lead us to suggest four key implications for future policy and design of family literacy programmes. These findings, and those described earlier in the chapter, are discussed in more detail in Hannon *et al.* (2005).

Building on existing relationships and familiarity

Given the success in recruitment and participation rates for this programme, we could ask, 'Is a 100% take-up rate the kind of response that should be expected in family literacy programmes?' Possibly, there are a number of features of this particular programme that may have been important in enhancing recruitment rates. A high response to family literacy programmes can be expected if they reach out sufficiently; programmes must not rely on a restricted approach. The invitation to participate came from the schools that children were waiting to attend; thus parents may have been more inclined to participate. Many parents with older children who had attended that school already knew the programme teacher. This factor was mentioned by a small number of parents in the responses they gave to some of the interview questions. When asked, for example, why they had agreed to participate in the programme, two parents said it was because the programme was associated with school and three said that they would not have liked a teacher visiting them at home it if it had been somebody they did not know. Several parents also stressed that they already had a good relationship with the teacher because their older children had been in their class.

Offering a programme at the right time

Another important factor in the recruitment success of this programme may be that it was offered at a critical stage of the child's education, that is, in the pre-school period, when parents may be particularly open to educational initiatives and want to do what they can to give their child a good start at school.

A non-stigmatising programme

This programme was non-stigmatising, in not being restricted to families who were perceived to be in the most need (by, for example, their entitlement to free school meals). Instead families were randomly selected from all those whose children were the appropriate age on school waiting lists. This could also be an important factor in influencing take-up. Non-stigmatising programmes in which there are clear links with local schools may have more sustained success than those which are targeted at parents perceived to have 'a problem'. Programmes routinely embedded in a wider programme of school activity may be more likely to attract and retain parents.

A highly flexible approach

Finally, and perhaps most crucially, this was not a 'restricted' family literacy programme (Hannon, 2000a). That is, parents were not obliged to undertake the adult education component; indeed, only nine chose to do so. Parents' interest in their own education may not always coincide with their being very ready to facilitate their children's development – making adult education a compulsory part of work with parents on children's literacy development may inhibit parent take-up and participation. Programmes need to be flexible and to 'fit' with families – home visiting makes it possible to tailor programmes to families' routines and literacy needs. The REAL programme was also designed to be highly flexible in that families could opt to have home visits in the early evening if necessary; in this way it was hoped to include as many families as possible, including those who were working.

In Chapter 8 we presented the perspectives of the practitioners who developed and delivered the family literacy programme and, in this chapter we have considered the views of parents and the implications of those views for practice. In Chapter 10 we consider young children's views of family literacy.

10 Children's perspectives on family literacy

Chapter summary
- Introduction
- Should we ask the children?
- How might we ask the children?
- What do the children say about home literacy?
- What can we learn from young children to help us improve family literacy programmes?

Introduction

This chapter looks at literacy in families from the perspectives of their 5-year-old children.[1] The chapter first considers whether children's views are important in understanding literacy in families. Second, issues of research process are discussed, with suggestions about the best methods to use in eliciting children's views, ways of resolving important ethical issues (such as obtaining permission and ensuring the children are content to give their views), and the validity of children's views. The chapter moves on to illustrate and discuss the perspectives of children who participated in the REAL Project family literacy programme, revealing what some children say about literacy in their homes. These children's perspectives are compared with those from the REAL Project control group who had not been part of the family literacy programme. In conclusion, the chapter suggests what can be learned by listening to children's views about the design and development of family literacy programmes.

Should we ask the children?

This chapter is concerned with finding out about family literacy practices as viewed by children, but first we should consider whether we should, indeed, 'ask the children'. As Chapter 2 has shown, research into family literacy (both practices and programmes), has, over the past two decades, involved three main approaches. Researchers have:

- found ways of observing and recording literacy practices in the home (Clay, 1975; Bissex, 1980; Tizard and Hughes, 1984; Schickedanz, 1990; Nutbrown, 1999b; and Chapter 4 in this book)
- solicited views and reports from parents (Parker, 1986; Hannon and James 1990; Weinberger, 1996; Hirst, 1998; and Chapter 9 of this book)

● evaluated learning outcomes for adults and children (Tizard *et al.*, 1982; McNaughton *et al.*, 1981; Edwards, 1994; Whitehurst *et al.*, 1994; Brooks *et al.*, 1996; Brooks *et al.*, 1997; and Chapters 5 and 11 in this book).

What so far has been generally overlooked has been the children's views of what is happening. Though family literacy programmes have been developed with the aim of helping parents to enhance their children's literacy development, the children have been the 'sleeping partners' when it comes to evaluation of such programmes. They have been given little opportunity to express an opinion about what is happening. It is unrealistic, of course, to expect young children to provide comprehensive reports of all the home activities that researchers and theorists now consider to comprise family literacy, but what may well be possible is for young children to tell us something about who and what is most salient in their literacy experiences.

But, *should* we ask the children? This question gives rise to many more. Is it right to expect young children to be involved in such enquiry? Would such research be intrusive? Is it wasteful of children's time? How do we know they are giving us a true picture? Can we really rely on information they give? How can we ensure that young children understand what they are being asked? What if children are upset by the research process?

Recent discussions in research methodology argue that children's perspectives are becomingly increasingly important as the focus (or an element) of research and children's perspectives are valuable. Therefore, appropriate ways need to be created to find out and understand their views (Holmes, 1998; Aubrey *et al.*, 2000; Christensen and James, 2000; Greig and Taylor, 1999; Lewis and Lindsay, 2000; Nutbrown and Hannon, 2003).

Arguably, the involvement of children as research participants rather than research subjects should be afforded them as a matter of right (Nutbrown, 1996) in order that their voices are heard and their viewpoints are taken into account in the development of policy and the evolution of practices which are designed to involve them. Some of the methodological considerations in such research (such as those raised in the questions above) can therefore be situated within the study of 'voice' in social science research in general, which has emerged in recent years as a politically and morally positioned research response to issues faced by oppressed and silenced minorities, black women, people with AIDS, students with disabilities and learning difficulties, disaffected youths and parents with disabled children (Fine, 1994; Tierney, 1993; Clough, 1998; Pereera, 2001). Tierney (1993, p.111) writes that differences of (for example) race, class, gender and sexual orientation: 'ought to be honoured and brought into the centre of our discourses about education and its purpose'.

To Tierney's list of differences we could add 'age'. Perhaps educational research is one of the last arenas in society where it is still the case that children – especially young children – are seen but not heard. Including children as research informants brings them into the centre of discourses about education and its purposes.

How might we ask the children?

Although recent studies have shown that exploring children's perspectives on their own learning can be illuminating, this approach does present some methodological challenges

(Marsh and Thompson, 2001; Critchley, 2002; Burnett and Myers, 2002). So, if we agree that it is right and appropriate to involve children in studies of family literacy practices, the next question is one of process – how exactly might we go about finding out what young children think about literacy at home, how might we find out who they share literacy with and what activities they enjoy?

Research methods to understand children's learning have mainly relied on observation, and techniques of observation have proliferated (Drummond *et al.*, 1992; Nutbrown, 2001) but far less attention has been given to listening to children and soliciting their views on matters of daily life and learning. It is the case that the 'voices' of vulnerable children have sometimes been attended to with the pioneering of specifically designed interview techniques, mainly in areas of difficulty, such as child protection and child witnesses in court (thus reflecting the interest in 'voice' in relation to oppressed and minority groups). But until recently there has been relatively little interest in understanding the perspectives of children on what we might call the 'ordinary, everyday aspects' of their own lives (Dyer, 2002; Filippini and Vecchi, 2000). Some studies have begun to develop ways of seeking children's views. Methods include: asking children to take photographs of spaces and events in their homes, communities and schools (Leslie, 2005) and forms of visual ethnography are being developed for use with children (Pink, 2001; Pahl, 2002).

What do the children say about home literacy?

In the REAL Project we asked: 'what do children say about literacy at home?' and had to develop appropriate processes by which to find out children's responses to questions about home literacy.

Interviewing young children: some concerns

Several studies have provided detailed impressions of individual children's literacy at home and these have helped researchers and practitioners to understand how children's literacy develops (Bissex, 1980; Burnett and Myers, 2002; Nutbrown, 1999b; Kirkpatrick, 2002; Schickedanz, 1990). The REAL Project study of children's perspectives aimed to do something different: to survey a relatively large sample of 5-year-old children in order to obtain a broad picture of their perspectives on family literacy. The survey we carried out has made it possible to develop brief literacy profiles of a large number of children and to develop generalisable findings about children's views on several aspects of literacy.

In deciding to interview all the children in the project (a total of 148 participated), interviews had to be brief, with a small number of short, clear questions. A team of ten early childhood professionals (seven teachers, three nursery nurses) worked with the research team to develop appropriate strategies for interviewing the children, and to devise an interview schedule. As part of their preparation, the concerns some members of the team had about interviewing 5-year-old children were considered. These could be summarised as: unreliability; misunderstanding; and fear. Members of the team voiced some of the worries mentioned earlier in this chapter such as, the children may: 'give you the answers they think you want'; 'not understand the questions'; 'feel overwhelmed by the situation'.

Of course, these are exactly the same concerns that need to be addressed when interviewing adults but when such young children are involved the issues come more sharply into focus. Again, the literature on 'voice' and interviewing those who traditionally have not been heard in social science research was useful in identifying and resolving difficulties by devising an approach that would best suit the young research participants. Such an approach is now well established in feminist studies with women participants (Oakley, 1993) and in advocacy work with adults with learning difficulties (Booth and Booth, 1994; Goodley, 2000). Our decision to proceed was based on a number of assumptions; namely, that:

- the children would be willing to give their perspective on family literacy
- 5-year-olds can be much better at saying 'no' than many adults, should they not wish to proceed
- children would know they were being asked questions
- interviewers could put children at their ease, just as they would if the interviewees were adults.

And we had to acknowledge and accept that

- despite all the thinking and planning – the children may not say anything at all.

Ethical considerations

The ethical considerations of our study of children's perspectives centred largely on issues of informed consent – both from parents and children – and of ensuring, to the best of our ability, that children were at no time uncomfortable or unhappy. The issue of taking up children's time for our own research purposes was also considered. The following steps were taken:

- Parental permission to interview the children was obtained.
- Interviewing protocols were developed which included a clear explanation to the children about the interview and ensured that they understood that they did not have to participate. The children were also told that they could stop whenever they wished. No interview began until children's explicit agreement was given.
- Children were interviewed in familiar surroundings.
- Data remained anonymous by the allocation of an identification number, with the children's names known only to the interviewing team.
- Interviewers worked with children in their usual roles of teachers and nursery nurses within the same LEA and had therefore undergone necessary legal checks in relation to child protection legislation.
- Full briefing, training, de-briefing and a telephone help-line was provided for all interviewers.

The interviewing team was sensitive to the needs and comfort of the children and prioritised the well-being of the children over data collection. Concerns about taking up or 'wasting' children's time were addressed by piloting the specifically designed interview schedule and finding out from children how it felt, whether they 'liked it', if they understood what they were being asked, and if they 'minded'.

The schedule was piloted by the team with 30 children (each member of the team interviewing three children in ten different settings). Children responded positively to being interviewed and interviewers reported that the style and scope of the interview was broadly appropriate. The team noted:

No parent objected.

Children seemed to enjoy the individual attention.

Children liked the idea of talking to someone different who was interested in them.

Children had no difficulty with being withdrawn from their larger group for the short period of the interview.

Children understood the questions.

Children said they 'didn't mind' talking to the interviewers.

Interviews took around ten minutes to complete.

Interview questions were mostly understood by the children, though some points of clarification were needed.

Following the pilot it was decided that the process and procedures worked, but some adjustments were needed to the interview schedule to ensure, as best we could, that all children understood the questions. Some questions were rephrased to make them clearer and some additional prompt questions were added.

Many aspects of family literacy could have been investigated but questions had to be limited due to constraints of time and concern to ensure that the experience was not too demanding of young interviewees. Difficult choices had to be made, which meant that some aspects of literacy were omitted (such as storytelling, talk about literacy, media literacy, computer use and ownership of books). Finally, six questions (with prompts) were chosen which focused on four strands of literacy (reading, writing, phonological awareness and environmental print) that Nutbrown and Hannon (1997) have suggested are key in early literacy development work with parents. Though the term 'interview' is used throughout this chapter, in reality, the experience for each child took the form of a one-to-one conversation about literacy at home.

After a preamble which followed the protocols detailed above, in which the interviewers explained about the interview and checked that the child understood and was happy to participate, they asked the questions on the schedule in Figure 10.1, noting children's responses.

Where children only mentioned school and their teachers, the prompt questions (in brackets) were asked to focus children's thinking on home literacy interactions. Asking 'Who?' and 'What?' questions was not intended to uncover a full picture of children's literacy experiences. It cannot be relied upon to generate an exhaustive list of everybody involved in literacy practices with the child and what they do. But it seems reasonable to infer from their responses something about the salience of certain individuals, certain literacy interactions and aspects of literacy from children's perspectives.

1. Who do you write with? *(Do you write at home?)* *(Who writes with you?)*

2. Who do you read with? *(Do you read at home?)* *(Who reads with you?)*

3. What's your favourite book? *(Is there one you like a lot?)*

4. There is a lot of writing in books, but can you think of anywhere else where you see words? *(Where is that?)*

5. Have you got a favourite nursery rhyme? *(What is it?)*

6. Who sings rhymes with you? *(Do you sing/say them at home?)* *(Who with?)*

Figure 10.1   Interview schedule for children

The interviewing experience

Interviews were carried out at the children's schools after the children had been in their reception classes (the first class attended by children of statutory school age in England) for half a term (about six weeks). The interviewing team found the experience interesting and reported that most of the children were happy to talk, responsive and not inhibited by the situation. Not all the interviews were completed in full. Interviewers never persisted if they felt the child showed the slightest sign of anxiety (two interviews were curtailed by the interviewers for this reason).

The groups studied

Two groups of children were studied: the children in the family literacy programme, (the 'programme group'[2]), and the group of children who had not participated in the family literacy programme (the 'control group'). The programme group consisted of 77 children (33 girls, 44 boys) and the control group consisted of 71 children (31 girls, 40 boys). In the programme group there were nine (out of 78) lone parents, in the control group 14 (out of 71) families had lone parents, all mothers.

Children's responses

The first task was to review each completed interview schedule to develop brief individual profiles of each of the children. The following examples show the types of profiles which were developed and use pseudonyms – Curtis and Beatrice were in the family literacy programme; Connor and Millie were in the control group.

Curtis

Curtis was five years old when he was interviewed. He had been in the first class of school, full time, for five weeks, and prior to that had attended the nursery class in the school, full time. Curtis lived with his mother, father and younger brother Neil. The family had been involved in the family literacy programme since Curtis was three and a half years old.

Curtis told us that he wrote at school 'with Miss Waters'.

He said he wrote with his mother too, telling us:

> I wrote loads of things with my mum and once I wrote loads on my own – even one big page.

Curtis said that he read with:

> my mum and Neil, at night and sometimes in the afternoon, that's when I go to my caravan on holiday to Skegness but that one was old and I'm at a new one now.

The book Curtis said he liked a lot was 'about Action Man'.
Curtis talked about print in the neighbourhood.

> outside on signs, on posters, on crisp packets. When there is some writing at home on lolly sticks – I can read it and it might be a joke on.

He told us that his favourite rhyme was 'Twinkle Twinkle', which he said he sang with his brother Neil, 'and Nannan when she comes up'.

Beatrice

Beatrice was five years and three months old when she was interviewed. She had been in the first class of school, full time, for six weeks, and prior to that had attended the nursery class in the same school. Beatrice lived with her mother, father and sister. The family had been involved in the family literacy programme since Beatrice was three and a half years old.

Beatrice said that she wrote:

> at school and at home . . . with my mummy, my daddy and my sister and on my own.

She told us that she read:

> with my teacher, my daddy and my mummy. A bit at home. I read at school for my teacher.

Beatrice did not give the title of her favourite book but said that she had one that she liked a lot 'about Christmas and Jesus'.
Thinking about examples of print, Beatrice said:

> on boxes and numbers on houses, doors, and on trousers and on letters.

Beatrice told us that her favourite nursery rhyme was 'Twinkle, twinkle' and that she sang rhymes with:

> my daddy and mummy . . . at home and school, but with my daddy really.

Connor

Connor was five years and two months old when he was interviewed. He had been in the first class of school, full time, for seven weeks, and prior to that had attended a nursery near his present school. Connor lived with his mother and father close to the school.

Connor reported that he wrote with his teacher at school and at home he wrote and read with: 'mum and dad and grandma and my grandad and uncles and aunties'.

Connor told the interviewer that you can also read at school with: 'Your friends who can read, or your teacher.'

The books he said were his favourites at the time were *The magic school bus* and *The times of the dinosaurs.*

He gave some examples of print in school: 'On some boards, on charts that stick on the wall, and on cards.' And he also said that there were lots of words 'at home'.

Connor talked about singing rhymes at home, saying his favourite was 'Baa, baa black sheep', and he usually sang them with:

> Nobody. They only clap at me when I'm done. Sometimes they do sing with me.

Millie

Millie was five years and one month when she was interviewed. She had been in the first class of school, full time, for six weeks, and prior to that had attended a nursery class in the same school. She lived with her mother and father and twin sisters.

Millie reported that she wrote with:

> Leah, my friend, at school – we write about things like animals.

and she said she wrote at home too:

> sometimes . . . but I have two sisters who get the pen and write on the sofa.

Millie mentioned reading with several people:

> Leah and Amber, my friends. I read to Louise and Mia (my sisters – they're one).

She also told the interviewer something about busy family lives, saying that she read with:

> Mummy or daddy sometimes, mummy has to do the ironing and daddy has to paint the conservatory.

Pocahontas was the book Millie named as her favourite book at the time.

Millie gave some examples of neighbourhood print:

> On a sign, in the middle of the street, and at the bus stop.

At home, 'while mummy is making tea', Millie and her sisters sang nursery rhymes, her favourite being 'Humpty Dumpty'.

All the children interviewed had their own personal literacy stories to tell and the data were sufficiently rich to continue analysis for generalisable findings across the sample. All children (in both programme and control groups) reported some literacy activity at home. From the children's perspectives, literacy took place in their homes and was supported by their families and reading and writing were common activities at home. Over 95% of children in the programme group said they read and wrote at home (over 90% in the control group). Singing and saying rhymes were also seen as a home activity though less

Table 10.1 Children in each group who said that they wrote, read and said nursery rhymes at home

		Programme (n = 77) %	Control (n = 71) %
Do you write at home?	Yes	95	94
	No	5	6
Do you read at home?	Yes	96	90
	No	4	7
Do you sing/say nursery rhymes at home?	Yes	83	69
	No	16	23

Note: Totals of responses less than 100% indicate some responses could not be coded.

so than reading and writing (83% of programme children, 69% of the control group – see Table 10.1).

It is important to remember that virtually all of these young children were from poor areas of a northern English city, where (according to national reports) school measures of literacy were low, as were parallel expectations of parental involvement in school literacy. However, contrary to those expectations, the children reported that they did engage in reading and writing at home.

The next stage of analysis was to explore the detail of their responses to see what they said about reading, writing and sharing nursery rhymes at home and whether there were any differences when programme and control group responses and responses according to gender were compared. In terms of REAL Project evaluation, a key question was whether it might be possible to add to such pre-existing literacy practices (as illustrated in the children's profiles earlier in this chapter) through the family literacy programme described in Chapter 4.

What difference does a family literacy programme make?

The responses of children in the programme and control groups were compared in order to determine what difference, if any, children's experience in the programme made to their perspectives on family literacy. As the children had been allocated strictly at random to two groups, the only difference was that children in the programme group had been part of a family literacy programme for the previous 18 months, and their parents had worked with teachers both in their own homes and in occasional small-group sessions on aspects of children's literacy development. The same interview schedule was used for both groups and the interviewers did not know which children had been involved in the family literacy programme. None of the teachers involved in the programme was involved in interviewing the children.

Figure 10.2 shows the proportions of children in each group who said that they wrote, read or said nursery rhymes at home. The responses indicate that children in both groups shared literacy with a range of family members. A greater proportion of children in the

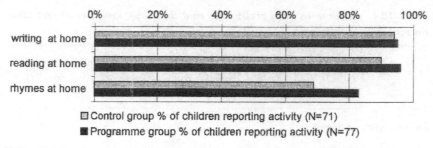

Figure 10.2 *Children's reported experience of reading, writing and sharing nursery rhymes at home*

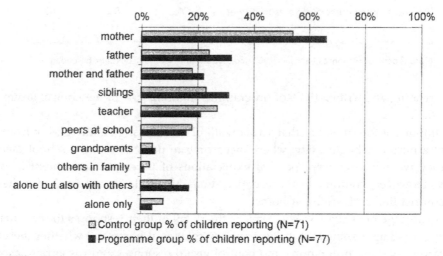

Figure 10.3 *Responses to 'Who do you write with?'*

programme group mentioned that they wrote, read and said rhymes at home but the differences were not statistically significant. It is worth probing a little deeper, however, in comparing the two groups.

Comparing children's family experiences of writing

In response to the question 'Who do you write with?', children in both groups listed a variety of people known to them: mother, father, siblings, teachers, peers at school, grandparents, other family members, and some also said that they wrote by themselves. Figure 10.3 shows the responses from all the children (control and programme) to the question.

Responses from children in the control group included:

'Aran, my bestest friend'

'My dad'

'Mrs Hudson, my teacher'

'Mrs Aston, you put your hand up and she comes'

'My mummy and Ben'

'Leah (my friend) at school. We write about things like animals'

'My nanan. We write numbers'.

Responses from children in the programme group to the same question were similar:

'By myself, mummy watches me and helps me a little bit'

'I wrote loads of things with my mum and once I wrote loads by my own – even one big page'

'My mummy, she doesn't know how to write so I help her out'

Sometimes on my own, my mummy, dad, friends, sister and brother'

'My nannan when my mum goes to the pub'.

Children in both groups reported active engagement in writing with others at home, with a slightly greater proportion of programme children reporting writing with their mother, father, siblings and grandparents and a slightly higher percentage of children in the control group reporting writing with their teachers and peers at school. None of these differences, however, was statistically significant.

Lynch (2002) examined the role of gender in parent–child reading relationships, one of few studies of family literacy to include separate discussion of 'parents' roles' as they relate to 'mothers' and 'fathers'. Most research refers to 'parents' (Brooks *et al.*, 1997; Benjamin and Lord, 1997) even when the majority of participants appear to be women (McNaughton, 2001; Wood, 2002). It is therefore difficult to distinguish the specific roles played by mothers and fathers. However, it is acknowledged that mothers play a prominent role in literacy with their pre-school children (Harrison, 1996) and are in the majority in family literacy programmes (Mace, 1998). The children in the survey reported in this chapter see it this way too, but around a quarter mentioned, for example, their father writing with them. This perhaps provides some indication that, though relatively under-reported, fathers are involved in their children's writing at home. Grandparents and other family members seem to have less salient roles in the writing lives of these young children. A small number of children said that they only ever wrote alone, or sometimes wrote alone but also wrote with others, perhaps indicating developing independence in writing.

Findings in relation to gender were of interest because of continuing concern, in England, over the school literacy achievement of boys (Qualifications and Curriculum Authority, 1998; Frater, 2000). This finding is consistent with that of Brooks *et al.* (1997) who found that girls outperformed boys in writing.

Comparing children's family experiences of reading

When asked, 'Who do you read with?', both groups listed a variety of people known to them: mother, father, siblings, teachers, peers at school, grandparents, other family members, and some also said that they read by themselves. The control-group children again listed a variety of people known to them: mother, father, siblings, teachers, peers at school, grandparents, other family members, and some also said that they read by themselves. Some responses were:

'Lewis, my friend from Scotland'

'Loads of books with daddy and mummy'

'Your friends who can read or your teacher'

'My teacher, Mrs Day'

'My sister Lily, she's Y4'

'Mummy, my dad can read but I learn with my mummy'

'My brother Ewan'

'Mrs Bingham, she's at school but she's not my teacher'

'Me grandad and me nanan'.

Children in the programme group gave similar responses, such as:

'Daddy and mummy'

'Upstairs with my sister Emma'

'My brother, Alex, my little brother'

'My teacher'

'Mummy at bedtime'

'I've got a big story book with Snow White in it and on my video and my mum and me Nanan reads it me'.

Figure 10.4 shows the responses from both groups to the question 'Who do you read with?' Children reported active engagement in reading at home with others but – as with writing – a greater proportion of programme children mentioned reading with their mother, father and siblings. The only differences, however, to be statistically significant[3]

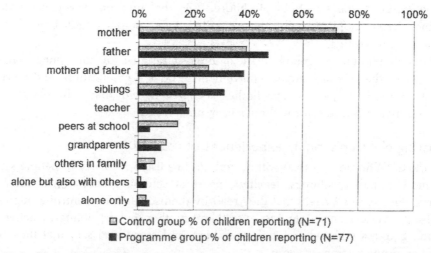

Figure 10.4 Responses to 'Who do you read with?'

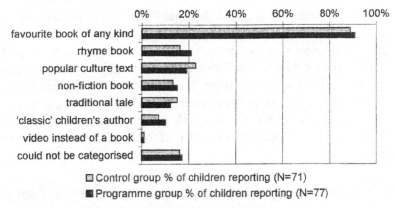

Figure 10.5 Children's favourite books ranked in order of programme group

were programme children's greater likelihood of mentioning reading with siblings at home and their lesser likelihood of mentioning reading with peers in school.

The children were also asked to name a favourite book and responded with a variety of types of book, as shown in Figure 10.5. None of the differences between groups was statistically significant although programme children appeared slightly more likely to name a favourite book, and to name rhyme books, non-fiction books and books written by well-known modern classic children's authors (such as Shirley Hughes or Eric Carl). In the control group the percentage response appeared slightly greater for popular culture texts (such as those produced to accompany Disney films or TV programmes) and traditional tales (such as *The Three Bears*) but the difference was not statistically significant.

Titles reported by children in the control group included: *Aladdin, Toy Story, Bugs Life, The Little Mermaid, Go, Go Power Ranger, Fireman Sam, Spot, Barbie, Grandpa, Goldilocks, What a Mess!, Thomas the Tank Engine, Dumbo, Hansel and Gretel.* Some children said:

'Can't remember the name of the story, I have the telly when I go to bed to watch videos, Bambi'

'My reading book from school "The Sausage" '

'I spy with my little eye – a book beginning with the one about A for Alice'

'One that opens things up'

'That police book that makes a noise'

'One about a dog. It has a sheep and a dog that talks'

'Me and Eric like Baa Baa Black Sheep book best'

'Goldilocks and the 3 bears, I've got it at Nanny Anne's'

'Houses – it's a book at school'.

Some of the titles reported by children in the programme group were: *Tom Kitten, The Dream, Thomas the Tank Engine, Butterflies, Three little pigs, Humpty Dumpty, Go, Snow White and the Seven Dwarves, Mickey Mouse, Spot, Jack and Jill, Peter the Tractor, We're going on a Bear Hunt, Teddy Bears' Picnic, Bugs Life.*

Weinberger (1996) found that the ability to name a favourite book at age five was a predictor of later literacy achievement. The majority of children (from both groups) were able to do this, and in keeping with findings from studies of literacy and popular culture (Marsh and Thompson, 2001), many texts named were those relating to popular culture such as Disney films (for example *Toy Story, The Little Mermaid, Mickey Mouse* and *Bugs Life*) and children's television programmes (such as *Teletubbies, Fireman Sam* and *Thomas the Tank Engine*).

Comparing children's family experiences of sharing rhymes and songs

Children listed a variety of people known to them: mother, father, siblings, teachers, peers at school, grandparents and other family members when we asked them 'Who do you sing or say rhymes with?' Responses from children in the control group included:

'Grandad'

'Mummy and on my own'

'I sing them on my own'

'I don't need anyone to help'

'Courtney, my cousin'

'With our Toni'

'Mummy and daddy'

'My mummy and she likes Robbie Williams'

Children in the programme group said things like:

'Mummy, daddy, brother and Jakey the dog'

'Emma, my sister, my big brother Joe'

'My teacher, Mrs Hatton'

'My grandad'

'Teachers and everybody'

'Nanan Shirley, Grandad One'

'Neil does and Nanan when she comes up'

Figure 10.6 indicates the active involvement of mothers and fathers in sharing rhymes with their children and also indicates the part some siblings played in sharing rhymes.

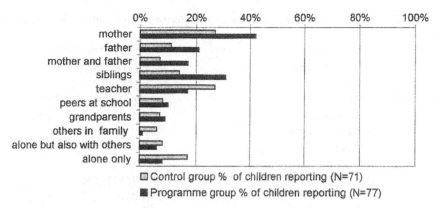

Control group % of children reporting (N=71)

Programme group % of children reporting (N=77)

Figure 10.6 Responses to 'Who do you sing or say rhymes with?'

Comparing children's family experiences of environmental print

Finally, when children were asked about environmental print, children in both groups responded with examples from four print domains: the community, school, home and on clothing. Responses from children in the control group included:

'A list on the side of food'

'Sweet shop'

'Where you play football'

'Bus stop'

'On the wall at Manor Top – people draw on the wall – it's naughty'

'On the floor on my road'

'White board'

'Letters outside in the yard'

'Name cards'

'Charts on the wall'

'A poster on my wall'

'Colouring books'

'In my kitchen behind the fruit basket'

'My brother's clothes'.

Print in school was mentioned by some 27% of control group children: 'teddy words', 'words on drawers', 'labels on coat pegs' being typical examples of such print. 'Teddy words' relate directly to teaching strategies being promoted nationally as part of the literacy hour (DfEE, 1998) and clearly had an impact on these children's concept of print.

Responses from children in the programme group are listed in Table 10.2 and include:

Table 10.2 *Children's comments in response to the question 'Can you think of anywhere else you see words?'*

	Programme group	Control group
Neighbourhood	Tesco	on my road where I live
	crisp packets	at shopping
	bread in the shop	down the street
	at shops	a list on the side of food
	at the bank	on tins
	at the shops, my big brother lifts me up	outside the shop
	at the library	shop sign
	shops have words	in the car
	on your credit card	sweet shop
	on a poster	where you play football
	at Asda	Netto
	on a newspaper	newspaper
	at the pictures	on my wall
	on windows	on my bike
	in signs	Co-op
	in town	bus stop
	MacDonalds	signs
	KFC	toyshop
	on a roof	television
	on a lollipop (crossing)	on the wall at Manor Top – people
	on a shop poster	draw on the wall – it's naughty
	on birthday cards	on the floor on my road
	on letters and envelopes	outside Crystal Peaks
	on food tins	Asda
	on ingredients	
	on the road and the path – I writed it	
	and I got done but me Mam don't	
	know	
	work signs on the road side	
	on the road	
	on walls near my house	
	on boxes, shops, baskets trolleys	
	on lolly sticks I can read it and it might	
	be a joke	
	video shops	
	sweets	
School	on the walls	ABC on my classroom wall
	in 'words and pictures' letters	in the corridor
	on a board	on the wall
	on a drawer	at school when it's someone's birthday
	on our meal boxes	labels of drawers
	on the box of letters	whiteboard
	on doors at school	letters outside in the yard

Table 10.2 Continued

	Programme group	Control group
School (*continued*)	on paper on the floor in the hall on work playground tuck shop	name cards milk label box on a jigsaw on the door at school on paper at school on the calendar at my school on pencil cases charts on the wall labels on paintings
Home	in an envelope in the cupboard I've got a poster that says words my dad put words on the back gate in a letter on a cake we've got a sign up because we're moving house on my walls in my bedroom in my bedroom newspapers magazines on an invitation sometimes	I have a number on my door a poster on my wall colouring books in letters in my kitchen behind the fruit basket Action Man pad and pencil
Clothing	on clothes school uniform on my jumper	my brother's clothes

'Tesco'

'At the shops, my big brother lifts me up'

'On your credit card'

'On a newspaper'

'MacDonalds'.

Figure 10.7 shows responses of both groups to the question '(Apart from books), can you think of anywhere else where you see words?' The programme group children provided more examples of family literacy in their neighbourhood, on clothing, in their homes and in school, and control group children were less likely to be able to think of examples of environmental print or they provided obscure responses. However, these differences were not statistically significant.

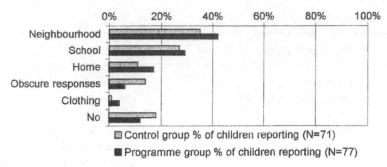

Figure 10.7   Responses to 'Can you think of anywhere else where you see words?'

The quality of children's responses in the two groups is worth further comment. Table 10.2 lists the responses from children in each group in each of the categories of print reported in Figure 10.7. Although many children gave similar responses, each is listed here only once. Table 10.2 suggests a more diverse set of responses from children in the programme group, who tended to give more examples of print in the neighbourhood and in their homes. Children in the control group, however, appeared to draw on a wider variety of print in the school environment.

Overall comparison of control and programme groups

Responses of children in the two groups to questions about writing, reading, rhymes and environmental print have been compared. The findings suggest that there are differences in so far as children in the programme group were slightly more likely to mention literacy involvement at home, and slightly less likely to mention school literacy than their control-group peers. Taken singly, these differences were not statistically significant. Taken collectively, however, an interesting pattern emerges.

Table 10.3 presents 43 different family literacy activities in two columns: those more often reported by control group children and those more often reported by programme-group children. The table further distinguishes literacy activities promoted by the family literacy programme from activities that were not actively promoted by the programme (because they fell outside the conceptual framework on which the programme was based or were more 'school' oriented). Over three-quarters (29 out of 36) of the activities promoted by the programme were cited more often by the programme group. As this difference is statistically significant,[4] it indicates that there was an overall programme effect in terms of children's perspectives on family literacy. Given that the two groups of children were equivalent as a result of random allocation, with the only difference being that children in the programme group were participants in a family literacy programme, one is forced to conclude that the family literacy programme had a discernible impact from the children's perspective.

Table 10.3 *Comparison of family literacy activities reported by children according to whether or not promoted in the family literacy programme*

	More often reported in programme group	More often reported in control group
Promoted in family literacy programme	writing at home reading at home rhymes at home	writing with others in family reading with grandparents reading with others in family
	writing with mother writing with father writing with mother and father writing with siblings writing with grandparents writing alone (and with others)	naming a traditional tale rhymes with others in family rhymes alone (and with others) rhymes alone (only)
	reading with mother reading with father reading with mother and father reading with siblings reading with teacher reading alone (and with others) reading alone (only)	
	naming a favourite book naming a rhyme book naming a non-fiction book naming book by 'classic' author	
	rhymes with mother rhymes with father rhymes with mother and father rhymes with siblings rhymes with grandparents	
	print in the community print on clothing print in the home print in school	
Not promoted in programme	rhymes with peers at school	writing with teacher writing with peers at school writing alone (only)
		reading with peers at school
		named a popular culture book
		rhymes with teacher

What can we learn from young children to help us improve family literacy programmes?

This study demonstrated that young children can give their perspectives on family literacy, and findings suggest that what children have to say is illuminating – we should ask them for their views. Four key findings emerge.

All children do some literacy at home

The children in this study were attending schools in very deprived communities where it would not be surprising to find low levels of literacy activity. If deficit assumptions about such family literacy practices are held by some educators, it is perhaps because home literacy is not as clearly visible (in school contexts) as school literacy. Studies such as this are needed to make visible home literacy practices. Family literacy practices are also sometimes different from school literacy and so there is the possibility that such literacy is not always recognised and valued as the kind of literacy which holds currency in school.

Fathers *are* involved in literacy at home

Relatively little is known about fathers' roles in their children's pre-school literacy, but – according to their children – the fathers in this study appeared to play an important role. Further research into fathers' roles would illuminate this neglected aspect of family literacy practice and could influence the development of family literacy programmes. If few fathers attend literacy events and programmes in pre-school and school settings, it should not be assumed that fathers have no involvement in their children's literacy at home.

Boys are involved in literacy at home

At the age of five, the boys in this survey reported that they were active in literacy, even if studies and national testing raise concerns about literacy not being a masculine pursuit and boys' lower achievement in literacy later (Office for Standards in Education, 1993; Qualifications and Curriculum Authority, 1998; Frater, 1997, 2000).

A programme *can* make some difference to family literacy

The programme outlined in Chapter 4 can – according to the children in this study – help parents build upon their existing home literacy practices with their children.

There are perhaps three implications from this study for the future development of family literacy programmes:

1   *Family literacy programmes need to start from a positive position.* They are building on existing knowledge and skills, not starting with 'blank slates', as Chapter 2 has shown (Auerbach, 1989; Taylor, 1997; Hannon and Nutbrown, 1997). Programmes can maximise children's literacy repertoires by offering a broad range of literacy activities continuous with, but also extending, those they experience at home.
2   *Family literacy programmes need to be reviewed in order to maximise the involvement of fathers.* For example, where home visiting forms part of the programme, fathers may become

more involved than they would in programmes which require regular group attendance. Emphasis on the roles both parents can play to support their children may well help fathers to enhance their roles in their children's literacy. Such interactions may be hidden, taking place in the home and not observed by family literacy workers who run group sessions. Fathers' participation in literacy at home may not be witnessed but this does not mean that such involvement does not happen.

3   *The content and delivery of programmes may need to be reviewed* (along the lines suggested in Chapter 4) in order to maximise the benefits to children and their families. The content of family literacy programmes may need to be adjusted so as to focus on particular strands of literacy and parents' roles in developing their children's early literacy. The delivery of the programme may need to include flexible home visiting (which can reach both fathers and mothers) as well as group sessions and *optional* adult learning opportunities.

The children's views reported in this chapter have enabled us to make clear suggestions for family literacy programme development. Young children are able to share their perspectives and their voices deserve to be heard in the future development of family literacy programmes. Added to the views of their parents (Chapter 9) and practitioners running family literacy programmes (Chapter 8) and considered alongside measures of children's early literacy development (Chapter 11), children's views can make an important contribution to understanding family literacy.

Notes

1   This chapter draws on a previously published paper, Nutbrown, C. and Hannon, P. (2003) Children's perspectives on family literacy: methodological issues, findings and implications for practice. *Journal of Early Childhood Literacy*, 3(2), 115–145.
2   This study of children's perspectives does not include the 8 children in the bilingual sample.
3   At $p < .05$ (according to chi-squared tests).
4   $[\chi^2(1) = 16.0, p < .001]$.

11 Making a difference?

Chapter summary
- Introduction
- Measuring the effects of the programme in children's early literacy development

Introduction

So far it is clear that, through what they said and through what they did, the adults most closely involved – parents and teachers – valued the programme. In Chapters 8 and 9 we saw how the teachers and parents in the REAL Project viewed the programme and the effects of that involvement on them and the children. In Chapter 10 we saw how the programme appeared to make a difference to aspects of children's literacy experiences according to their own reports. However, such findings are rarely sufficient to convince practitioners, policy-makers and researchers of the value of a new approach. Therefore, the multi-method evaluation of the REAL Project included a randomised control trial (RCT) because it is by measuring children's literacy development after the programme and comparing those measures to those of other children (in a truly comparable control group) that it becomes possible to evaluate, quantitatively, the impact of the programme on children's literacy achievement. In this chapter we explain briefly how the RCT was designed and carried out, and present and discuss some key findings. Further, technical details are reported by Hannon *et al.* (2005).

Measuring the effects of the programme on children's literacy development

In order to incorporate an RCT of the programme into the evaluation, we had a control group from the beginning of the study. When eight children were selected for the programme at each school they were actually part of a larger group of 16 children who had been randomly selected from school waiting lists. The 16 children were then randomly allocated to 'programme' or 'control' groups (parents understood, and knew in advance, that they might or might not be picked for the programme). We were therefore able to compare programme children's literacy development to that of within-school controls.

One of the biggest challenges facing us in the early stages of the project was how to measure literacy development in the 3–5 age range. We knew that existing methods of assessment were not adequate (Nutbrown and Hannon, 1993; and Chapter 7 in this

Table 11.1 Pre-programme measures

Measure	Groups	
	Programme	Control
SELDP		
Mean	14.6	14.8
SD	7.1	7.9
N	87	88
BPVS (raw)		
Mean	25.6	25.9
SD	9.6	11.6
N	84	85

book). Cathy Nutbrown therefore devised the Sheffield Early Literacy Development Profile (SELDP) and we used this as our principal pre-programme and post-programme outcome measure. It is an individual, 60-point scale, assessment of children's knowledge of environmental print, books and early writing (Nutbrown, 1997). Children were assessed before the programme began, using the SELDP and the British Picture Vocabulary Scale (BPVS; Dunn et al., 1997), a test of receptive vocabulary.

As children had been randomly allocated to programme and control conditions, the programme and control groups should have had similar scores on pre-programme measures. Table 11.1 shows this was the case – mean scores were virtually identical and there was no difference in language development as measured by the BPVS.

We hoped that, after the programme, children who had been in it would be ahead of the control group on the main assessment (the SELDP) by which we had chosen to measure literacy outcomes. As all the children were by then almost five years old, we also used a standard letter recognition test (Clay, 1985) that other studies have shown to be a powerful predictor of later attainment (Wells, 1985; Tizard et al., 1988; Riley, 1996; Weinberger, 1996). Testing of children was done by an independent team of assessment teachers.

Post-programme gains

At the end of the REAL Project, the programme group was very definitely ahead (Table 11.2). The difference between the programme and control groups was statistically significant (at $p < .005$) and there was a satisfactory effect size[1] of 0.41, typical of much more intensive early childhood intervention programmes. Given the RCT design it is difficult to see what factor, other than the programme, could possibly account for the difference. There was also a significant difference in another measure of literacy development, the number of letters children were able to recognise (effect size 0.30).

The programme did not seek directly to change children's vocabulary but Table 11.2 shows that there was a slight (but not statistically significant) difference in BPVS scores favouring the programme group.

Table 11.2   *Post-programme measures*

Measure	Groups		Difference in means	Significance	Effect size
	Programme	Control			
SELDP					
Mean	33.6	30.2	+3.5	$p < 0.005$	0.41
SD	7.5	8.6			
N	85	80			
Letter recognition					
Mean	18.1	13.4	+4.7	$p < 0.05$	0.30
SD	17.3	15.9			
N	85	79			
BPVS					
(standardised)					
Mean	97.4	95.6	+1.8	n.s.	–
SD	11.2	12.6			
N	85	79			

Two further points are worth noting about the data in Table 11.2. First, the comparison is between all the programme children and all the within-school control children. It includes all children whose parents were invited to join the programme, regardless of how involved they actually became. This is what medical researchers call the 'intention-to-treat' group. (Our further analyses showed that if we were to consider only those families who joined in most fully in the programme, e.g. those where parents gained accreditation or those who participated in the programme at high levels, then those children's literacy measures were very much higher than the controls, suggesting effect sizes greater than 0.8. Such comparisons would not, of course, be valid, however, for we need to compare 'like with like' and a control group including a proportion of 'low participating' families is not like a programme group excluding such families.)

Second, it is worth reflecting that this programme did not set out to teach children directly but to work with parents. The parents were also seen as facilitators of children's learning rather than instructors. The gains did not result from a teaching or training programme as normally understood but through providing parents with ways of thinking about their roles and, as needed, resources such as books to help their children's literacy development (see Chapter 4). The differences in a row of figures in Table 11.2 therefore reflects socio-cultural change in family literacy – produced through teacher–parent interaction and parent–child interaction. It is remarkable that something so subtle should have effects detectable at all by quantitative methods.

As well as analysing programme effects for the whole group, we also examined pre-programme and end-of-programme assessment scores for children in three sub-groups likely to underachieve in literacy: children whose mothers reported no education-al qualifications; children whose parents were in lower SES groups; and boys. The details are, again, reported elsewhere in full (Hannon *et al.*, 2005). We found that while scores for programme and control sub-groups were similar before the programme, the end-of-programme scores showed large gains for programme children whose mothers reported no educational qualifications.

The programme had a significant impact, too, on boys and children of mothers from lower SES occupations – especially the latter. Gains for children in receipt of free school meals were not statistically significant.

Persistence of gains after school entry

It is not uncommon in pre-school intervention studies to find that gains achieved at the end of a programme are not maintained after children enter school, at least not in any measurable form. One of the methodological problems here is that ways of measuring development before school entry may differ considerably from those appropriate in the school years, i.e. we may not be measuring the same thing. Nevertheless, programme effects, in pre-school intervention studies – even when positive and educationally significant effect sizes have been found – generally fade as children progress through school (Lazar and Darlington, 1982; McKey et al., 1985). We were curious to know how the children fared at the age of seven, and in particular we wanted to see whether the gains made by children of mothers with no formal educational qualifications had been sustained. We investigated children's literacy achievement at age seven in the school follow-up stage of the study by analysing achievement on national tests. For the programme group as a whole, there was little or no evidence of persistence of gains; results did favour the programme group, but the differences were small and statistically insignificant. However, analyses of the sub-groups showed a different picture. The most striking results related to gains by children of mothers who had reported no educational qualifications, these being both statistically and educationally significant (Hannon et al., 2005).

Chapters 8, 9 and 10 showed how the REAL Project family literacy programme was valued by teachers and parents and how it appeared to make a difference to what children said about family literacy. In this chapter we have seen evidence that views of parents and teachers (that children's literacy had been influenced by the programme) were borne out by quantitative findings from the RCT part of the evaluation. Children in the programme outperformed their control-group peers on early literacy and letter recognition assessments after the programme. It is clear that the programme had an educationally significant impact on children's literacy, particularly for sub-groups where children tended to have low achievement in school literacy. Furthermore, the programme effects persisted for one such sub-group (children whose mothers had no educational qualifications) to age seven.

In the final chapter we shall see how aspects of family literacy work developed in the REAL Project have influenced the development of other family literacy projects internationally.

Note

1   Effect size is the difference in means between the two groups expressed as a proportion of the standard deviation of the control group. It is used as a measure of the educational, rather than statistical, significance of a programme.

PART IV

The Future for Early Childhood Education and Family Literacy

So far we have examined family literacy policy context, explained the ORIM framework and the experiences of working with it and evaluated the REAL Project from the perspectives of its participants. In Chapter 11 we showed how children in the REAL Project family literacy programme made and sustained gains in their literacy achievements. Other family literacy projects, small and large scale, have been carried out in different parts of the world, drawing on the ORIM framework. In the final chapter we summarise some of these studies and demonstrate how aspects of family literacy work developed in the REAL Project have influenced other family literacy projects internationally.

12 Developing practices and processes

Chapter summary
- Introduction
- Using the ORIM framework
  - in planning and evaluation
  - in family literacy programmes
- Learning from the REAL Project: issues in design and implementation of family literacy programmes

Introduction

This chapter looks at how other practitioners and researchers have used the REAL Project's ORIM framework (Chapters 3 and 4) to design and develop their own early literacy work with parents. Studies in the UK and overseas which have used the ORIM framework are summarised. Small-scale programmes are included here to show that some family literacy initiatives need not be large scale or (even) well funded to be effective; careful planning, monitoring and evaluation are key elements in successful programmes whatever the scale. The chapter ends with an attempt to identify the key strengths of the REAL Project, the factors that may have contributed towards successful outcomes, as they have emerged throughout this book. We also suggest how these factors might influence future work in early childhood education.

Using the ORIM framework

A central feature of the REAL Project was the ORIM framework and, although ORIM was first developed and used by the REAL Project, it has been adapted and used in subsequent literacy work in a range of settings and situations. In this section we review other studies that have used the ORIM framework, first in planning and evaluation, and second to develop family literacy programmes and small-scale projects.

Using the ORIM framework for planning and evaluation

Several studies have evaluated the usefulness of the ORIM framework in a variety of settings and for a variety of purposes. Having devised the framework, Hannon and Nutbrown (1997) assessed its usefulness in practice by seeking views of teachers in 24 schools. All thought the ORIM framework made sense and all but one school said that ORIM had helped in their work with parents and that they would use it again. Teachers said ORIM was useful in helping to clarify their thinking and as an aid to planning. Virtually all teachers appeared to find the framework meaningful and useful, and many schools reported changes in their practice as a result of their use of the ORIM framework.

In Australia, Rigo-Toth and Ure (2000) reviewed the ORIM framework in terms of its effectiveness for evaluating pre-school literacy provision in two contrasting settings. A teacher in one setting believed that readiness was the most influential factor in children's acquisition of literacy, while a teacher in the other setting was a proponent of emergent literacy. Use of the ORIM framework illustrated that both settings provided literacy opportunities, but that the two teachers differed markedly in their use of recognition and interaction; indeed, no examples were observed for the teacher who advocated readiness while several were observed for the emergent literacy advocate. Both teachers modelled literacy behaviours. The authors argue that on the basis of the equipment available to the children (or opportunities), it might be concluded that the literate environments were equally enriched. However, the 'RIM' (recognition, interaction and model) attributes of the framework demonstrated that there were marked differences in teacher practice of the two pre-schools. Rigo-Toth and Ure concluded that the framework was an effective tool for pre-school professionals and may help them to guide their own practices.

Turnbull (1998) investigated whether the ORIM framework could inform nursery nurses' understanding of early literacy development and change their practice in their work settings. She found that the six participants in the study felt that ORIM did help with planning a language and literacy education programme and changed their practice. In another study, the literacy provision in eight pre-schools in Ireland was evaluated using a literacy evaluation scale based on the ORIM framework. Delaney (1997) investigated how teachers supported literacy development in the pre-school and the level of support given to parents with regard to their child's literacy development at home. Use of the framework highlighted the fact that little recognition was given to the importance of literacy in the early years curriculum and that there was very little direct parental involvement in the process. In a similar study, Preece (1999) used the ORIM framework to investigate parents' roles at home in relation to their children's literacy. She also explored what teachers thought was happening at home, and found a lack of knowledge about home literacy and its difference from school literacy.

The ORIM framework has also been adapted for use in other contexts. In the UK, Barton and Hamilton (1998) expanded ORIM to describe home practices of adults other than parents and for a wider age range of literacy learners. Leibowitz (2001) investigated South African students' access to academic literacy in higher education, extending ORIM for use with this group and including the provision of resources such as books and attitude towards literacy.

Using the ORIM framework in family literacy programmes

One of the largest programmes to use ORIM is the Peers Early Education Partnership (PEEP), a programme – based in Oxfordshire, England – aimed at facilitating children's learning through work with parents. Box 12.1 summarises the programme, the main outcomes and some successful features of the programme. Some 2000 children under five have been involved, with promising results, believed to be at least partly attributable to the use of the ORIM framework (Roberts, 2001). According to Roberts,

The ORIM approach could be part of every teacher training course. It really works. It helps parents to value themselves as their children's first educators, and to realise that they do not need any particular skills to help their child learn.

(Roberts, 2001, p.138)

Box 12.1 PEEP (Peers Early Education Partnership) (Roberts, 2001)

Overview

The Peers Early Education Partnership (PEEP) is an early intervention which aims to improve the life chances of children in disadvantaged areas. PEEP was set up in 1995 and is located in a housing estate of Oxford. Its purpose is to raise educational attainment, especially literacy, by supporting parents and carers in their role as first educators, giving their children a flying start at school. PEEP has developed a five-year programme of support for parents (from birth to five years), which complements pre-school provision. It offers materials, group sessions and home visits to parents. The focus is on listening, talking, playing and singing together and sharing books every day. The aim is to lay foundations for later learning. In PEEP, the ORIM framework is utilised across the curriculum. The curriculum areas are self-esteem, disposition (perseverance, curiosity and confidence), listening, talking, reading, writing and numeracy.

Outcomes

One of the intended outcomes of PEEP for parents is to know about, understand and use ORIM to support their children's learning. Gains have been reported in children's verbal comprehension, vocabulary, concepts about print, phonological awareness, writing, early number concepts and self-esteem (Evangelou and Sylva, 2003).

What worked well?

1 **The emphasis on songs and rhymes and stories.** These have an impact on language development, they have wide appeal across cultures and language barriers and are enjoyed by children and adults alike. PEEP provided audio-tapes and song-books for every family, which Roberts (2001) believes was a particularly sound investment.

2 **The book and play-pack borrowing scheme.**

3 **An investment in quality support staff, particularly group leaders.** Although resources are important, the work of the staff was crucial to the effective implementation of the project.

4 **Monitoring, evaluation and research.** These are fundamental to the continued existence of the programme, and studies have been set up to provide answers to the question 'Is PEEP making a difference?' Only by finding answers to such questions can PEEP be developed further and taken up more widely.

5 **The programme's emphasis on acceptance and its availability to all families.**

A family literacy programme in Canada successfully used a slightly adapted version of ORIM. The PRINTS (Parents' Roles Interacting with Teacher Support) family literacy programme (see Box 12.2) has proved effective in involving parents and enhancing the literacy development of children. The Clare Family Learning Project (2000), based in Ireland, aimed to provide family learning courses which support the educational needs of families who were marginalised from the education and employment sectors by low income and low educational attainment. The literacy and numeracy courses which formed part of this project were based on the ORIM framework. FAST (Families And Schools Together) (Cook, 1994) originated in Sefton, England. This programme worked with families and schools to raise awareness of the role of parents in children's learning, particularly in the early years. Its core programme included home visiting and a range of family learning courses, based mostly in schools and with a specific focus on literacy and numeracy skills. FAST worked in partnership with Sefton Sure Start and was also supported by funding from a number of agencies.

Box 12.2 PRINTS (Parents' Roles Interacting with Teacher Support) (Fagan, 2000)

Overview

The PRINTS programme was developed from the REAL model and incorporates 'steps' (strands of literacy) and 'roles' (ORIM). The programme was extended slightly, so that there were five steps, the four strands of literacy identified in REAL plus 'play'. ORIM was extended so that parents engaged in five (rather than four) roles: opportunities; interaction; feedback (recognition); modelling; and 'setting guidelines'. 'Setting guidelines' includes activities that help children develop responsibility such as putting away materials.

'Adjusting/modifying' was also included to help parents to think through how an activity could be best used given the age and maturity of their children.

The programme consisted of 12 centre-based sessions and did not include home visiting. The sessions consisted of an introductory session, two sessions on each 'step', and a concluding session. Each session lasted for two hours.

Outcomes

An evaluation showed that the programme was effective: parents showed a strong commitment to it and children showed considerable progress in book and print knowledge. The programme was very successful and is now widely used in Canada. Children's literacy development and self-confidence increased. An interesting outcome was that the parents involved in the programme made an effort on their own to invite other parents to participate in future versions of the programme when offered. Parents became facilitators of the programme for other parents in their neighbourhood, making PRINTS a community-based programme.

What worked well?

1   **The comprehensive nature of the programme.** Activities were provided for literacy development in five contexts: books and book sharing; talk/oral language; play; environmental print; scribbling drawing, writing.

2 **A structured and systematic approach.** This ensures that parents were clear
   on how they could best help their children. Parents learned to take five roles
   (adapted from ORIM) in assisting their children's literacy development.

3 **The emphasis on parent participation** in developing or acting out activities
   ensured they were confident in understanding and using them.

The PEEP, CLARE and FAST programmes described above have all been implemented on a relatively wide scale, but several much smaller-scale programmes (mostly based
in one setting) have also used ORIM successfully. For example, Evans (2003) carried out
a small-scale action research project based on the REAL Project model in the primary
school in which she worked (see Box 12.3). REAL Project ideas were modified for use in
a school setting, with reception-aged children and their parents. Evans' work demonstrates what can be achieved even without funding.

Jones' (1998) study evaluated a family literacy programme, 'Literacy begins at home',
in her school using the ORIM framework (Box 12.4). She found the ORIM framework
to be a useful tool for examining two things: parents' involvement in their children's
literacy and provision for parents offered by the school. Cigman (1996) used the ORIM
framework successfully to create a 'literacy pack' for families (see Box 12.5). The pack
worked well as a partnership project by identifying and supporting nursery parents as
co-educators.

Box 12.3 'Parent partnership' programme (Evans, 2003)

Overview

This programme was delivered in a primary school through eight weekly
workshops for parents, rather than home visiting, which is more costly and
time-consuming. The programme began with environmental print (three sessions)
followed by books (one session), early writing (one session), language for literacy
(two sessions, one of which was led by a storyteller) and a final session on parental
views of the project. A leaflet for parents detailing one of the workshop sessions,
'Sharing books', is illustrated below:

Parent Partnership Project: Sharing Books

The aim of today's session is to think about the many different ways
children can be introduced to books and be encouraged to enjoy reading
without the pressures of racing through a reading scheme.
   We want our children to become life-long readers!

Parent/Child Activity (9:00–9:15)

Choose a 'book' activity to share with your child. You can:

● Think about things that make your favourite book special
● Use a shape to make a book
● Make a zig-zag book

- Make a number book
- Draw a favourite character from a book
- Make an alphabet book
- Add to our 'lift the flap' panel
- Add a favourite nursery rhyme
- Make a book about YOU!
- Play out a story in the puppet theatre
- Dress up and pretend to be 'Little Red Riding Hood' characters
- Act out 'The Three Bears' story.

Parent Activity (9:15–9:45)
Learning to read
Supporting our children

At Home
Look at a photograph album together – talk a lot! Can you make a book all about things that are special to you?

Next Session
Early writing

Outcomes

The programme was largely successful: parents and staff valued the programme and parents reported benefits for children. They also felt that participating in the study had enhanced their relationship with practitioners. Overall, the impact of the programme was considered to be significant, and increasing the provision for parental involvement, based on the REAL model, was included in the school's development plan for the following year.

What worked well?

1 **The storyteller.** Parents appreciated observing a storyteller using props when telling stories to the children. They also felt they had been shown some good ideas on how to develop skills in storytelling.

2 **Using an unfamiliar script in the session for parents on sharing books.** This helped parents to appreciate how difficult it is for children to learn to read.

3 **Taking photographs in each workshop session.** This helped to keep a record of what happened and to evaluate the sessions.

Box 12.4 'Literacy begins at home' programme (Jones, 1998)

Overview

Jones (1998) investigated parents' involvement in the literacy development of their pre-school children through three different programmes; a 'family information booklet' (FIB), a short-term tutored course for parents and a book borrowing scheme. Many of the ideas for activities in the FIB were based on the ORIM framework to ensure coverage of all areas of literacy and parents' roles. The following extract is taken from the page of the FIB relating to language for literacy.

Young children learn through talking and listening

Children will:

- Listen to you reading them a story
- Talk on the telephone and listen to the other person
- Talk to themselves and their toys
- Tell you what is the matter when they are unhappy or upset
- Listen to the rules and instructions when you are playing games together
- Ask questions when they are out and about with you and the family
- Talk when they are pretending to be other people or animals.

Children can be encouraged to talk and listen by:

- Playing a 'telephone game' – you could talk on the toy or real telephone encouraging them to take turns and listen to what you say
- Asking your child to deliver messages, e.g. 'Please see if Jane wants a cup of tea.'
- Singing songs and nursery rhymes together – make up different actions and have fun.
- Playing a 'silly word' game, e.g. 'Humpty Dumpty sat on a cow'
- Discussing events that happened yesterday, today and what may happen tomorrow

Evaluation of the FIB included a parent questionnaire in which questions were designed to investigate whether parents were providing all four aspects of ORIM, including increased opportunities and resources for literacy.

Jones based the parental involvement programme on an earlier programme run by the school (which had not been designed using ORIM), which she evaluated using the ORIM framework. The new programme used material adapted from the REAL Project manual (Nutbrown and Hannon, 1997). Parents used the ORIM framework to keep a check on their involvement in their children's learning.

Outcomes

Jones found that the children of families who had attended the course had made significant gains according to baseline literacy assessments. Both the booklet (FIB) and the parental involvement programme were developed using the ORIM framework, ensuring that parents were aware of all aspects of literacy and their own roles in children's learning.

Jones concluded that the parents as educators course was the most effective of the three involvement programmes and that the ORIM framework was a useful tool for examining both the parents' involvement in aspects of their children's literacy development and also the school's provision for parents. Weaknesses in earlier course designs were much easier to analyse when mapped on to the ORIM framework.

What worked well?

1 **The Teddy Bears' Picnic**
2 **Making story books and story tapes**
3 **The library visits**
4 **Children enjoyed receiving a new book each week**
5 **Taking photographs** for monitoring and evaluation

Box 12.5 'Creating links between home and school literacies' programme (Cigman, 1996)

Overview

Cigman (1996) used the ORIM framework to design and evaluate a literacy pack for parents and children at a nursery school. The pack was designed to create opportunities for writing, parental recognition of the validity of their children's attempts at early writing, interaction around writing between parents and children and for children to witness their parents modelling writing. Thirteen families with 3- or 4-year-old children participated in the project.

The literacy pack consisted of a plastic wallet containing stationery items: paper, old unused diaries, pens and pencils, envelopes, forms, a tape for recording children's told stories, an information leaflet for parents and a list of things to do with the pack.

Ideas for things to do:

- Keep the folder somewhere that is easy to reach
- Write letters to friends and relations
- Make books to read together
- Write messages
- Make labels and stick them around the house
- Write messages on the postcards and post them to a friend
- Make shop signs with coloured card
- Write shopping lists
- Write menus for tea
- Make tickets for games
- Use the scrapbook at nursery
- Bring some drawings and writing in to nursery to show us!

A recording sheet was also included in the packs. This asked parents to tick what they had used, write what the child did and what they did together. This acted as a focus for parents to record interactions and recognition of their child's achievement but was also designed to be helpful in evaluating the usefulness of the pack later.

Outcomes

Cigman found that parents used the literacy pack in a variety of ways which matched the ORIM framework. The literacy pack provided a context within which information about early literacy development could be discussed with parents while the methods of developing and introducing the pack enabled parents to discuss their concerns and expectations relating to their child's literacy learning.

What worked well?

1 **Involving parents in writing information leaflets.** Two parents helped develop a leaflet for other parents, including ideas and suggestions for what to do. Another parent helped by producing the leaflet on a word-processor.

2 **Using the comments made by parents about their children's literacy** in a second leaflet that later became part of the literacy pack.

Other small-scale projects have concentrated on just one area (or strand) of literacy. In Tameside, England, for example, several early years practitioners have based small-scale family literacy work on aspects of ORIM. Hickson (2003) used the ORIM framework to encourage parents to become effectively involved in the early writing experiences of their children. This has already been outlined in Chapter 1. In another example, Barker (2003) attempted to raise the profile of early writing with parents in a the nursery setting where she taught (see Box 12.6).

Box 12.6 'Raising the profile of early writing with parents' programme (Barker, 2003)

Overview

In Tameside, Barker (2003) attempted to increase children's opportunities for writing through the use of home writing packs (provided by the nursery). The packs included writing materials and a focus and there were nine packs in total. The titles of the packs were: message pack (containing a phone and message pads), shopping pack (containing plastic play food cartons and shopping list paper), letter writing pack (complete with stamps), café pack (with play food and crockery) and card pack (with a variety of cards to make and write). Over a five-week period the children borrowed up to five packs, taking a different one home each week. Each time the packs were returned, Barker collected the children's mark-making together and glued it into a scrapbook for each child to take home at the end of the project.

Outcomes

The aim to increase the amount of mark-making done in school by children was achieved.

What worked well?

1 **The literacy packs** were enjoyed by both parents and children.

2 **Collecting feedback** from parents, both verbally and using a simple questionnaire included in each pack.

As we have seen, several programmes, in various parts of the UK and internationally have made effective use of the ORIM framework to develop family literacy practices in their educational and community settings. Taken together, what can be learned from these programmes about future work in family literacy?

The most successful family literacy programmes may be those which have adopted a facilitative approach. These programmes offer ideas, not instructions; the professionals who work with families do so not as distant 'experts' but as supportive 'partners'; ideas and knowledge are exchanged between parents and professionals – not transmitted from professional to parent. This philosophy acknowledges parents as their children's first and most important teachers: parents know their own children better than any professional. Others also agree that a facilitative approach to family literacy programmes is the most appropriate. The director of PEEP, Rosie Roberts (2001) put it like this:

> It seems that a respectful offering of relevant and appropriate information and ideas has been far more effective than a more didactic, instructional approach. In using the University of Sheffield's ORIM structure to build up the programme with parents and carers in the pilot groups, and in focusing on children's play-patterns we have been acknowledging and valuing and building on what is already there.
>
> (Roberts, 2001, p.148)

Learning from the REAL Project: issues in the design and implementation of a family literacy programme

This chapter has demonstrated how one of the key features of the REAL Project family literacy programme, the ORIM framework, has been adapted and used in other family literacy work. But what else can be learned from the REAL Project? The design, implementation and evaluation of the REAL Project have been described in Chapters 3 to 6, while Chapters 7 to 10 gave the different perspectives of those involved in the programme. The effects of the programme on children's literacy development, using measures of early literacy development have been presented and discussed in Chapter 11.

Three main points emerged:

- The programme was effective as indicated by the overall scores of the programme group compared with the controls at the end of the programme.
- The programme was particularly effective for children in certain sub-groups: children where mothers reported no educational qualifications; children in lower SES groups; and boys.
- There were long-term effects to age seven for children whose mothers reported no educational qualifications.

We suggest there are several likely reasons for why programme children showed gains as identified in the RCT (Chapter 11), which could prove useful in the development of future policy and practices in family literacy. From the outset three key factors were in place: methods, funding and evaluation.

Careful development of methods within a conceptual framework

The methods and activities used in the programme had been developed over several years and piloted in schools with parents and children (Nutbrown and Hannon, 1997). This meant that the project used tried-and-tested methods and activities. The ORIM framework for planning, implementing and evaluating work with parents had also been evaluated (Hannon and Nutbrown, 1997) and the systematic use of ORIM also contributed to the success of the programme – allowing for comprehensive coverage of strands of literacy and parents' roles alongside flexibility of pace and depth.

Sufficient funding

Funding enabled quality resources (such as children's books) to be used, and ensured that REAL Project teachers were released from their teaching duties half a day per week to work with families and for ongoing professional development and support throughout the project.

Evaluation

The experimental design (using a programme and a control group for evaluation) showed that gains made by the programme group could only have arisen as a result of the REAL programme (Chapter 11). As we have seen, evaluation included: levels of take-up, participation and drop-out; outcomes for children using measures of literacy; parents', children's and teachers' views and experiences. Few family literacy programmes have the resources to implement such a rigorous design, but (as we have argued in Chapter 7) some evaluation – however modest – should be built into all family literacy work.

As we have seen in earlier chapters, evaluation has helped us to identify some key factors for programme success from the perspectives of the three main groups of participants: teachers, parents and children, which we summarise here.

For the teachers who developed and ran the programme (Chapter 8) successful family literacy work depends upon:

- **Appropriate and sufficient professional development experiences which augment their knowledge and skills and create a network of support** – The professional development programme ensured that teachers were comfortable working with families at home and confident in developing and implementing family literacy work. Teachers' involvement in the development of the programme meant that their ideas and experiences were valued and their contribution was crucial.
- **Time to carry out such work properly** – working at the pace each family found right for them, fostering positive and trusting relationships with and respectful attitudes towards families.
- **Flexibility through home visiting** – meant that the programme could be fitted to families. Home visiting was a central component of the programme and may well have contributed to success, especially as home visiting was viewed favourably by parents.

From parents (Chapter 9) we concluded that important features of the programme were:

- **Building on existing relationships and familiarity** – working with someone they got to know well.
- **The right time** – having an opportunity to join a programme during their child's pre-school years
- **A non-stigmatising programme** – which was not restricted to families who were perceived to be in the most need and with clear links with local schools.
- **A highly flexible approach** – which built upon families' existing literacy practices and allowed families to rearrange visits to suit their own situations.
- **An available (but non-compulsory) adult education component** – Those who took up the opportunity valued it but many said that it was not right for them at that time. The imposition of an assessed adult learning element may well have effected take-up and participation (Chapter 9).

From interviews with the children (in Chapter 10) we concluded that family literacy programmes should:

- **Start from a positive position** – maximising children's literacy repertoires by offering a broad range of literacy activities continuous with – but also extending – those they already experience at home.
- **Maximise the involvement of fathers** – making it possible for them to participate and emphasising the roles both parents can play to support their children.
- **Ensure that the content and delivery of programmes maximise the benefits to children and their families** – focusing on particular strands of literacy and parents' roles in developing their children's early literacy, and including flexible home visiting (which can reach both fathers and mothers) as well as group sessions and optional adult learning opportunities.

We hope that, in sharing our work on the REAL Project, we have done justice to the contribution of all those involved and encouraged practitioners to develop their own work to promote and evaluate early literacy development with families. There continues to be great interest around the globe in family literacy and we hope that this book will contribute to future policy in developing and supporting flexible, non-stigmatising and effective family literacy programmes.

References

Adult Literacy and Basic Skills Unit (ALBSU) (1993a) *Family literacy news, No. 1.* London: Adult Literacy and Basic Skills Unit

Adult Literacy and Basic Skills Unit (ALBSU) (1993b) *Framework for family literacy demonstration programmes.* London: Adult Literacy and Basic Skills Unit

Adult Literacy and Basic Skills Unit (ALBSU) (1993c) *Parents and their children: the intergenerational effect of poor basic skills.* London: Adult Literacy and Basic Skills Unit

Ahlberg, A. and Ahlberg, J. (1986) *The jolly postman.* London: Heinemann

Anning, A. and Edwards, A. (2003) Language and literacy learning. In J. Devereaux and L. Miller (eds) *Working with children in the early years.* London: David Fulton/Open University

Applebee, A.N., Langer, J.A. and Mullis, I.V. (1988) *Who reads best? Factors related to reading achievement in grades 3, 7 and 11.* Princeton, NJ: Educational Testing Service

Armstrong, F. and Moore, M. (eds) (2004) *Action research for inclusive education: changing places, changing practice, changing minds.* London: RoutledgeFalmer

Arnold, C. (2001) Persistence pays off: working with 'hard to reach' parents. In M. Whalley and the Pen Green Centre Team, *Involving parents in their children's learning.* London: Paul Chapman Publishing

Athey, C. (1990) *Extending thought in young children, a parent–teacher partnership.* London: Paul Chapman Publishing

Aubrey, C., David, T., Godfrey, R. and Thompson, L. (2000) *Early childhood education research: issues in methodology and ethics.* London: RoutledgeFalmer

Auerbach, E. (1989) Toward a social-contextual approach to family literacy. *Harvard Educational Review,* 59(2), 165–181

Auerbach, E. (1995) Which way for family literacy: intervention or empowerment? In L.M. Morrow (ed.) *Family literacy: connections in schools and communities.* Newark, DE: International Reading Association

Auerbach, E. (1997a) Family literacy. In V. Edwards and D. Corson (eds) *Encyclopaedia of language and education. Vol. 2: Literacy.* Dordrecht, Boston, London: Kluwer

Auerbach, E.R. (1997b) Reading between the lines. In D. Taylor (ed.) *Many families, many literacies: an international declaration of principles.* Portsmouth, NH: Heinemann

Auerbach, E. (ed.) (2002) *Community partnerships.* Alexandria, VA: TESOL

Baghban, M. (1984) *Our daughter learns to read and write.* Newark, DE: International Reading Association

Baker, A., Piotrowski, C. and Brooks-Gunn, J. (1998) The effects of the Home Instruction Program for Preschool Youngsters (HIPPY) on children's school performance at the end of the program and one year later. *Early Childhood Research Quarterly,* 13(4), 571–588

Baker, L., Sonnenschein, S., Serpell, R., Fernandez-Fein, S. and Scher, D. (1994) *Contexts of emergent literacy: everyday home experiences of urban pre-kindergarten children. Reading*

Research Report No. 24. Athens, GA/College Park, MD: National Reading Research Center

Barker, J. (2003) Raising the profile of early writing with parents in the nursery. In *Summaries of action research reports.* Tameside LEA/University of Sheffield School of Education

Barton, D. and Hamilton, M. (1998) *Local literacies: reading and writing in one community.* London: Routledge

Baz, P., Begun, L., Chia, K., Mason, G., Nutbrown, C. and Wragg, L. (1997) Working bilingually with families. In C. Nutbrown and P. Hannon (eds) *Preparing for early literacy education with parents: a professional development manual.* Nottingham/Sheffield: NES Arnold/University of Sheffield School of Education

Benjamin, L.A. and Lord, J. (eds) (1997) *Family literacy: directions in research and implications for practice.* Washington: US Department of Education/Office for Educational Research and Improvement

Bissex, G. (1980) *GYNS AT WRK: a child learns to write and read.* Cambridge, MA: Harvard University Press

Blackledge, A. (2000) *Literacy, power and social justice.* Stoke-on-Trent: Trentham

Booth, T. and Booth, W. (1994) *Parenting under pressure: mothers and fathers with learning difficulties.* Buckingham: Open University Press

Brizius, J.A. and Foster, S.A. (1993) *Generation to generation: realizing the promise of family literacy.* Ypsilanti, MI: High/Scope Press

Brooks, G., Cole, P., Davies, P., Davis, B., Frater, G., Harman, J. and Hutchison, D. (2002) *Keeping up with the children: evaluation for the Basic Skills Agency by the University of Sheffield and the National Foundation for Educational Research.* London: Basic Skills Agency

Brooks, G., Gorman, T., Harman, D. and Wilkin, A. (1996) *Family literacy works: the NFER evaluation of the Basic Skills Agency's family literacy demonstration programmes.* London: Basic Skills Agency

Brooks, G., Gorman, T., Harman, J., Hutchison, D., Kinder, K., Moor, H. and Wilkin, A. (1997) *Family literacy lasts: the NFER follow-up study of the Basic Skills Agency's demonstration programmes.* London: Basic Skills Agency

Brooks, G., Harman, J., Hutchison, D., Kendall, S. and Wilkin, A. (1999) *Family literacy for new groups: the NFER evaluation of family literacy with linguistic minorities, Year 4 and Year 7.* London: Basic Skills Agency

Bryant, P. and Bradley, L. (1985) *Children's reading problems.* Oxford: Basil Blackwell

Bruner, J. (1987) The transactional self. In J. Bruner and H. Harste (eds) *Making sense: the child's construction of the world.* London: Methuen

Burke, C. (1982) *Redefining written language growth: the child as informant.* Paper presented at the 8th Australian Reading Association Conference, Adelaide

Burnett, C. and Myers, J. (2002) 'Beyond the frame': exploring children's literacy practices. *Reading,* 36(2), 56–62

Bus, A.G., Van IJzendoorn, M.H. and Pellegrini, A.D. (1995) Joint book reading makes for success in learning: a meta-analysis on intergenerational transmission of literacy. *Review of Educational Research,* 65(1), 1–21

Bushell, R., Miller, A. and Robson, D. (1982) Parents as remedial teachers. *Journal of the Association of Educational Psychologists,* 5(9), 7–13

Cairney, T. (2002) Bridging home and school literacy: in search of transformative approaches to curriculum. *Early Child Development and Care*, 172(2), 153–172

Cairney, T.H. and Munsie, L. (1995) *Beyond tokenism: parents as partners in literacy.* Portsmouth, NH: Heinemann

Cairney, T.H. and Ruge, J. (1998) *Community literacy practices and schooling: towards effective support for students.* Canberra: Department of Employment, Education, Training and Youth Affairs

Christensen, P. and James, A. (eds) (2000) *Research with children: perspectives and practices.* London: Falmer Press

Cigman, J. (1996) *Creating links between home and school literacies: working with parents to develop and evaluate a literacy pack for children starting at nursery.* Unpublished M.Ed Thesis: University of Sheffield School of Education

Clare Family Learning Project (2000) *Family learning resource guide.* Ennis: Clare Family Learning Project

Claverie, J. and Price, M. (1993) *Peek-a-boo.* Harmondsworth: Penguin

Clay, M. (1972) *The patterning of complex behaviour.* Auckland, New Zealand: Heinemann

Clay, M. (1975) *What did I write?* Auckland, New Zealand: Heinemann Educational

Clay, M. (1985) *The early detection of reading difficulties: a diagnostic survey.* Portsmouth, NH: Heinemann

Clough, P. (1998) *Articulating with difficulty: research voices in inclusive education.* London: PCP

Clough, P. and Nutbrown, C. (eds) (2001) *Voices of Arabia: essays in educational research.* Sheffield: University of Sheffield Papers in Education

Cook, M. (1994) Growing into literacy: an approach to home visiting. *Family Literacy News*, 4, November, 6–7

Critchley, D. (2002) Children's assessment of their own learning. In C. Nutbrown (ed.) *Research studies in early childhood education.* Stoke-on-Trent: Trentham

Darling, S. (1993) Focus on family literacy: the national perspective. *NCFL Newsletter*, 5(1), 3

Davie, R., Butler, N. and Goldstein, H. (1972) *From birth to seven: a report of the National Child Development Study.* London: Longman/National Children's Bureau

Delaney, P. (1997) *A study of the provision for literacy development in early-childhood education in Ireland.* Unpublished M.Ed Thesis: University of Sheffield School of Education

Delgado-Gaitan, C. (1990) *Literacy for empowerment: the role of parents in children's education.* London: Falmer Press

Department of Education in Northern Ireland (DENI) (2004) *Review of preschool education in Northern Ireland.* Department of Education, Bangor: Co Down

DfEE (1998) *The National Literacy Strategy.* London: DfEE

Dickinson, D. (ed.) (1994) *Bridges to literacy: children, families and schools.* Oxford: Blackwell

Douglas, J.W.B. (1964) *The home and school: a study of ability and attainment in primary school.* London: MacGibbon and Kee

Drummond, M., Rouse, D. and Pugh, G. (1992) *Making assessment work: values and principles in assessing young children's learning.* Nottingham: NES Arnold/National Children's Bureau

Dunn, L.M., Dunn, L.M., Whetton, C. and Burley, J. (1997) *British Picture Vocabulary Scale* (2nd edition) (BPVS-II) Windsor: NFER Nelson

Dyer, P. (2002) A box full of feelings: emotional literacy in a nursery class. In C. Nutbrown (ed.) *Research studies in early childhood education.* Stoke-on-Trent: Trentham

Edwards, P.A. (1994) Responses of teachers and African-American mothers to a book-reading intervention program. In D. Dickinson (ed.) *Bridges to literacy: children, families and schools.* Oxford: Blackwell

Evangelou, M. and Sylva, K. (2003) *The effects of the Peers Early Education Partnership (PEEP) on children's developmental progress.* DfES Research Report. Retrieved 4 September 2004 from http://www.dfes.gov.uk/research/data/uploadfiles/RR489.pdf

Evans, L. (2003) *Working with parents: a REAL partnership.* Unpublished MA Thesis: University of Sheffield School of Education

Fagan, W.T. (2000) Family literacy: five steps to success. *Literacy Today,* 24, 26

Ferreiro, E. and Teberosky, A. (1989) *Literacy before schooling.* Oxford: Heinemann

Filippini, T. and Vecchi, V. (eds) (2000) *The hundred languages of children: exhibition catalogue.* Reggio Emilia: Reggio Children

Fine, M. (1994) Dis-stance and other stances: negotiations of power inside feminist research. In A. Gitlin (ed.) *Power and method: political activism and educational research.* London: Routledge

Finlay, A. (1999) Exploring an alternative literacy curriculum for socially and economically disadvantaged parents in the UK. *Journal of Adolescent and Adult Literacy,* 43(1), 18–26

Firth, R. (1997) Brunswick Primary School 'Parents in Partnership' Project. In C. Nutbrown and P. Hannon (eds) (1997) *Preparing for early literacy education with parents: a professional development manual.* Nottingham/Sheffield: NES Arnold/University of Sheffield School of Education

Frater, G. (1997) *Improving boys' literacy.* London: Basic Skills Agency

Frater, G. (2000) *Securing boys' literacy: a survey of effective practice in primary schools.* London: Basic Skills Agency

Glass, N. (1999) Sure Start: The development of an early intervention programme for young children in the United Kingdom. *Children and Society,* 13, 257–264

Goelman, H., Oberg, A. and Smith, F. (eds) (1984) *Awakening to literacy.* Portsmouth, NH: Heinemann

Goodhall, M. (1984) Can four year olds 'read' words in the environment? *Reading Teacher,* 37(6), 478–489

Goodley, D. (2000) *Self-advocacy in the lives of people with learning difficulties.* Buckingham: Open University Press

Goodman, Y. (1980) The roots of literacy. In M.P. Douglas (ed.) *Claremont Reading Conference forty-fourth yearbook.* Claremont, CA: Claremont Reading Conference

Goodman, Y. (1986) Children coming to know literacy. In W.H. Teale and E. Sulzby (eds) *Emergent literacy: writing and reading.* Norwood, NJ: Ablex Publishing Corporation

Goodman, K., Goodman, Y. and Burke, C. (1978) Reading for life – the psycholinguistic base. In E. Hunter-Grundin and H.U. Hunter Grundin (eds) *Reading: implementing the Bullock Report.* London: Ward Lock

Goswami, U. and Bryant, P. (1990) *Phonological skills and learning to read.* Hove: Lawrence Erlbaum Associates

Grant, A. (1997) Debating intergenerational family literacy: myths, critiques, and counterperspectives. In D. Taylor (ed.) *Many families, many literacies: an international declaration of principles.* Portsmouth, NH: Heinemann

Green, C. (1987) Parental facilitation of young children's writing. *Early Child Development and Care,* 28, 31–37

Gregory, E. (1996) *Making sense of a new world: learning to read in a second language.* London: Paul Chapman Publishing

Greig, A. and Taylor, J. (1999) *Doing research with children.* London: Sage

Griffiths, A. and Edmonds, M. (1986) *Report on the Calderdale pre-school parent book project.* Halifax: Schools Psychological Service, Calderdale Education Department

Haggart, J. (2000) *Learning legacies: a guide to family learning.* Leicester: National Institute of Adult and Continuing Education

Hall, N. (1987) *The emergence of literacy.* London: Hodder and Stoughton

Hannon, P. (1987) A study of the effects of parental involvement in the teaching of reading on children's reading test performance. *British Journal of Educational Psychology,* 57, 56–72

Hannon, P. (1995) *Literacy, home and school: research and practice in teaching literacy with parents.* London: Falmer Press

Hannon, P. (1996) School is too late. In S. Wolfendale and K. Topping (eds) *Family involvement in literacy: effective partnerships in education.* London: Cassell

Hannon, P. (1998) How can we foster children's early literacy development through parent involvement? In S.B. Neuman and K.A. Roskos (eds) *Children achieving: best practices in early literacy.* Newark, DE: International Reading Association

Hannon, P. (2000a) Rhetoric and research in family literacy. *British Educational Research Journal,* 26(1), 121–138

Hannon, P. (2000b) *Reflecting on literacy in education.* London and New York: Routledge Falmer

Hannon, P. and Jackson, A. (1987) *The Belfield reading project – final report.* London/ Rochdale: National Children's Bureau/Belfield Community Council

Hannon, P. and James, S. (1990) Parents' and teachers' perspectives on preschool literacy development. *British Educational Research Journal,* 16(3), 259–272

Hannon, P. and Nutbrown, C. (1997) Teachers' use of a conceptual framework for early literacy education with parents. *Teacher Development,* 1(3), 405–420

Hannon, P. and Nutbrown, C. (2001) *Outcomes for children and parents of an early literacy parental involvement programme.* Paper presented at the British Educational Research Association Annual Conference, Leeds, September 2001, Symposium on Parents and Early Literacy Development

Hannon, P., Nutbrown, C. and Fawcett, E. (1997) Taking parent learning seriously. *Adults Learning,* 9(3), 19–21

Hannon, P., Nutbrown, C. and Morgan, A. (2005) *Effects of a family literacy programme on children and parents: findings from the REAL Project.* Manuscript submitted for publication. School of Education, University of Sheffield

Hannon, P., Weinberger, J. and Nutbrown, C. (1991) A study of work with parents to promote early literacy development. *Research Papers in Education* 6(2), 77–97

Harrison, C. (1996) Family literacy: evaluation, ownership an ambiguity. *Royal Society of Arts Journal* (November), 1–4

Harste, J.C., Woodward, V.A. and Burke, C.L. (1984) *Language stories and literacy lessons.* Portsmouth, NH: Heinemann Educational Books

Heath, S.B. (1982) What no bedtime story means: narrative skills at home and school. *Language in Society,* 2, 49–76

Heath, S.B. (1983) *Ways with words: language, life and work in communities and classrooms.* Cambridge: Cambridge University Press

Hebbeler, K.M. and Gerlach-Downie, S.G. (2002) Inside the black box of home visiting: a qualitative analysis of why intended outcomes were never achieved. *Early Childhood Research Quarterly,* 17(1), 28–51

Hedge, N. (1996) *Going the distance: teaching, learning and researching in distance education.* USDE: University of Sheffield

Hewison, J. (1988) The long term effectiveness of parental involvement in reading: a follow-up to the Haringey Reading Project. *British Journal of Educational Psychology,* 58, 184–190

Hewison, J. and Tizard, J. (1980) Parental involvement and reading attainment. *British Journal of Educational Psychology,* 50, 209–215

Hickson, H. (2003) Developing the role of parents in early writing experiences of their children. In *Summaries of action research reports.* Tameside LEA/University of Sheffield School of Education

Hiebert, E.H. (1981) Developmental patterns and inter-relationships of preschool children's print awareness. *Reading Research Quarterly,* 16, 236–259

Hirst, K. (1998) Pre-school literacy experiences of children in Punjabi, Urdu and Gujerati speaking families in England. *British Educational Research Journal,* 24(4), 415–429

Hirst, K. (2001) *Preschool literacy and home-school links in Pakistani origin bilingual families in the United Kingdom.* Unpublished PhD Thesis, University of Sheffield

Hirst, K. and Nutbrown, C. (eds) (2005) *Perspectives on early childhood education: essays in contemporary research.* Stoke-on-Trent: Trentham

Holmes, R. (1998) *Fieldwork with children.* London: Sage

Hutchins, P. (1971) *Rosie's walk.* London: Macmillan

Hurst, V. and Joseph, J. (eds) (1998) *Supporting early learning: the way forward.* Buckingham: Open University Press

Jones, B. (1998) *Literacy begins at home: combining parental involvement programmes to develop pre-school children's literacy competences.* Unpublished M.Ed Thesis: University of Sheffield School of Education

Jones, M. and Hendrickson, N. (1970) Recognition by preschool children of advertised products and book covers. *Journal of Home Economics,* 62 (4), 263–267

Jordan, G.E., Snow, C.E. and Porche, M.V. (2000) Project EASE: the effect of a family literacy project on kindergarten students' early literacy skills. *Reading Research Quarterly,* 35(4), 524–546

Karran, S. (2003) 'Auntie-Ji, please come and join us, just for an hour.' The role of the bilingual education assistant in working with parents with little confidence. In J. Devereaux and L. Miller (eds) *Working with children in the early years.* London: David Fulton/Open University

Karther, D. (2002) Fathers with low literacy and their children. *The Reading Teacher,* 56(2), 184–193

Kenner, C. (2000) *Home pages: literacy links for bilingual children.* Stoke-on-Trent: Trentham

Kirkpatrick, A. (2002) Preschool writing development and the role of parents. In C. Nutbrown (ed.) *Research studies in early childhood education.* Stoke-on-Trent: Trentham

Kirkpatrick, A. (2004) *Shared reading interactions: identifying and developing behaviours between parents and preschool children.* Unpublished PhD Thesis, University of Sheffield

Lazar, I. and Darlington, R. (1982) The lasting effects of early education: a report from the Consortium for Longitudinal Studies. *Monographs of the Society for Research in Child Development,* 47(2–3), Serial no. 195

Leibowitz, B. (2001) *Students' prior learning and their acquisition of academic literacy.* Unpublished PhD Thesis: University of Sheffield School of Education

Leslie, R. (2005) Seeing gender through young girls' eyes. In K. Hirst and C. Nutbrown (eds) *Perspectives on early childhood education; essays in contemporary research.* Stoke-on-Trent: Trentham

Lewis, A. and Lindsay, G. (eds) (2000) *Researching children's perspectives.* Buckingham: Open University Press

Lloyd, T. (2001) *What works with fathers?* London: Working With Men

Lynch, J. (2002) Parents' self-efficacy beliefs, parents' gender, children's reader self-perceptions, reading achievement and gender. *Journal of Research in Reading* 25(1), 54–67

Mace, J. (1998) *Playing with time: mothers and the meaning of literacy.* London: UCL Press

Maclean, M., Bryant, P. and Bradley, L. (1987) Rhymes, nursery rhymes, and reading in early childhood. *Merrill-Palmer Quarterly,* 33(3), 255–281

Manning, K. and Sharp, S. (1977) *Structuring play in the early years.* London: Schools Council

Marsh, J. (2000) Teletubby tales: popular culture in the early years, language and literacy curriculum, *Contemporary Issues in Early Childhood,* 1(2), 119–136

Marsh, J. and Thompson, P. (2001) Parental involvement in early literacy: using media texts. *Journal of Research in Reading,* 24(3), 266–279

McIvor, M.C. (1990) *Family literacy in action: a survey of successful programs.* Syracuse, NY: New Readers Press

McKey, H.R., Condelli, L., Ganson, H., Barrett, B., McConkey, C. and Plantz, M. (1985) *The impact of Head Start on children, families and communities.* Head Start Bureau, Administrtion of Children, Youth and Families, Office of Human Development Services. Washington, DC: CSR Incorporated

McNaughton, S. (1995) *The patterns of emergent literacy.* Oxford: Oxford University Press

McNaughton, S. (2001) Co-constructing expertise: the development of parents' and teachers' ideas about literacy practices and the transition to school. *Journal of Early Childhood Literacy* 1(1) 40–58

McNaughton, S., Glynn, T. and Robinson, V. (1981) *Parents as remedial tutors: issues for home and school.* Wellington: New Zealand Council for Educational Research

Meek, M. (1982) *Learning to read.* London: The Bodley Head

Meek, M. and Dombey, H. (1994) *First steps together: home–school early literacy in European contexts.* Stoke-on-Trent: Trentham

Millard, E. (2001) *It's a man thing! Evaluation report of CEDC's Fathers and Reading project.* Coventry: CEDC

Moll, L., Amanti, C., Neff, D. and Gonzalez, N. (1992) Funds of knowledge for teaching: using a qualitative approach to connect homes and classrooms. *Theory Into Practice*, 31(2), 132–141

Morrow, L.M. (ed.) (1995) *Family literacy: connections in schools and communities*. Newark, DE: International Reading Association

Morrow, L.M. and Paratore, J. (1993) Family literacy: perspectives and practices. *The Reading Teacher*, 47, 194–200

Morrow, L.M., Tracey, D.H. and Maxwell, C.M. (eds) (1995) *A survey of family literacy in the United States*. Newark, DE: International Reading Association

Moss, B.J. (ed.) (1994) *Literacy across communities*. Cresskill, NJ: Hampton Press

Moss, E. (1977) What is a good book? The peppermint lesson. In M. Meek, A. Warlow and G. Barton (eds) *The cool web: the pattern of children's reading*. London: The Bodley Head

Nash, A. (1987) *English family literacy: an annotated bibliography*. Boston: English Family Literacy Project, University of Massachusetts

National Center for Family Literacy (NCFL) (1994) Communicating the power of family literacy. *NCFL Newsletter*, 6(1), 1

Newson, J. and Newson, E. (1977) *Perspectives on school at seven years old*. London: Allen and Unwin

Nickse, R.S. (1990) *Family and intergenerational literacy programs: an update of 'Noises of Literacy'*. Columbus, OH: ERIC Clearinghouse on Adult, Career and Vocational Education, Ohio State University

Nutbrown, C. (ed.) (1996) *Respectful educators – capable learners: children's rights and early education*. London: Paul Chapman Publishing

Nutbrown, C. (1997) *Recognising early literacy development*. London: Paul Chapman Publishing

Nutbrown, C. (1999a) Learning about literacy in the earliest years: Alex's story. In E. Millard, *Enquiries into literacy*. Sheffield: University of Sheffield Papers in Education

Nutbrown, C. (1999b) *Threads of Thinking: young children learning and the role of early education* (2nd edition). London: Paul Chapman Publishing

Nutbrown, C. (2001) Watching and learning: the tools of assessment. In G. Pugh (ed.) *Contemporary issues in the early years: working collaboratively for children* (3rd edition). London: Paul Chapman Publishing

Nutbrown, C. (2002) Early childhood education in contexts of change. In C. Nutbrown (ed.) *Research studies in early childhood education*. Stoke-on-Trent: Trentham

Nutbrown, C. and Hannon, P. (1993) Assessing early literacy – new measures needed. *International Journal of Early Childhood*, 25(2), 27–30

Nutbrown, C. and Hannon, P. (eds) (1997) *Preparing for early literacy education with parents: a professional development manual*. Sheffield/Nottingham: NES Arnold/University of Sheffield REAL Project

Nutbrown, C. and Hannon, P. (2003) Children's perspectives on family literacy: methodological issues, findings and implications for practice. *Journal of Early Childhood Literacy*, 3(2), 115–145

Nutbrown, C., Hannon, P. and Collier, S. (1996) *Early literacy education with parents: a framework for practice* (Video). Sheffield: The REAL Project/University of Sheffield, Sheffield University Television

Nutbrown, C., Hannon, P. and Weinberger, J. (1991) Training teachers to work with parents to promote early literacy development. *International Journal of Early Childhood*, 23(2), 1–10

Oakley, A. (1993) Interviewing women: a contradiction in terms. In H. Roberts (ed.) *Doing Feminist Research* (2nd edition). London: Routledge

Office for Standards in Education (OFSTED) (1993) *Boys and English.* London: The Stationery Office

Pahl, K. (2002) Ephemera, mess and miscellaneous piles: texts and practices in families. *Journal of Early Childhood Literacy*, 2(2), 145–166

Parker, C. (2002) Working with families on curriculum: developing shared understandings of children's mark making. In C. Nutbrown (ed.) *Research studies in early childhood education.* Stoke-on-Trent, Trentham

Parker, S. (1986) 'I want to give them what I never had'. Can parents who are barely literate teach their children to read? *Times Educational Supplement*, 10 October, p.23

Payton, S. (1984) *Developing awareness of print – a child's first steps towards literacy.* Birmingham: Educational Review Occasional Papers No. 2, University of Birmingham

Pereera, S. (2001) Living with special educational needs: mothers' perspectives. In P. Clough and C. Nutbrown (eds) *Voices of Arabia: essays in educational research.* Sheffield: University of Sheffield Papers in Education

Pfannenstiel, J.C. and Seltzer, D.A. (1989) New parents as teachers: evaluation of an early parent education program. *Early Childhood Research Quarterly*, 4, 1–18

Pink, S. (2001) *Doing visual ethnography.* London: Sage

Poulson, L., Macleod, F., Bennett, N. and Wray, D. (1997) *Family literacy: practice in local programmes.* London: Basic Skills Agency

Preece, V. (1999) *Bridging the gap: investigating parents' and teachers' perspectives on parental involvement in the development of literacy.* Unpublished M.Ed Thesis: University of Sheffield School of Education

Purcell-Gates, V. (1995) *Other people's words: the cycle of low literacy.* Cambridge, MA: Harvard University Press

Purcell-Gates, V. (2000) Family literacy. In Kamil, M.L., Mosenthal, P.B., Pearson, P.D. and Barr, R. *Handbook of reading research, Volume III.* Mahwah, NJ: Lawrence Erlbaum Associates

Qualifications and Curriculum Authority (QCA) (1998) *Can do better: raising boys' achievement in schools.* London: The Stationery Office

Qualifications and Curriculum Authority (QCA) (1999) *The National Numeracy Strategy.* London: The Stationery Office

Qualifications and Curriculum Authority (QCA) (2000) *Curriculum guidance for the Foundation Stage.* London: The Stationery Office

Qualifications and Curriculum Authority (QCA) (2003) *Birth to three matters.* London: The Stationery Office

Qualifications Curriculum and Assessment Authority for Wales (QCAAW) (2004) *The Foundation Phase in Wales: a draft framework for children's learning.* Cardiff: National Assembly for Wales

Rigo-Toth, R. and Ure, C. (2000) Evaluating literacy in the preschool: a review of Hannon's ORIM framework. *International Journal of Learning*, 7

Riley, J. (1996) The ability to label the letters of the alphabet at school entry: a discussion on its value. *Journal of Research in Reading,* 19(2), 87–101

Roberts, R. (ed.) (2001) *PEEP voices: a five year diary.* Oxford: PEEP

Ross, D. and Brondy, E. (1987) Communicating with parents about beginning reading instruction. *Childhood Education,* 63(4), 270–274

Schickedanz, J. (1990) *Adam's righting revolutions.* Portsmouth NH: Heinemann

School Curriculum and Assessment Authority (1996) *Desirable outcomes of nursery education on entry to compulsory schooling.* London: The Stationery Office

School Curriculum and Assessment Authority (1997) *National Framework for baseline assessment.* London: The Stationery Office

Scottish Executive (2003) *Integrated strategy for early years – consultation document.* Edinburgh: Children and Young People's Group – Scottish Executive

Siraj-Blatchford, I. (1994) *The early years: laying the foundations for racial equality.* Stoke-on-Trent: Trentham Books

Smith, F. (1976) Learning to read by reading. *Language Arts,* 53, 297–299

Stenhouse, L. (1975) *An introduction to curriculum research and development.* London: Heineman

St. Pierre, R., Swartz, J., Gamse, B., Murray, S., Deck, D. and Nickel, P. (1995) *National evaluation of the Even Start family literacy program.* Washington, DC: US Department of Education, Office of Policy and Planning

Styles, M., Bearne, E. and Watson, V. (eds) (1992) *After Alice – exploring children's literature.* London: Cassell

Taylor, D. (1983) *Family literacy: young children learning to read and write.* Exeter, NH: Heinemann

Taylor, D. (ed.) (1997) *Many families, many literacies: an international declaration of principles.* Portsmouth, NH: Heinemann

Taylor and Dorsey-Gaines (1988) *Growing up literate: learning from inner city families.* Portsmouth, NH: Heinemann

Teale, W.H. (1986) Home background and young children's literacy development. In W.H. Teale and E. Sulzby (eds) *Emergent literacy: writing and reading.* Norwood, NJ: Ablex Publishing Corporation

Teale, W.H. and Sulzby, E. (eds) (1986) *Emergent literacy: writing and reading.* Norwood, NJ: Ablex Publishing Corporation

Tett, L. (2000) Excluded voices: class, culture, and family literacy in Scotland. *Journal of Adolescent and Adult Literacy,* 44(2), 122–128

Tierney, W. (1993) Self and identity in a postmodern world: a life story. In D. McLaughlin and W. Tierney (eds) *Naming silenced lives.* New York: Routledge

Tizard, B. and Hughes, M. (1984) *Young children learning: talking and thinking at home and in school.* London: Falmer

Tizard, B., Blatchford, P., Burke, J., Farquhar, C. and Plewis, I. (1988) *Young children at school in the inner city.* London: Lawrence Erlbaum Associates

Tizard, J., Schofield, W.N. and Hewison, J. (1982) Collaboration between teachers and parents in assisting children's reading. *British Journal of Educational Psychology,* 52, 1–15

Topping, K. and Lindsay, G.A. (1991) The structure and development of the paired reading technique. *Journal of Research in Reading,* 15(2), 120–136

Topping, K. and Lindsay, G.A. (1992) Paired reading: a review of the literature. *Research Papers in Education*, 7(3), 199–246

Tough, J. (1976) *Listening to children talking*. London: Schools Council Publications

Tucker, N. (1993) The 'good book': literacy and developmental aspects. In R. Beard (ed.) *Teaching literacy: balancing perspectives*. Sevenoaks: Hodder and Stoughton

Turnbull, C. (1998) *How valuable is the ORIM framework as a tool for nursery nurses developing the early literacy skills of pre-school children?* Unpublished M.Ed Thesis: University of Sheffield School of Education

Voss, M. (1996) *Hidden literacies: children learning at home and at school*. Portsmouth, NH: Heinemann

Wade, B. (1984) Story at home and school. *Educational Review Publication Number 10*. Birmingham: University of Birmingham, Faculty of Education

Wagner, M., Spiker, D. and Linn, M. (2002) The effectiveness of the parents as teachers program with low-income parents and children. *Topics in Early Childhood Special Education*, 22(2), 67–81

Wasik, B.H. (ed.) (2004) *Handbook of family literacy*. Mahwah, NJ: Erlbaum

Wasik, B.H., Dobbins, D.R. and Hermann, S. (2001) Intergenerational family literacy: concepts, research, and practice. In S.B. Neuman and D.K. Dickinson (eds) *Handbook of early literacy research*. New York: The Guilford Press

Waterland, L. (1992) Good for any age. In M. Styles, E. Bearne and V. Watson (eds) *After Alice – exploring children's literature*. London: Cassell

Webster (2002) Cinderellas in lonely castles? Perspectives of voluntary preschool supervisors in rural communities. In C. Nutbrown (ed.) *Research studies in early childhood education*. Stoke-on-Trent: Trentham

Wedge, P. and Prosser, H. (1973) *Born to fail?* London: Arrow Books/National Children's Bureau

Weinberger, J. (1996) *Literacy goes to school: the parents' role in young children's literacy learning*. London: Paul Chapman Publishing

Weinberger, J., Hannon, P. and Nutbrown, C. (1990) *Ways of working with parents to promote early literacy development*. Sheffield: University of Sheffield

Wells, G. (1985) *Language development in the preschool years*. Cambridge: Cambridge University Press

Wells, G. (1987) *The meaning makers: children learning language and using language to learn*. London: Hodder and Stoughton

Whalley, M. and the Pen Green Centre Team (2001) *Involving parents in their children's learning*. London: Paul Chapman Publishing

Whitehurst, G.J., Epstein, J.N., Angell, A.L., Payne, D.A., Crone, D.A. and Fischel, J.E. (1994) Outcomes of an emergent literacy intervention in Head Start. *Journal of Educational Psychology*, 86(4), 542–555

Wolfendale, S. and Topping, K. (eds) (1996) *Family involvement in literacy: effective partnerships in education*. London: Cassell

Wood, C. (2002) Parent–child pre-school activities can affect the development of literacy skills. *Journal of Research in Reading* 25(3), 241–258

Wray, D., Bloom, W. and Hall, N. (1989) *Literacy in action – the development of literacy in the primary years*. London: Falmer Press

Index

Adult Literacy and Basic Skills Unit (ALBSU) 21, 26, 27, 28, 134
Ahlberg, A. 42
Ahlberg, J. 42
Anning, A. 16
Armstrong, F. 114
Arnold, C. 14
Athey, C. 14
Aubrey, C. 148
Auerbach, E. 21, 22, 26, 27, 30, 116

Baghban, M. 11, 45
Baker, L. 19, 28
Barker, J. 183
Barton, D. 124, 176
Baz, P. 14
Benjamin, L.A. 157
Bissex, G. 45, 147, 149
Blackledge, A. 30
Booth, T. 150
Bradley, L. 23
Brizius, J.A. 31
Brondy, E. 44, 45
Brooks, G. 25, 29, 30, 124, 134, 138, 148, 157
Bruner, J. 49
Bryant, P. 23, 47, 48
Burke, C. 39
Burnett, C. 148, 149
Bus, A.G. 23
Bushell, R. 25

Cairney, T. 19, 21, 26, 30, 124
Christensen, P. 148
Cigman, J. 179, 182
Claverie, J. 42
Clay, M. 48, 49, 147, 169
Clough P. 114, 148
Cook, M. 178
Critchley, D. 149

Darling, S. 21, 27, 171
Davie, R. 23, 49

Delaney, P. 176
Delgado-Gaitan, C. 27, 30
Department of Education in Northern Ireland (DENI) 3
DfEE 4
Dickinson, D. 25, 123, 124
Dorsey-Gaines 19, 124
Douglas, J.W.B. 49
Drummond, M. 149
Dunn, L.M. 169
Dyer, P. 149

Edmonds, M. 28
Edwards, A. 16
Edwards, P.A. 25, 148
Evangelou, M. 14
Evans, L. 179

Fagan, W.T. 178
Ferrerio, E. 44
Filippini, T. 149
Fine, M. 148
Finlay, A. 29
Firth, R. 13
Foster, S.A. 31
Frater, G. 157, 166

Gerlach-Downie, S.G. 134, 136
Glass, N. 3, 11
Goelman, H. 23
Goodhall, M. 39
Goodley, D. 150
Goodman, Y. 11, 12, 39, 44, 45, 47
Goswami, U. 47, 48
Grant, A. 26
Green, C. 11, 25
Greig, A. 148
Griffiths, A. 28

Haggart, J. 30
Hall, N. 23, 41
Hamilton, M. 124, 176

Hannon, P. 15, 19, 21, 23, 24, 25, 26, 27, 28, 29, 30, 31, 35, 36, 49, 104, 106, 108, 118, 121, 122, 123, 124, 128, 134, 138, 145, 147, 148, 150, 166, 168, 170, 171, 175, 181, 185
Harrison, C. 157
Harste, J.C. 44, 45, 47
Heath, S.B. 19, 23, 124
Hebbeler, K.M. 134, 136
Hedge, N. 114
Hewison, J. 23, 29
Hickson, H. 15, 16, 17
Hiebert, E. H. 39, 183
Hirst, K. 11, 19, 30, 114, 124, 147
Holmes, R. 148
Hughes, M. 24, 148
Hurst, V. 13
Hutchins, P. 41

Jackson, A. 134, 138
James, A. 148
James, S. 19, 23, 148
Jones, B. 179, 180, 181
Jones, M. 41
Jordan, G.E. 28
Joseph, J. 13

Karran, S. 14
Karther, D. 30
Kenner, C. 30
Kirkpatrick, A. 138, 149

Lazar, I. 171
Leibowitz, B. 176
Leslie, R. 149
Lewis, A. 148
Lindsay, G. 25, 148
Lloyd, T. 30
Lord, J. 157

Mace, J. 157
Maclean, M. 23, 47, 48
Manning, K. 114
Marsh, J. 42, 149, 157
Maxwell, C.M. 21
McIvor, M.C. 21, 25, 26
McKey, H.R. 171
McNaughton, S. 19, 25, 148, 157
Meek, M. 41, 42, 49

Millard, E. 30
Moll, L. 27
Moore, M. 114
Morrow, L.M. 21, 22, 124
Moss, E. 19, 43
Munsie, L. 124
Myers, J. 149

Nash, A. 19
National Center for Family Literacy (NCFL) 31
Newson, E. 23, 49
Newson, J. 23, 49
Nutbrown, C. 4, 5, 11, 14, 24, 30, 31, 35, 36, 42, 45, 49, 104, 106, 108, 111, 114, 121, 122, 123, 124, 128, 147, 148, 149, 150, 166, 168, 169, 175, 181, 185

Oakley, A. 150
Office for Standards in Education (OFSTED) 11, 166

Pahl, K. 149
Paratore, J. 1, 22
Parker, C. 14, 148
Payton, S. 148
Pellegrini, A. D. 134
Pereera, S. 148
Pfannenstiel, J. C. 134
Pink, S. 149
Poulson, L. 134
Preece, V. 176
Price, M. 42
Prosser, H. 49
Purcell-Gates, V. 22

Qualifications and Curriculum Authority (QCA) 3, 4, 5, 12, 46, 157, 166
Qualifications Curriculum and Assessment Authority for Wales (QCAAW) 4

Rigo-Toth, R. 176, 177
Riley, J. 169
Roberts, R. 176, 184
Ross, D. 44, 45
Ruge, J. 19

Schickedanz, J. 45, 147, 149

School Curriculum and Assessment Authority (SCAA) 4
Scottish Executive 4
Seltzer, D. A. 134
Sharp, A. 114
Siraj-Blatchford, I. 14
St. Pierre, R. 29, 134
Stenhouse, L. 118
Styles, M. 42
Sulzby, E. 23
Sylva, K. 14

Taylor, D. 19, 21, 22, 166
Taylor, J. 26, 27, 124, 148
Teale, W. H. 19, 23, 124
Teberosky, A. 44
Tett, L. 21, 27, 29
Thompson, P. 149, 157
Tierney, W. 148
Tizard, B. 23, 24, 25, 147, 148, 169
Topping, K. 25, 123, 124
Tough, J. 114

Tracey, D. H., 21
Tucker, N. 43
Tumbull, C. 176

Ure, C. 176

Vecchi, V. 149

Wade, B. 25
Wagner, M. 28, 29
Wasik, B. H. 21, 22
Waterland, L. 42
Webster, S. 11
Wedge, P. 49
Weinberger, J. 36, 43, 44, 48, 49, 124, 143, 147, 157, 169
Wells, G. 23, 48, 169
Whalley, M. 14
Whitehurst, G.J. 24, 134, 148
Wolfendale, S. 21, 22, 25, 123, 124
Wood, C. 157
Wray, D. 46